SE

SI

SEX IN MIDDLESEX

Sex in Middlesex

POPULAR MORES IN A

MASSACHUSETTS COUNTY, 1649–1699

ROGER THOMPSON

FOREWORD BY DAVID D. HALL

THE UNIVERSITY OF MASSACHUSETTS PRESS

AMHERST, 1986

Printed in the United States of America
Set in Linoterm Bembo at The University of Massachusetts Press
Printed by Cushing-Malloy and bound by John Dekker & Sons
LIBRARY OF CONGRESS CATALOGING-IN-PUBLICATION DATA
Thompson, Roger, 1933–
    Sex in Middlesex.

    Includes bibliographical references and index.
    1. Sex customs—Massachusetts—Middlesex County—History—17th century.
2. Sexual ethics—Massachusetts—Middlesex County—History—17th century. 3. Sex
crimes—Massachusetts—Middlesex County—History—17th century. 4. Puritans
—Massachusetts—Middlesex County—History—17th century. 5. Family
—Massachusetts—Middlesex County—History—17th century. I. Title.
HQ18.U5T49   1986   306.7′097444   85–24630
ISBN 0–87023–516–8 (alk. paper)

Contents

vi   Contents

Foreword

THERE ARE certain Dutch paintings from the seventeenth century that make vividly real the texture and tone of everyday life. Similarly, certain documents from that far-away period are unusually revealing of how ordinary people felt and acted. Such are the records of the county court in Middlesex County of the Colony and Province of Massachusetts Bay. These records include not only the formal proceedings of the court but also the depositions made by hundreds of witnesses and those charged with criminal behavior. Out of these depositions Roger Thompson has woven a story of individuals in search of freedom and security, of love and intimacy—individuals such as Sarah Crouch of Charlestown, Christopher Grant of Watertown, and Samuel and Hannah Hutchinson of Reading. In bringing these forgotten, faceless people to life Thompson has performed one of the classic services of the social historian.

The Middlesex records allow Thompson to perform another service for us, that of finding pattern and meaning in the past. The voices that remain so vivid in these documents disclose to us attitudes and actions of which we know too little. Collectively these voices instruct us on the relationship between social order and disorder. Men and women in seventeenth-century Massachusetts could make some choices, but not others, and the hundreds of cases that Thompson has studied allow him to infer persistent structures. The records strongly suggest that the puritan social system was not so rigid and the relationships between the sexes not so regulated as some historians have suggested. The argument of *Sex in Middlesex* is revisionist: the "puritans" and "theocrats" who throng its pages do not behave in accordance with popular stereotype or conform to the interpretations of major historians.

The puritans, it is commonly said, were bent on "order." Puritans wanted and got system and discipline; theirs was a tightly structured society. So goes the conventional wisdom. In support of this interpretation, twentieth-century historians cite beliefs and institutions. Surely these people valued order and obedience, for the leaders of Massachusetts said so time and again. Surely they created a powerful network of institutional controls: a covenant among residents of the town and another among members of the congregation, each of them giving fellow residents and members the privilege and responsibility of keeping "brotherly watch" upon neighbors; a court system and a legal code that, among its harsh provisions, specified the death penalty for children who disobeyed their parents; schools that combined a child's A.B.C.'s with lessons on the importance of self-control and obedience; and as the linchpin of the whole system, a family structure that enabled parents to reign over the lives of their children even after they had reached adulthood. No privacy, no ameliorating love, no autonomy—such is the picture of family and community life as some historians have described it in early New England and early modern Europe.

There is more to the story, for certain historians tell us that puritanism originated in England as a campaign for the "reformation of manners." Those who led this movement set out to impose their concept of the good life, or godliness, upon other social groups. The puritan version of godliness promulgated a work ethic and, of particular importance here, an ethic of sexual restraint. Enemies of the "easier-going sexual habits of traditional society," these reformers wanted to impose new moral rules and new sanctions against idleness. Hence the sabbatarianism of the puritans, hence their railings against maypoles and carnival. Hence too, in New England, the restriction of the franchise to church members, for only the godly could be trusted with political power, and hence the close alliance between magistrates and ministers in what some historians still refer to as a "theocracy."

Sex in Middlesex puts several of these propositions to the test and finds them wanting. Let me voice my own skepticism. Church records indicate that members who were censured for flouting moral rules or causing other trouble frequently did not take their punishment to heart. From court records we learn that severe penalties were usually commuted into lesser ones; the most severe of all, the death penalty for such crimes as disobeying parents or committing adultery, was imposed only once. The town covenant is as much myth as fact; many towns, and perhaps the majority of them, came into being without the services of a covenant. A famous law of 1636 commanding everyone to reside within a short distance of a meetinghouse quickly became a dead issue as the colonists spread outward onto farms. No maypoles graced New England villages, but the reformation of manners waxed and waned with the passing of the decades. Some colonists began to stay away from church, finding Sundays a good time to frolic. The suppression of religious dissent faltered, for the brethren who became Baptists or Quakers were protected by neighbors and kinfolk who refrained from enforcing the letter of the law. At the highest levels of authority, magistrates fell to quarreling among themselves and with the clergy, who divided into factions on key issues. The deputies in the Massachusetts General Court, though presumably among the "godly," obstructed the alliance of the magistrates and clergy and threw their weight on the side of weaker government. Rituals of reconciliation, like the fast day, became enmeshed in politics. On rare moments the "theocracy" lashed out boldly against perceived sin and disorder, but in doing so it provoked criticism and created a fresh sympathy for the persons it pursued. Indeed, the colonists were highly sensitive to the exercise of power and their ideology of order coexisted with principles of voluntary consent and "liberty" from unjust authority. The founders of Massachusetts deliberately chose not to reproduce in New England most of the appointive offices, church courts, and privileged corporations they had resented in their native land. Fearing "tyranny" on the one hand and "anarchy" on the other, these people worked out in practice and theory a mixture of strong leadership and voluntary participation.

How misleading it can be, therefore, to conceive of Massachusetts as a static social system organized according to a rigid set of principles policed by a host of social agencies. The crucial agency of order in seventeenth-century Middlesex was undoubtedly the family, although other agencies—church, court, and civil government—played useful roles. A fundamental discipline arose from the hardships of earning a livelihood, and in family units that were also small-scale economic systems, children became accustomed to certain rules and limits. Yet as Thompson demonstrates, the family system contained surprising amounts of room for personal expression. Moreover, the colonists soon learned that anarchy did not ensue if families moved away from the immediate vicinity of the meetinghouse or if a merchant charged more than a "just price" for his goods. For that matter, they discovered that a society in which many persons were but partial church members worked reasonably well—as did a society in which the children of church members sometimes became pregnant before they married.

In other words, the colonists experienced and came to accept compromise. We should not exaggerate the significance of their complaints about the process of adjustment. The transition out of perfect order (which never really existed) to a more patchwork system occurred without real crisis. Historians have made much of trends in criminal behavior, interpreting, for example, a rising rate of bastardy as a signal that social breakdown was occurring. According to conventional wisdom, illicit behavior is a function of stress and strain as the social system undergoes deep change. Although *Sex in Middlesex* describes people who broke the law and got in trouble, it reveals a society in which there were remarkably *few* crimes against the family—and therefore no real crisis. Thompson's argument to this effect deserves greater emphasis, and we need to reflect on its implications. I would propose that the extraordinarily low rate of sexual offenses in seventeenth-century Middlesex, at least as these are known to us through the court records, serves to disprove assertions that the colonists were experiencing profound strain or dislocation. A commonsense explanation is at hand for many of the cases of bastardy. Is it also common sense to suggest that the mechanisms of social order, including the family, functioned adequately throughout the period Thompson has surveyed? After 1660 the political system became disrupted as the Stuart kings extended their authority across the Atlantic. But disturbances in the political system do not necessarily translate into disturbances in social structure.

The substance of *Sex in Middlesex* is the speech of ordinary people. This is speech that informs us richly about popular religion ("God sees in the dark") and youth culture, about sex and love, about family and community. Tangible, immediate, and compelling, the speech of these people resists any simple black or white interpretation. It is the great strength of Roger Thompson's narrative that he has responded so imaginatively to the nuances of everyday life, and in doing so has enriched the social history of early New England.

DAVID D. HALL
BOSTON UNIVERSITY

Acknowledgments

MANY PEOPLE have helped me in practical and scholarly ways during my research and writing; to all of them I express my gratitude: John Ashworth, Charles Cohen, Peter Cole, Ann Cook, Richard Crockatt, David Dearborn, Toby Ditz, David Hall, Joe Illick, Martin Ingram, John Kneeland, Edmund Leites, Michael Macdonald, Richard Martin, Jim Monahan, Norman and Bici Pettit, David Quinn, Jim Sharpe, Kit Thompson, and Muriel Utting.

I also wish to thank the Research Grants Committee of the School of English and American Studies of the University of East Anglia, Norwich, for two grants for research in Cambridge and Boston, Massachusetts.

Preface

A DISTINGUISHED pioneer of Middlesex County, Massachusetts, Captain Edward Johnson, depicted a herald of Christ Jesus stirring up volunteers with an "Oh yes! Oh yes! Oh yes!" to "be shipped for his service, in the Westerne World, and more especially for planting the united Colonies of new England."[1] More than three centuries later a rather more earthbound herald issued a similar clarion call to social historians in England and America to volunteer for the service of recovering that "World we have Lost." Peter Laslett's manifesto for "sociological history" demonstrated the potential of the "scientific historical demography" developed by Louis Henry and also by French scholars of the *Annales* School.[2] Instead of the letters, diaries, conduct books, sermons, and autobiographies normally used in the writing of family or community history, he and his Cambridge colleagues showed how analysis of neglected town and parish vital records, wills, census and tax listings could overthrow long-held assumptions about "the man in the village lane" in the early modern period.[3]

Suddenly, it seemed, all Anglophone social historians were becoming "cliometricians" or quantifiers and immersing themselves in microcosmic studies. By the mid-1970s, the results of this "torrential outpouring" of research had produced important revisions on such topics as household and community structure, literacy, fertility, bastardy and mortality rates, geographical mobility, and wealth transmission.[4] Many of these new studies, especially of townships and counties in colonial America, reached impressive but often divergent findings. As these were digested all sorts of shortcomings became apparent. There were problems with the incompleteness of registers, the class bias of

wills, and the "snapshot" nature of listings. There were methodologi-
cal difficulties in family reconstitution which could obscure the intrica-
cies of family life and kinship networks. In censuses, for instance,
"married sisters living next door to each other will go undetected." The
most serious criticism, however, was that demographic analysis could
not "unlock the inner life of the family." So far as past attitudes, relationships, family and community dynamics were concerned, the cliometricians served up "a thin and watery gruel." Laslett had to admit
that "the emotional pattern of that society has vanished for ever" from
the particular slides under his microscope. It slowly came to be realized
that "all the possible statistics about age of marriage, size of family,
rates of illegitimacy will not add up to the history of the family."[5]

Many of these criticisms had been raised by more traditionalist social
historians whose sources threw more light on *mentalité*. Yet they faced
problems too. "Plebeians" rarely wrote letters, kept diaries, or left
autobiographies. Sermons and conduct books were prescriptive, but
were they descriptive? William Lamont recently exemplified the dangers of relying on such evidence in the case of Richard Hooker. That
"greatest spokesman of the patriarchal ideal" was discovered by former
pupils tending sheep, "which he was forced to do then, for that his
servant was gone home to dine, and assist his wife to do some necessary
household business . . . But when his servant returned and released
him . . . Richard was call'd to rock the cradle: and the rest of their welcome was so like this, that they staid but till next morning which was
time enough to discover and pity their tutors condition."[6] If there
were such discrepancies between the preachments and the practices of
Hooker, could any historical trust be placed in the great puritan instruc-
tors on marriage and the family, let alone in the compliance of their
readers? Other potential sources for mentalité, like folklore and popular
literature, posed similarly intractable problems of interpretation, of
distinguishing the ideal from the real.[7]

What was plainly needed by the late 1970s was a pulling together and
an ordering of this huge and exciting, but uncoordinated and specialist
body of research. Such a synthesis was attempted in 1977 by Lawrence
Stone in his *Family, Sex and Marriage in England 1500–1800*. Variously
described as "a monument in more senses than one" and "a *ballon d'essai*
of more than dirigible proportions,"[8] this vast work of scholarship
ranged widely over the English-speaking world, incorporating into its
thesis findings from early American history. Adapting some ideas originally propounded in Edward Shorter's *The Making of the Modern
Family* (1974), Stone argued that from medieval to modern times the

family progressed from an "Open Lineage Family 1450–1630" through a transitional "Restricted Patriarchal Nuclear Family 1550–1700" to the "Closed Domesticated Nuclear Family 1640–1800" which is the foundation of the modern family. From a group dominated by the clan (past, present, and future), and by the community, the family first cast off these extraneous influences and became a little church and a little commonwealth under its priest and king, the all-powerful father. Then, thanks to the rise of affective individualism, patriarch and subordinate laborers in the family business gave way to the affectionate couple nurturing their beloved children in the family nest. This new bourgeois family, according to Stone, spread its influence upward to the aristocracy and then downward to the lower classes.

Stone's depiction of the transitional phase, the restricted patriarchal nuclear family, especially among what he calls "plebeians," deserves closer study. In the strictly hierarchical societies of Stuart England and puritan America, according to Stone, functions previously performed by the extended family, like care of aged or poor relations, godparenthood, marriage negotiations, estate transmission, or protection of the family reputation, were either institutionalized or conferred upon the nuclear family, which became the primary unit of society. No longer limited by the kinfolk (or by the priest), the father became the "priest-ruler of his microcosmic empire, the family despot." The household, in most cases a farm or small-holding, was a unit of production as well as reproduction. In this "phallocentric social system" the father-farmer was the boss, and the family a weapon of oppression.

Under the demigod patriarch were ranged wife, children, and servants. All owed him deference and unquestioning obedience. That symbol of the age, the whip, exacted fealty where necessary. The wife, chosen for economic rather than personal assets, was required to love her oppressor. She must produce heirs and young workers in the family enterprise as well as contribute to the backbreaking slog of survival. As daughters of Eve, all wives were potentially subversive; they needed to be kept on a tight rein. Their kinfolk could no longer intercede for them. The death of a cow or a horse might well cause the patriarch greater grief than the loss of a replaceable wife.

As for the children, many were quickly dead, some not accidentally. Emotional bonding between parents and infants was thus too often disrupted to be ever worthwhile. Those who survived were "dangerous little animals" diseased with original sin. Like colts or puppies they had to be broken in with cuffs and beatings and the psychological threat of early death so that they could become useful chattels. Their labor was owned by the boss. Relationships in this harshly punitive prison were predictably cold, quietly hostile, and withdrawn. Children, battered and deprived, grew into desexed and cowed adolescents; any sense of personal autonomy was undermined by their transfer to another household. The patriarch's ultimate weapon was his control of the family assets. Thus was generational conflict crushed. The household was more like a common room than a home; there was little privacy or opportunity for personal development. "After marriage fairly brutal treatment of wives by husbands was normal." Sexual relations were instrumental or exploitive rather than affective. Coital pleasure was the prerogative of the patriarch; the act was nasty, brutish and short.

Within isolated rural communities, nuclear family faced nuclear family with suspicion and hostility. Cooperation had given way to competition. Life was like Hobbes's state of nature, a war of all against all. "The average peasant was a short-tempered, malicious character, who flared into physical violence on the flimsiest excuse." In such groupings defamation and witchcraft accusations flourished; communal obligations, previously voluntary, now had to be enforced by such statutes as the poor laws.[9]

Stone attributed the emergence of the restricted patriarchal nuclear family to specific causes: the rise of possessive individualism and the rise of the patriarchal nation state. Yet the primary cause was the protestant reformation. Indeed, the new family structure was for him its "most far-reaching consequence." Puritanism, the radical reformist wing of the movement, placed greatest stress on patriarchalism by its "spiritualisation of the household."[10] In an anxious world ruled by a patriarchal predestinating divinity, "many puritans, on both sides of the Atlantic, clearly believed that God held all members of the nuclear family as hostages for the good behaviour of any one of them." In its passion for purity and its terror of pollution by "the world," puritanism required the father to become the minister of his dependents, disciplining them, catechizing them, praying with them, reading the Bible to them, generally putting the fear of God into them. To the economic power of the family boss, puritanism added the potent psychological power of the priest.

Logically the transitional patriarchal family structure should appear in its purest form in seventeenth-century puritan New England.

The initial reaction to Stone's synthesis was awe and approval. The range of his scholarship and the imposition of order on widely diverse findings impressed reviewers. The history of the family would never be the same again.[11] To general or partisan readers the Stone thesis became the new paradigm. Feminists and psychohistorians, for instance, grasped the symbol of the oppressive family despot as an explanation of female and child neuroses in the past and a welcome scapegoat for the present.[12] But to specialists in family history, Stone's work presented an important challenge. Ever since the publication of *Family, Sex and Marriage,* his methodology and conclusions have been subjected to testing and review.[13] The 1982 Anglo-American Conference on the Family saw almost every speaker implicitly evaluating some aspect of the new model. As well as trenchant criticisms of Stone's use of evidence, scholars generally agree that his work is least satisfactory in its consideration of the lower end of the social scale—a weakness he readily admits.[14] Nonetheless he stands by his major conclusions about the transformation of the preindustrial family, and some historians have been persuaded of their plausibility.

This, then, is the historiographic context in which the present study of sexual misdemeanors and family and community life has been written. The testing ground of the Stone paradigm is the county of Middlesex in Massachusetts between 1649 and 1699. Sexual relationships have been singled out not because "the dedicated social historian [is] second cousin to the tabloid journalist" as G. R. Elton claims,[15] but because the norms, values, aspirations, and inhibitions of ordinary people can be vividly exposed in such intimate situations and crises. As Stone has recently written: "The problem of assessing the quality of family life among the poor [and, we might add, the not so poor] in the past, of penetrating their bedrooms, hearing them talk and understanding how they felt about their wives, their children, their relatives, their mothers-in-law" remains a major challenge to the social historian.[16]

The main source for this study is the Middlesex county court records, buttressed by town, church, and genealogical records. Many historians of the family have come to realize the immense value of such sources. They provide "the best available portrayal of the prevailing system of values." They "can throw a flood of light on lineage ties, household loyalties, family relations, and sexual behaviour, even at a very remote period in time. . . . It may be that this will turn out to be the single most important untapped body of information about the quality of family life in the past. The documents provide precisely the kind of information that historians of mentalité are looking for, and work upon them is likely to bring rich rewards in the 1980s." "Depositions are the only source of the words of the [ordinary] women and men themselves."[17]

There are, of course, serious difficulties to be faced in the use of court records. It is tempting to project on to the majority of the population the behavior and attitudes of the minority who appeared before the magistrates. The historian has to try to determine from his material whether that minority is a criminal subculture rejecting prevailing mores or the tip of an iceberg, the unlucky few who got caught. He must allow for the possibilities of ineffective law enforcement, private conflict- and crisis-resolution, and skillful evasion. He must be alert to the fact that people may behave abnormally under the stress of examination or trial, saying what they think the authorities wish to hear rather than revealing their true feelings. He must never forget the remarkable human aptitude for rationalization and outright deceit. Court proceedings are often adversarial; they may give a false reflection of normal relationships. Some cases are far better documented than others, giving them a weight, perhaps, that they do not deserve. Certain individuals are hard or impossible to trace. The records rarely tell the researcher such vital details as what people looked like or how they presented themselves. Finally the analyzer must be sensitive to the official nature of court records and the sieving process which evidence may have undergone before it appeared in writing. Without observing and avoiding such potholes in his path, the interpreter may well end up with "officially acceptable morality" rather than genuine popular morality.

Nevertheless the advantages of careful use of court records greatly outweigh these difficulties. As we shall discover, the large array of witnesses ranges across social classes, age bands, and genders. Frequently they are a random selection. They just happened to hear or see something relevant to a particular case. Their statements were often taken down verbatim by village constables or magistrates and have the authentic ring of seventeenth-century speech. As such they provide us with invaluable listening posts on the past, that mysterious "other country." Given both the intrinsic fascination of hearing our lost ancestors speaking and the fact that the Middlesex records have yet to be published, I make no excuse for frequent and sometimes extended quotation in the case studies in each chapter. The use of county records gives the added benefit of studying a wider range of experience than the detailed town studies. Within Middlesex there were varied communities: a seaport, a college town, country villages with or without resident magistrates, frontier settlements, "peaceable kingdoms," and feud-wracked settlements. From this variety we may arrive at a greater typicality.[18]

The half-century covered by this study starts with the earliest surviv-

ing records in the county courthouse in Cambridge. In 1649, the year of
John Winthrop's death, many of the first generation pioneers of Massachusetts Bay and Middlesex County were still alive. By 1699, the year
of Thomas Danforth's death (he arrived in Cambridge in 1635 at the age
of eleven), the third generation had grown to maturity. The fifty-year
time span (dictated by the mass of materials within the archive) gives us
an opportunity to examine change over time. Was the "declension," or
decline in spiritual and moral standards, which many contemporaries,
and their greatest interpreter Perry Miller, saw as the key movement of
New England in the seventeenth century a historical reality or the outcome of a romanticization of the past? Did it affect all classes and per-
suasions equally or were some groups more prone to following primrose paths than others? Was Middlesex relatively homogeneous in its
values or were two cultures diverging during the period: one godly,
"tribal," and conservative, the other pleasure-loving, earthly, and materialistic, reflecting the role models of popular literature with their self-
serving tricks and their cult of merriment? How did the behavior and
popular morality of New Englanders compare with those of the mother
country? Did the inexorable drawing of the quasi-independent colony
of 1649 into the ambit of the English nation after 1660—and particularly after 1686—give added impetus to social change? Did it have any
noticeable effect on sexual mores or family and community dynamics?

After an introductory description of the sources and the setting, this
study moves in a logical progression. The first section deals with extramarital sexuality among adolescents (defined throughout as people
between the ages of puberty and marriage): fornication, bridal pregnancy, breach of promise cases, and sexual deviancy. Was such behavior restricted to a criminal subculture or was it spread across the
social scale? Were the children of church members as prone as the nonelect? What was the life of adolescents like, and what does it tell us about
patriarchal power? The second section focuses on married people. It
analyzes marital problems and mismatched or unfaithful spouses in an
effort to discover what people expected of marriage and what their
standards of marital behavior were. Was marriage the inherently unequal relationship that many historians have depicted? The third section
looks at family dynamics by examining the treatment of dependents,
the relations with kin, and the nature of community interaction and
control. The conclusion assesses comparisons with contemporary
England, the reality and extent of declension, and the validity of the
Stone paradigm for the Middlesex area.

SEX IN MIDDLESEX

Introduction / Middlesex County and Its Records

THE county of Middlesex in Massachusetts was instituted in May 1643,[1] along with Suffolk and Essex. They replicated in the new world the major unit of local government and law enforcement in England, though their populations were comparatively minute. Middlesex covered the area to the north and west of Boston and originally included the towns of Cambridge and Charlestown (which alternated as the seats of the county court), Sudbury, Chelmsford, Reading, Concord, Woburn, and Watertown. By the end of the century Malden, Marlborough, Lancaster, Billerica, Groton, Framingham, Dunstable, Newton, Stow, Sherborn, Tyngsborough, Dracut, Worcester, and Medford had been incorporated or settled.[2] It was, of course, predominantly agricultural, but Charlestown, the largest town in the county, had a good harbor and Cambridge was the seat of Harvard College and, from 1639 to 1675, of the only printing press.

Various geographic, social, and economic factors during the period 1649 to 1699 led to the dispersal of the county's population away from its original base along the north bank of the Charles River to increasingly far-flung inland settlements. The relative shortness of the rivers in the bay area, the pressure of population, the need for good mixed farming land (meadow, arable, upland, and timber), the search for beaver pelts, and disagreements about town policies, all conditioned this process. Concord in 1635 was the first foundation away from the Charles River, and Sudbury, on the great trail westward to the Connecticut Valley, continued this process in 1637. By the end of the century the original three river settlements had subdivided into eight, while inland settlements had swelled to eleven. In 1690 their estimated populations totaled

MIDDLESEX COUNTY   1649–1699

5,555, compared to the 2,300 of the river towns.[3] Until new counties were instituted, the Middlesex County Court had cognizance of cases in distant settlements. Thus, in the 1650s, it dealt with serious cases in far western towns like Northampton and Springfield, and in the 1690s with cases in Worcester, forty miles west of the bay.

The county court met four times each year like English quarter sessions. The April and October sessions were customarily held at Cambridge, those in June and December at Charlestown. It had power "to hear and determine all causes, civil and criminal, not extending to life, member or banishment (which, with causes of divorce, are reserved to the Court of Assistants)."[4] The number of magistrates and associates on the bench varied from three to eight, but averaged five.[5] Thomas Danforth, Daniel Gookin, Simon Willard, Richard Russell, and his son James Russell dispensed justice and administered the county for several decades each.[6] This they did not only in court but also day by day in overseeing their localities; issuing warrants and recognizances; examining complainants, suspects, and witnesses; ensuring execution of judgments; arbitrating in minor disputes; and dealing summarily with petty causes such as swearing, idleness, or petty theft.[7] Such men were the "sword" of puritanism, the godly magistrates, to complement the "word" as preached by the divines. In reaction to English puritan criticism of "dumb dogges on the bench," the magistrates in Middlesex "embraced the duty of punishing all crime, of maintaining the integrity of the family and imposing rigorous moral standards on the community." They were active interventionists, "God's deputies," or "the Lord's gardeners, keeping the good plants watered, the weeds and stones thrown out that hinder growth, the hedge kept strong and good about it."[8] The court records are an eloquent tribute to their industry, dedication, public spirit, and judiciousness. As well as the magistrates, the grand jury (responsible for presentments of "any misdemeanours or breaches of such wholesome laws" to the court) and the jury of trials (all men of substance elected by their peers) were listed at the head of each sessions record.

Sexual misdemeanors represented only a small part (about five percent on average) of the business of the court. The Charlestown session which met on 2 April 1663 was fairly typical. The order book records:

1. Four civil actions for debt, non-performance of contract, trespass, &c.
2. Four grants of administration of estates of people recently dead.
3. Two men released from militia training because of infirmity or age.
4. Man fined for non-appearance at court. Two others forfeit £5 recognisances for non-performance.
5. Three criminal cases: disorderly conduct, lying, drawing away affections of a maid.
6. Two settlement disputes between towns. People likely to become a burden to their adopted town are ordered to return to permanent place of residence.
7. Three people released from bonds for good behaviour; one continued.
8. County, town appointments approved; licensees also approved.
9. Charlestown selectmen to oversee house repairs of poor family.
10. Date of next session set.

The justices also administered guardianship of minors, upkeep of highways and bridges, church attendance, probate, school provision, pounds, the county rate, and the treasurer's expenditure and accounts.

Much of this business would have been familiar to anyone acquainted with English quarter sessions, but the Massachusetts county courts were burdened with two additional types of cases which in the old country would have been handled by the civil courts or the hierarchy of ecclesiastical courts. English county benches would not normally have heard suits of trespass, debt, or defamation, nor would they have dealt with testamentary business, sabbath breaking, or moral offenses.[9]

During the period 1649 to 1663 the Court almost always completed its business in the time set, usually two days. By the end of the 1670s the increase of work, especially testamentary matters in the wake of King Philip's War and disputes between towns over settlement of paupers, led to the need for adjournment meetings. At times during the 1680s the pressure of court business was so great that one session might go on by weekly adjournments to within a week or two of the next session. The county court became a regular feature of life rather than an occasional one. A serious accumulation of cases caused considerable inconvenience to plaintiffs, complainants, and witnesses; it increased the costs of legal action by requiring hearings to be adjourned and people to leave and then return a week or two later.

The judicature act passed by the Dominion of New England in March 1687 had the effect of centralizing the administration of justice and separating equity and criminal proceedings.[10] The 1692 division of the county court into an Inferior Court of Pleas dealing with the often highly complex civil cases and a Court of General Sessions of the Peace similarly hastened criminal proceedings and improved the efficiency of county administration.[11] Nonetheless, the habit of adjournment had become so deeply ingrained that it was a common feature of the sessions in the 1690s.

In the early years of the Massachusetts Bay Colony, the magistrates had used their discretion in the handling of criminal cases. Winthrop defended this ad hoc approach on the grounds that the bench could make the punishment fit the crime and, more importantly for him, the criminal. Yet from the mid-1630s onward he was fighting a losing battle against the demands of the people and their deputies for "known laws to live by . . . in resemblance to Magna Charta." After Nathaniel Ward's *Body of Liberties* had been drawn up in 1641, *The Laws and Liberties of Massachusetts* were adopted in 1648, the year before the start of the Middlesex records. This insistent demand for codification of the law shows that the ideas that New Englanders carried over from England were very much those of the legal reformers—Ward and Winthrop among them—who had for decades sought radical changes in the tangled mess of English jurisprudence. Many of their proposals were adopted in the Massachusetts code and were the laws and practices followed by the Middlesex bench: hence the existence of a simplified code and the fact that all documents were written in English. Justice and probate business were decentralized; magistrates were annually elected as were juries; equity and canon law cases were incorporated in county courts with juries. Capital punishment for crimes against property was abolished, but moral enormities like adultery incurred the biblical penalty of death. In such ways Massachusetts achieved the revolution in English law which eluded the Barebones Parliament in England in 1653.[12]

Despite these striking improvements on the English legal system (which helped to obviate the need for a tribe of parasitic lawyers), criminal cases, unlike the civil actions which preceded them on court days, were normally tried by summary justice from the bench. It was very rare for the accused to elect to be tried by jury. Often, of course, the verdict was a foregone conclusion; an unmarried woman who had already given birth or a couple whose first child had arrived shortly after marriage could hardly plead not guilty of fornication. On the other hand there were, as we shall discover, plenty of contentious cases, especially over paternity, where the bench had to decide between conflicting evidence.

Much groundwork would have been done before the trial; the accused would have been examined by a magistrate, usually face to face with the complainant; depositions of witnesses would have been collected in writing. Since magistrates combined this inquisitorial role with the judicial, the examination might often act as the real trial when the examining magistrate decided in his own mind on the guilt or innocence of the accused. This is the explanation for the high conviction rate, around 90 percent, not only in Middlesex but in the other county courts, and for the rarity of appeals to the Court of Assistants.[13]

In sentencing, all judges should seek to strike a balance between retribution and reclamation. The attitude of those convicted will naturally weigh heavily with them. As one witness put it: "The more sensible you are of sin, the more hopes there is of marcy." In Middlesex, those who persisted in denying guilt against compelling evidence, or demanded jury trial, or offended persistently could expect harsher penalties than contrite confessors. We shall meet individuals who stuck to their stories until the last moment and then fulsomely admitted deceit, or who, after sentence, petitioned the court in self-abasing terms for reduction of punishment. In both kinds of cases, the bench reacted mercifully. "By repentance and forgiveness, the sinner could be brought back into full fellowship and the authority of the community reasserted." Thus in criminal as well as civil cases, the county court could and did perform a ritualized integrative function.[14]

Penalties for the commoner sexual offenses were quite varied in the early part of the period but tended toward greater uniformity in later decades. During the 1650s, for instance, punishments for premarital fornication ranged from forty shillings to ten pounds (five times as much) and from six stripes or lashes to fifteen. By the 1680s fines were commonly forty shillings, with ten stripes as an alternative; this was always the punishment imposed after 1692. Sanctions against fornication declined from five pounds or twenty stripes to forty shillings or ten stripes between 1681 and 1686. Weekly maintenance levied on reputed fathers was usually 2s. 6d. per week. Sexual abuse against a woman was almost always dealt with very severely. Men would receive at least twenty stripes, sometimes thirty or even forty. Often monetary alternatives were not offered; when they were, they were often at the stunning amount of fifteen or twenty pounds.

Male adultery was also harshly penalized;[15] in the 1680s an adulterer was offered the alternative of thirty stripes or a twenty pound fine. Promiscuous women could expect similar treatment. Corporal punishments were publicly administered as "dramatic spectacles of the consequences of crime" and ritual demonstrations of "publically established boundaries of acceptable behaviour." The shaming punishment of stocking was occasionally used for petty offenses like cursing and drunkenness. In some defamation cases public apology to the plaintiff was offered as an alternative to damages. All such punishments were meant to take place in an atmosphere of solemn soul-searching. One young man who was heard to invite his friends along to watch was rewarded with an extra ten strokes for his impertinence.[16]

The gradual change from varied to uniform sentencing arose from several causes. Although the codifications of the 1640s reduced the complete discretion that Winthrop had advocated, they still allowed considerable latitude. Thus, the penalty for fornication laid down in *The Book of General Laws and Liberties* of 1648 was "enjoyning to marriage, or fine or corporall punishment or all or any of these." With the new charter of 1692 and a consequent revision of Massachusetts laws, however, legislation laid down that offenders could either be fined five pounds or whipped up to ten strokes. There was much less room for judicial flexibility here. Another cause was more general. This was the almost inevitable routinization which an enlarged population and greater pressure of court business would produce. Furthermore David Grayson Allen has argued that after about 1660 "Massachusetts was becoming a legally rationalised system of government," leading to a loss of local discretion and a concomitant growth of uniformity of practice emanating from the central institutions of the colony. Finally, the magistracy was becoming more professionalized. English legal guides, notably Dalton's *Country Justice,* were consulted increasingly. Following such precedents would tend to reduce ad hominem sentencing.[17]

Massachusetts law of this period required "every judgment given in any court to be recorded in a book and all evidences (which are to be given in, in writing in fair and large papers) shall be kept."[18] In accordance with this, the court records consist of two types: court order or docket books and court files. The order books usually merely record judgments and sentences in civil and criminal cases, and the multifarious administrative decisions in running the county. Four order books, entitled "County Court Records," cover the period 1649 to 1692, with a gap between 1663 and 1671 because the second order book was destroyed in a fire in 1671. After 1692 the records dealing with sexual offenses are found in "Sessions Records 1692–1723." The county court records from 1686 to 1689 are also found at the back of this volume.[19]

The court files contain documents associated with individual cases, writs, arrest warrants, attachments, recognizances, deeds, wills, examinations, bills of cost, depositions, petitions, presentments, verdicts, and administrative documents like venires, testamentary papers, committee reports, warrants for payments, or selectmen's returns. One hundred seventy-two files cover the period 1649–1699, and each file averages about eighty documents.[20]

By extrapolating from Files 33 to 57 it has been possible to reconstruct to some extent the sexual misdemeanors in the destroyed order book covering the years 1663 to 1671. The verdicts and sentences have only occasionally survived. Nevertheless, the extrapolations have produced a reasonably accurate run of cases of sexual misbehavior for the second half of the seventeenth century in Middlesex County, with, in many instances, a large amount of revealing supporting evidence.

The incidence of sexual misdemeanors convicted in the Middlesex County Court between 1649 and 1699 is set out in table 1.[21] Although offenses are normally listed as the authorities perceived them, cases of male adultery, usually treated by the court in the same way as fornication, are here cited as adultery. Similarly bastardy cases where the alleged father denied responsibility are entered under both fornication or adultery and disputed paternity, and entries under separated spouses (wife-beating, scolding, and wife company-keeping) also involve some

Table 1 / Incidence of Conviction for Sexual Misdemeanors in Middlesex County, 1649–1699

	Court Record Book, 1 1649–63 (Pulsifer 1)	Files 33–57 1663–71	Court Record Book, 3 1671–80 (Pulsifer 3)	Court Record Book, 4 1681–86 (Pulsifer 4)	Sessions Records, 1 (Back) 1686–89 (Sessions Records A)	Court Record Book, 5 1689–92 (County Court Records 5)	Sessions Records, 1692–99 (Sessions Records I)	Totals
MARITAL								
Spouses living apart or contentiously	6	2	4	–	–	–	1	13
Wife-beating	7	1	1	1	–	–	1	11
Scolding	3	1	–	–	–	–	–	4
Wife company-keeping	3	1	2	1	–	–	1	8
Adultery	2	1	–	4	–	4	2	13
Bigamy	1	1	–	–	–	–	–	2
Irregular marriage	–	2	–	–	–	–	–	2
Incest	–	–	–	1	–	1	–	2

EXTRAMARITAL								
Fornication	12	9	22	11	4	13	25	96
Premarital sex	7	10	9	13	4	5	18	66
Promiscuous women	2	3	2	2	–	2	6	17
Disputed paternity	–	2	2	–	–	1	2	7
Sexual dalliance	7	1	3	2	–	2	1	16
VIOLENCE AND DEVIATION								
Sadism	2	1	1	–	–	2	–	6
Rape and sexual abuse	8	5	6	6	–	1	1	27
Sexual slander	5	6	1	3	–	1	–	16
Attempted abortion	–	1	1	2	–	–	–	4
Cases involving blacks	2	2	8	3	–	4	1	20

duplications. Sexual dalliance refers to cases in which various kinds of flirtation, petting, and philandering could be proved. Cases involving Negroes—occasionally misbehaving with whites—duplicate entries elsewhere. Instances of "adulterous carriages" are subsumed, for women, under the headings of "Wife company-keeping" and "Promiscuous women," and for men, under "Sexual abuse."

Cases from Sessions Records 1 (back), covering the years of the ill-fated Dominion of New England experiment, are notably low in the number of entries; this reflects a marked general decline in the business of the court during these years.[22] Some offenses neglected then may, however, have been taken up in the subsequent sessions after the so-called Glorious Revolution in the colony in April 1689. The cases listed from the files in column two may also be lower because evidence of conviction is not always available there.

The general trend of the statistics suggests a gradual increase in the commoner forms of sexual misdemeanor. Thus, the two convictions for adultery in the thirteen-year period covered by the first order book are doubled in the five-and-one-half year period in column four and trebled in the ten-and-one-quarter year period of the last two columns. Fornication averages only one case each year in the period 1649–71, doubles from 1671–86, and almost quadruples in the last decade covered by columns six and seven. The records thus mirror the 1665 comment that this "shamefull sin [is] much increasing amongst us." Seven cases of bridal pregnancy in the period 1649–63 have risen to twenty-six in the same time span at the end of the century. Convictions of sexually promiscuous women similarly quadrupled in number.

One reason for these increases was undoubtedly the growth of population, though the calculation of bastardy and bridal pregnancy ratios is bedeviled by the paucity of population figures for the county. From the figures assembled by Robert E. Wall, it appears that Middlesex numbered 2,990 in 1647 and 5,361 in 1666.[23] Assuming that the birthrate in the period 1649 to 1663 averaged forty births per annum per each thousand of population,[24] this would convert twelve fornication convictions recorded in the first book of court records into a mean bastardy ratio of 0.55 percent of all births per annum, and prenuptially conceived babies would represent an average 0.32 percent of all babies born each year. Using the militia lists of 1690 and Rossiter's calculation of a 29 percent decadal increase in population for the 1690s, the numbers of the county would have grown to 9,320 in 1690 and to 12,017 by 1699.[25] (See table 2.) With the same birthrate, the average bastardy ratio would have risen to 0.90 percent per annum,[26] and premarital conceptions to

0.54 percent.[27] It cannot be too strongly stressed that population figures for seventeenth-century New England can never be more than intelligent estimates. Nevertheless, two conclusions seem warranted. First, the ratio of fornication and premarital fornication did increase between 1649 and 1699, and second, these offenses were markedly rarer in Middlesex than they were in contemporary England.[28]

Table 2 / Estimated Town Populations—1647, 1666, and 1690

	1647	1666	1690
Watertown (1630)★	750	790	755
Charlestown (1630)	644	904	490
Cambridge (1631)	604	990	590
Sudbury (1639)	304	320	515
Concord (1635)	274	510	810
Woburn (1642)	274	424	710
Reading (1644)	140	304	375
Newton (1688)			385
Medford (1630)		240	100
Malden (1649)		300	365
Groton (1655)		30	290
Marlborough (1660)		55	340
Chelmsford (1655)		200	490
Dunstable (1673)			155
Billerica (1655)		240	525
Lancaster (1653)		54	290
Sherborn (1674)			315
Stow (1683)			145
TOTALS	2990	5361	9320

★Dates are for incorporation.

One category of sexual offense went against the trend: crimes of violence in either deed or word. Cases of rape and sexual harassment were very rare in the last decade of our period compared with twenty-five in the first thirty-six years. Similarly reduced were convictions for sexual slanders.[29]

Table 3 / Geographical Incidence of Sexual Misdemeanors

	1649–63	1663–71	1671–80	1680–86	1686–89	1689–92	1692–99	Totals
Watertown	6	2	5	4	4	1	6	28
Woburn	11	1	5	3	0	6	1	27
Charlestown	6	9	9	13	4	8	11	60
Malden	5	3	5	2	0	1	1	17
Cambridge	13	4	5	4	1	1	3	31
Chelmsford	1	1	1	1	0	1	2	7
Reading	1	1	2	0	0	1	1	6
Concord	3	2	4	2	0	0	3	14
Medford	2	1	1	0	0	0	0	4
Sudbury	1	4	3	2	0	0	4	14
Lancaster	1	1	0	1	0	3	0	6
Marlborough	0	2	0	1	0	2	2	7
Billerica	0	0	3	3	0	0	3	9
Groton	0	0	1	0	0	0	2	3
Worcester						1	0	1
Stow							1	1
Newton							4	4
Sherborn							1	1
Dracut							2	2
TOTALS	50	31	44	36	9	25	47	242

Table 3 shows the geographical spread of all but eleven sexual misdemeanors in the county, chronologically divided in the same way as table 1. Charlestown's eminence will be explained below. The breaking off into new settlements and the migration of youth to the frontier help account for the decreasing entries of some older towns, like Cambridge or Malden, and the increase in sexual crimes in the inland towns, notably in the 1690s. Small fluctuations in individual towns were probably due to complex local factors such as the quality of leadership, the discipline of adolescents, and the presence or absence of problem families.

Some 480 witnesses testified in cases of sexual misdemeanor. Women slightly outnumbered men as witnesses, notably in their official role as midwives.[30] Although miscreants could be depicted as not representative of puritan culture as a whole, the nearly five hundred witnesses, who frequently revealed attitudes and opinions about sexuality, are a remarkably varied sample of the county population. They range in age from seven to eighty-three and in social status from a Negro slave to the deputy-governor. As fortuitous witnesses they can be seen with some justification as a random selection of the population. As such they represent an invaluable source of evidence about sexual mores in a typical New England county.

The churches of Christendom might slaughter each other in their thousands, but they did agree that there was only one proper place for sexuality and that was the marriage bed. Newlyweds should enter it—"a thing undefiled"—unspotted virgins. The authority of biblical, canon, and statute law was reinforced with emphatic urgency by countless puritan sermons, moral tracts, and conduct books. All asserted that the primary agency for enforcing chastity was the family, buttressed where necessary by the community and its officials.

The major question we must confront in this part of the study is why, comparatively speaking, the ratios of bastardy and premarital fornication in Middlesex were low. Was it the result of patriarchal power within households isolated from the compensating influences of peer or gender or kinship groups? Did the puritanical "family governors" of the county, supported by a culture constantly stressing obedience, resistance to temptations, the need for conversion, and an obsession with purity, so dominate their offspring that these will-broken, guilt-laden, rule-conscious young people were forced into suppressing or repressing their sexual drives during the long wait from puberty to marriage? Was courtship, with its important element of property exchange and economic linkage between two families, considered far too serious to be left to the whim of the courters?

If these were indeed the reasons for the low levels of sexual offenses among the unmarried, then we should expect certain conclusions to follow. The bulk of cases should occur among those households which in one way or other were exceptional: families without fathers or with weak, lazy, or incompetent patriarchs; families with a background of problems or with nonpuritan beliefs. We should, in short, be able to detect "a sub-culture of the bastardy-prone." Among members of the dominant culture, and especially among those "born within the covenant of grace" we should anticipate widespread adult control of brainwashed, isolated adolescents. Young people should have been taught to prize their virginity, to abjure extrafamilial company and to sublimate flighty romantic ideas to the considerations of family economics. Where these chattels of their fathers occasionally erred, we should look for internalized guilt to induce full and candid penitence.

Before we examine in greater detail the circumstances in which extra- and premarital sexual activity took place, reactions to such breaches of the moral code, the typical backgrounds of such malefactors, and what the cases tell us about early-modern adolescence, we must first turn to the problem of numbers. Were the cases which came to court a true measure of the frequency of sexual activity among the unmarried, or were they just a suggestion of what remained undetected?

1 / Fornication: Detection and Evasion

EXUAL intercourse between couples when both were unmarried was a crime in seventeenth-century Massachusetts. The law did not formally require that pregnancy should occur or that an illegitimate child should be born before there was any prosecution. As we shall see, however, almost all the cases which came before the county court arose from the birth of a bastard. Yet modern fertility experts calculate that "the probability of pregnancy from a single act of coitus was about one in fifty" or, put another way, a couple needed to have slept together fifty times on average before impregnation took place.[1] It is therefore perfectly feasible that many more young people had engaged in sexual activity than those unlucky few who produced bastards. Furthermore, unmarried girls who found themselves pregnant might resort to abortion or even infanticide to conceal the fact of their crime. Even where unmarried mothers were convicted, the authorities still had the problem of finding the actual father and ensuring that he maintained the child. This chapter explores the means that were used to discover fornication among the unmarried and the means used to frustrate discovery and conviction. We shall attempt to arrive at a just estimate of successful detection and successful evasion. Only then will we have some measure of the actual as opposed to the convicted level of sexual activity among adolescents.

Means of Detection

There were two means of detecting fornicators before a pregnancy occurred: either catching the culprits in the act or spontaneous confession. It was, however, rare to suffer the fate of Thomas Abbott and Anne Williamson: on 1 June 1653 "being between eight and nine o'clock in the morning" Elizabeth Betts, their dame, "went into the kitchen where I saw Anne Williamson's clothes up her waist and the said Abbott with his body working and in motion towards her body with his armes encompassing her hipps and her arms encompassing Abbott's shoulders."[2] It was equally unusual for single people to behave like the nineteen-year-old Mary Edwards of Charlestown, who accused Samuel Starr "of having the carnall knowledge of her body . . . but she knew not whether she was with childe or no."[3] Throughout the records for our period there are only four eyewitness accounts of couples caught in flagrante delicto and only one spontaneous confession.

Nonetheless, evidence culled from confessions, examinations, and depositions suggests that amorously inclined adolescents could usually find opportune times and places to pursue their affairs. The commonest time was, not surprisingly, "in the night season." Robert Shepard's boast was not untypical: "He said it was not the first time he had been with maids after his master was abed."[4] John Grant of Watertown tried to allay suspicion by going out on watch and then climbing back into his father's house where Sarah Fiske was staying.[5] The elderly Elizabeth Pierce, who lived with her daughter Mary Tufts, "often heard somebody moving in the house late at night and doors opening. I told Goodman Tufts of it but he was weary and careless."[6] Examples of amorous servants upright when their masters and dames were supine could be multiplied many times.[7] If for some reason the cats were out during the daytime, mice might play in the empty house. Thus Susan Martin confessed to committing fornication with her fellow servant John Baker when they were left alone on the last general militia training day.[8] Days of private meetings of church members, election and court days, or sacrament days were mentioned as other opportunities of freedom from supervision.[9]

The place was presumably determined to a considerable extent by the seasons. One witness claimed to have seen a couple on the ground beside a barn in December, but a Massachusetts winter was hardly conducive to alfresco lovemaking.[10] Although there are several accounts of outdoor surprisals during the warm weather—for instance Moses Whitney's in late May 1674 of Thomas Loverun and Ruth Sawtle "in a secrett place under a great rock not farr from Bever brooke and not above sixty rod from old Sawtles house"—the commonest trysting places were the chambers or firesides of houses.[11]

Sometimes intimacy occurred while a man and woman were working together. In July 1668, for example, Elizabeth Wells and James Tufts were unloading a cart of wheat. He criticized the way she was stacking.

> He took hold of me about the middle and I took hold of the barn beam. He took hold of my hands and so drew me down. I said to him he was worse than Zacharee Hill and so he pressed upon me with his knees that I could not help myself. Then I desired him to let me rise for I laie at very little ease but he said he would not unless I would lie down in another place but he did take his will of me where I laie.[12]

More often outbuildings were refuges from the prying eyes and ears of master, dame, and other servants.[13] Even there lovers were not always safe. When visitors investigated the goings-on in William Everton's stable, they found Elizabeth Brown hiding in the corner, "like a woman surprised somewhat."[14] William Clark, a cooper, claimed an experience reminiscent of a Restoration whore story. In November 1665 he was lying with Hannah Green, servant of Charlestown, when "a noise affrighted him and made him run away & he then carried away in haste her petticoat instead of his britches & carried it aboard Capt Allen's ship & showed it to Sam Sherman."[15] Goodwife Grant discovered "after last training in Cambridge [that] Mary Grant was not in her bed." She found her "in the leanto barn with Daniel Smith, whom she chid for unseasonable company keeping and took sd. Mary in. She also found Daniel Smith and Mary Grant in the backroom at a very unseasonable hour."[16] Andrew Robinson's absence was likewise detected by his master and dame, who locked him out. He was discovered the next morning in the barn.[17] John Needham chose the entry to Samuel Frost's shop for his nefarious activities with Frost's daughter; Christopher Grant inveigled Sarah Crouch to an empty house,[18] and John Jones came after Mary Bell in the cellar and "wid a kiste her and wid a putt his handes under her apron."[19]

These examples and many more we shall encounter only emerged subsequently in court. How much more unsupervised lovemaking was going on is a matter of conjecture. Some statements suggest it may have been considerable. Thus John Phillips boasted that "he had to do with sundry young women whom he named."[20] Robert Shepard claimed to be a Cambridge Lothario. Abigail Blood confessed that "she had had to do with so many" that she could not tell who was the father of her bastard.[21] Zechariah Hill plainly had a reputation for meddling with the maids. From evidence similar to this, David Flaherty has argued that "the prosecuted cases were only the most visible manifestations of illicit sexual activity. Most immoral acts escaped the attention of the law."[22] Our conclusion must carefully weigh this possibility.

In the normal course of events it was only when the results of extra-marital sexual activity were betrayed by obvious pregnancy or even delivery that action was initiated. Delivery effectively convicted the unmarried mother, and the main problem of the authorities was to discover the father "that the sin may be punished and the town pre-vented from charge." For many selectmen these priorities seem to have been reversed, especially when questions of settlement and thus finan-cial responsibility were involved.[23]

Sometimes the father confessed and acknowledged paternity before or after the mother named him. Thus John Baker charged in April 1654 with fornication with his fellow servant Susan Martin frankly admit-ted, "I had the use of her body in a carnall way and did comitt fornica-tion with her." The couple were "to be severely whipped twelve stripes apiece upon their naked bodies before the public concourse and are also injoined to marry."[24] This injunction, not uncommon in the 1650s, Susan met with adamant refusal. Later she changed her mind, married Baker in May, and bore him twelve children at Woburn where they settled.

Sometimes the father would incriminate himself before witnesses. On 20 June 1665 Thomas Barrett and his wife "were discorsing Christopher Bannister about going up of the poste together . . . I said to said Bannister I heard one say he would be put[25] by [here, he paused], at which Bannister asked By whom, to which I answeared By one of Sudbury, but not willing to say whom. Thereuppon Bannister said Mary Parminter . . . This was spoken before I heard of any accusation made by Mary against him."[26] But what if the man named as reputed father denied paternity, as many did "vehemently" or "positively" or "as God is my witness"? Without witnesses to the act, self-incrimina-tion, or confession, the verdict depended on the unsatisfactory process of believing one person's word against another's.

New procedures similar to practice in England were introduced by the Massachusetts General Court in 1668 to improve the process.[27] Two witnesses in the Robinson and Wells case in 1669 described how "last winter there was talk of the new law whereby if any man were ac-cused with a bastard and the woman held to it in her labour he would be the reputed father."[28] For the rest of this period the word of the prospective mother during the agony of "travail" was normally ac-cepted as incontrovertible. Unfortunately this did not entirely solve the problem of correctly identifying the father nor did it put to rest bitter wrangles arising from disputed paternity cases.

However faulty, the new law added an extra element to crime detection: midwives and their assistants.[29] Until the Wells case, midwives had only been called on twice to testify. In 1661 four women of Providence assured the court that Abigail Grant's bastard had succumbed to "sickness & vomiting and looseness" thus dispelling any suspicion of infanticide.[30] The Sudbury midwives were asked the probable date of conception of the Bent's baby in 1667. They judged

> that the child was come to full maturity: we found these signes, viszt. nayles upon the fingers and tooes haire upon the head as long & thicke as most children we have seene, & the navell string dyed off which was about five or six dayes after her delivery and that it sucked hartily. . . .

The two women subsequently questioned Elizabeth Bent as to the father and the date of conception, but this was a *week after delivery*. As if to demonstrate the necessity of the new law, she lied to them blatantly, as we shall see.[31]

Midwives were still called upon after 1668 to adjudicate upon prematurity, to certify that mothers were too ill to attend court, or that the death of babies was through natural causes,[32] but their profession now, as in England, took on a quasi-judicial, inquisitorial role. In July 1689, Sarah Blake, a single woman, went into labor. When Hannah Wilson, in the presence of Mary Peirce and Frances Thompson, asked her to name the father, she refused. The midwife said that

> if she would not tell me I could not help her & she tould me yes I must help her: I tould her I would not if she would not tell me who was the father of the child . . . she tould me it was Joseph Winn, the young Joseph Winn . . . she said he promised her mariage before that time . . . I asked her had she had no temptation to make away with the child & she said it was past her skill . . . she said it was begat abroad.[33]

When Elizabeth Mellins, a widow, was brought to bed in 1698,

> Elizabeth Paine [the midwife] tould her that she was in a very dangros condition, that none would help her without she would tell us the right father . . . this might be her last breath . . . she must answer as she would before God another day and then she would have help . . . if any other man ever offerred her such abuse . . . Elizabeth Mellins was constant that it was Samuel Sprague.[34]

In the same year Elizabeth Frost's midwife reported:

In her extremity & thinking she was fetching her last breath she said if I dy this minute it was John Needhams. I said it would be a dreadfull thing to dy with a ly on your mouth, to which she replied as I look to Answer it another day I spak the truth.[35]

Sarah Ward's midwife questioned her "as in the presence of God . . . as she looked for help from Him in this her condition."[36]

Midwives were often elderly women, sometimes, like Anne Hutchinson, from leading families. Occasionally, there is evidence that they abused their power. For example, Susannah Coburn's 1696 childbed response of "I must perish for I do not know" the father, was explained by her subsequent charging of John Varnum.

Being at the house of old goodman Varnum [John's father] and few of my friends with me, and being in great pains the daughter of Goodman Varnum [Hannah Coburn] came to me and asked me who was the father. I then gave her to understand whose it was. Soon after she returned and told me John denied it. She charged me not to lay the child to any of her brothers. If I did her mother [the midwife] would not help me and therefore I should not own any father for it. Being in great fear that I should perish I did not tell who the father was though often asked. Joseph Varnum [John's brother] said that if any body laid a bastard child to any of them they would hand thair house blood.[37]

Another possible perversion of justice may have occurred in the Dunster prenuptial fornication case of 1693. The ancient Cambridge midwife Goody Bowers seemed genuinely forgetful in her evidence, but Sarah Swan's confusion about prematurity may have been more calculated. After the case against the scions of two leading families had been dropped, Gershom Swan worked Dunster land on highly preferential terms.[38]

Means of Evasion

The new law of 1668 also placed power in the hands of single women. Jane Bowen wrote to her lover, "I am a-child by you and I wil either kil it or lay it to another & you shal have no blame at all for I have had many children and have none of them placed to their [real] fathers."[39] Elizabeth Wells, during a discussion of the law of 1668, announced that "if shee should be with child shee would be fain to lay it on to one who was rich enough able to maintain it whether it were his or no." She spoke of "a maid in England with child [who] laid it to the wrong father. The midwife urging her to confess in a long sore travaill the maid said when the apple is ripe it will fall." When there was talk of "a maid who accused three different men, Elizabeth replyed I would hold unto the man I had first charged although he had never been near me."[40]

William Hudson, presented in April 1691, bewailed "the dangers that whores accuse rich single men or married men as the fathers of their bastards."[41] A man protesting his innocence was often asked if some other male might be responsible. Hudson produced evidence that "in August [1689] the soldier John Fay had been at the house of Ephraim Roper in Lancaster, in or on the bed with the sd. Mercy Rugg lying upon his belly with some violent motions towards her." Fay had, in the meantime, conveniently or coincidentally died. The protesting Hudson was eventually judged by the court to be the reputed father.[42]

Some suspects were alleged to have concealed an abortion or a birth. The Bloods were a leading but somewhat disreputable family of Groton. The father, Richard Blood (a selectman, large landowner, and Indian trader), had several convictions from the 1660s to the 1680s for illicitly selling liquor to Indians; his daughter-in-law Abigail, widowed in the Indian raid of 1692, fled to Andover in 1695 "to lay down her illegitimate burden."[43] In October 1678 four leading townsmen alleged that in the preceding April they had seen Richard's daughter Hannah looking "big like a woman with child . . . a little before the morneing preceding the loss of her great belly she was as big as a woman ready to lẏ in." "Some of Bloods family left their usuall lodging that night & lay in an empty house not far from there." A note adds: "Mr. [Henry] Willard can informe of her using savin [abortifacient] the last summer." Hannah herself had responded to rumors of her pregnancy with "she did not know but that she might." After the alleged delivery, she disappeared as did any offspring. The Bloods denied all knowledge of the affair.[44]

The dangerously indiscreet Elizabeth Wells displayed signs of pregnancy in 1668. Mary Tufts, her dame, "questioned her and she said nobody in New England ever had to do with her: she had been as fat as this for two years in England." Unconvinced, Tufts "did threaten to send her water to Dr. Snelling" at which Elizabeth confessed.[45] She had already taken savin boiled in beer. Had she not been thus cornered she might well have committed infanticide after a secret delivery. She boasted to one of her retentive young gossips how she had

left a boy of two years in bed in England & rann away up to London with her breasts full of milk to come to New England . . . her nurses little girl did often draw [the milk from] her breasts for her. . . . She and another buried four Bastards in a garden in England . . . she pulled a verie good handkerchief from her neck to bury one of them in.[46]

We know from testimony that knowledge of abortifacient herbs was widespread, yet evidence of the use of savin or other herbs was offered in only four cases, and in three of them the women later gave birth.[47] One would-be seducer claimed that he had some "steel powder" which would prevent conception, but he never got the chance to demonstrate its properties.[48] Only one Middlesex couple were charged with infanticide before the Court of Assistants during this period and they were acquitted.[49] In three other suspicious cases, the authorities were reassured by the evidence of midwives or by exhumation that the infant had died by natural causes.[50] Clandestine self-deliveries were not unknown. Thus Mercy Rugg evaded the questions of midwives and attendants by having her child in an old cellar a considerable distance from her father's house.[51]

A common means of attempting to evade detection lay in flight.[52] On the cover of a letter used in evidence in 1671 is written "Letter of Mary Ball to Michael Bacon her master by whom she saith she is with child." The contents, addressed from Rhode Island to Woburn, are a plea for money and a plaint about loneliness and neglect. There is both a veiled threat—"I will have to return to Massachusetts if I receive not timely relief"—and an appeal that "those promises which were made by you . . . I hope will not be forgotten by you." When Bacon was arrested on John Ball's complaint, he broke out of prison and fled. Thomas Danforth ordered a hue and cry.[53]

Abigail Grant, pregnant by Roger Rose, a seaman of Charlestown who was "contracted to Jamaca and could not gett cleare," likewise escaped to Providence to have her baby.[54] In 1674 one of the sureties for Elizabeth Cole reported "doubts that she may run away." She was taken into custody.[55] In 1690 Consider Sampson, servant maid to John Pratt, disappeared for a considerable period. She was convicted of fornication in February 1691.[56] In the same year the selectmen of Medford warned out or ordered out of town "Katherine Groce of Charlestown, singlewoman bigg with child."[57] Attempts were made in the late 1690s to bribe the pregnant Elizabeth Mellins to go away to have her illegitimate baby.[58] In 1698 the Deputy Sheriff had to go on two expeditions to Worcester to recapture Mary Middleton "with child with a bastard" and return her to Boston.[59] In the 1690s, constables' reports increasingly resembled that of Concord's in 1697: "I have inquiered dilligently after [an unmarried mother] but cannot finde her or hear anything of her." The birds had flown.[60]

If the mother stayed to face the consequences, there were nonetheless other ways of "saving the father harmless."[61] Sarah Baker of Woburn charged Sherebiah Roberts with fathering her bastard in April 1691. However "no such person is known." By May the forename had been changed to Archibald, but no one of that name was ever convicted.[62] Sarah Pore obstinately refused to name the father of her second child until a severe flogging was threatened.[63] Widow Mary Edes similarly stayed mute. Perhaps this procedure of identification lost its persuasive powers after the first experience of childbirth.[64] Dorothy Hildreth's premature delivery in 1697 was so sudden and quick that Mary Adams the midwife heard her cry out but by the time she entered the room the baby was born; "sd. Dorothy was in travail paines still and her life despaired of if not given present help." There was, in other words, no time or opportunity for the customary interrogation.[65]

Another, somewhat desperate, means of shielding the true father was a quick marriage to another man. The midwife and assistants at the confinement of Martha Dix in February 1698 assumed it was her husband's child and subjected her to no interrogation. Eight months later, after John Dix "asserted that he did not know who was the father and that he had nothing to do with her before marriage," Martha was fined forty shillings for fornication; no man was convicted with her.[66] In a letter to the court dated 8 May 1690 Captain John Wing of Worcester described how two servants of Major Thomas Savage had come to be married. "Mary suffered a negar to lie with her by whom she was with child and therefore she suffered Thomas Atherton her fellow servant to lie with her. She then told her master [about Atherton] and he forced Thomas to marry her." The mulatto to which she gave birth "is living yett at Hingham."[67] A few women like Abigail Blood were so free and easy that they might genuinely be unable to name one father.[68]

The father might also seek to enter into a private arrangement for support of the mother and child and thus escape legal involvement. In May 1692, James Russell examined Elizabeth Ross face to face with John Coller of Sudbury. Despite his denial that "ever he had to do with her," she "affirms that John Coller lay with her three times at her brother Eleazer Whitneys & she knew no other man and another time going from Whitneys to her mother Rosses in Sudbury." The testimony of her sister and brother-in-law help to explain Coller's denial.

The Deposition of Dorithe Whitene aged about twenty five years testifyeth that I meet with John Choler at Mr Flints farm about the third of May last past and I asked him if he cold safely say Befor God that he had never nothing to doe with my sister in that way of uncleaness and he said no he could not clear himself of that thing for if he did he should wrong his owne Conchance then I asked him John if you will not Deny it why will you not owne it and he answered that if he owned it he should then lye under the Laish of the Law.

At this point they met her husband, who takes up the story.

I called to him when I saw him and he said you Rog[u]e have you got your warant about you and I sad no for if I had I wold not come to him without serving it and he answered you Rog you have; but if you have, I have got a Good Clob and we came to gether, and he said he was sorree for my sister for she was one that he had a Great Love for and he told me he had given her a three shilling pece of mony and he asked me what we wold have more and I told that their was something to be considered for her lying in and he answered he would not have us nor her troble our selves about her for he said he wold help us or her to mony to provid for her lying in[69] for he had thirty shillings in his poket and if the child lived it should be no charg to her friends nor the Town for he wold maintain it and he wold provid for her as well as if she ware his own wife and if he and she could agree after she was delivered he wold maree her and he said he was not willing to owne it for then he should Lye under the Laish of the Law and if ever they com to court he wold pay her fine for what he had don was best known to himself. Then John Choler and I went and sate down together and he said Eelezer I will tell you what when I was a coming home from Canada that we ware like to be cast away and I made some vows to God that if he wold deliver me and bring me safe hom again that I wold mend my Life and forsake my evel way but I have broken my vows and theirfor it was just with God to leve me to what he had.

It is unclear whether Coller meant "the Laish of the Law" literally or figuratively. He plainly objected, however, to official involvement in what he wanted to keep as a private obligation. In July 1692 he was pressed for further military service, and the only sentence recorded is the customary forty shilling fine or ten stripes for Elizabeth Ross in October.[70]

John Needham of Billerica sought respite from the accusations of Elizabeth Frost in November 1698 by a calculated piece of bribery to her father.[71]

I am clear in conscience of the charges made against me concerning your dafter. . . . This dorty business for peas and quiatness sake I shal not be against giving a smal mater [£15] for to be quiat. . . . It were best for you for I can live in another place as well as this. . . . I shal not live long upon the land for I doe desire to go to se very speadily for I have disposed of my estate . . . you are not like to have one farding thereof if you wil not take som thing while you may. . . . Mr Joseph Crosby [will] talk with you about this thing . . . my desin is to go away the beginning of next week.

He complained in court about the "unjust odiom" he had borne and concluded:

I know according to the letter of the law that I am culpable being so charged by a woman (however innocent I am) . . . I acknowledge this humbling providence and crave your honours favour.

Their honors judged John Needham to be the reputed father of the child and ordered him to pay 2s. 6d. maintenance per week. Needham appealed to the superior court whose judgment is not known.[72]

Benjamin Cheney or China of Cambridge and Mercy Page of Watertown managed to elude the authorities for seventeen months after their bastard was born clandestinely in 1698.[73] Cheney's twenty pounds supported the mother and financed the child's long-term fostering. Only his boasting of his paternity incriminated him.[74]

Lies to the midwife or inducements for her to lie, concealed births or abortions, flight, tricked marriages, private accommodations or bribery—such were the evasive tactics practiced by male and female fornicators. Denial, deceit, desertion, and dissembling became more frequent within the period under study. In the twelve fornication cases recorded in the first court order book, covering the period 1649–63, ten of the fathers were convicted on their own confessions. In the other two cases, grounds for conviction are not recorded, but there is no suggestion that the men involved attempted to evade their responsibilities. In all these early cases the men received punishment in the form of fines or whippings similar to their female partners.

The files covering the second phase, 1663–71, present a striking change in the response to accusations. Instead of the straightforward admissions of previous years, dishonesty is rampant. In three cases, couples confessed that their initial statements were false: in two, the wrong man was named as father; in the third, the father was caught in his lying denial. Three more cases involved disputed paternity; in the nature of such cases someone must have been lying. Another two couples blatantly misled magistrates about their freedom to marry. The ninth case involved a girl's trenchant accusation being met by equally trenchant negation.

By the time the third order book starts in 1671 and sentences are regularly recorded again, the new law of 1668 was in force. Men who denied paternity but were reputed by the bench to be fathers of bastards escaped punishment but had to enter recognizances to support the child. There are more convictions in the period 1671–80—twenty-two—than in the preceding twenty-two years, and attempts to escape responsibility correspondingly increase. In eight cases one of the accused lied; in seven there is evidence of absconding. Only one man ran away in the eleven cases between 1681 and 1686, but seven men or women attempted to deceive the court. Flight by one or both parties grew in popularity between 1689 and 1699. In the fifteen accusations made between 1689 and 1691, seven suspects tried to escape; twenty-two people involved in thirty-one accusations made between 1692 and 1698 absconded. In twenty-two cases between 1689 and 1699 either the unmarried mother or the alleged father lied. Attempts to keep knowledge of illegitimate children from the authorities while privately maintaining them was a new development of the 1690s. Indeed, by this decade, it had become exceptional for the man named as father by the mother to admit his guilt by a frank confession as had been the norm forty years before.

An area of reported behavior where there are strong grounds for skepticism is the frequency of sexual intercourse admitted in some confessions. Usually only one or two acts of coition are mentioned, often with specific circumstantial detail.[75] Sarah Dawes[76] owned to making love twice within the space of fifteen weeks; Susan Martin[77] once, on a given day; Anne Williamson[78] twice, "the first time a good space since." When Elizabeth Bent[79] was asked by the midwife if James Taylor had "to do with her over once," she answered, "Severall times." Elizabeth Wells carefully specified two times; Sarah Crouch, with similar detail, "three times he had the use of her body."[80] Elizabeth Cole, Mary Pike, and Rachel Smith were quite insistent that they had only succumbed once.[81] Susannah Woodward was unique in reeling off a long list of bouts with Thomas Hastings "for all of which miscarriages . . . she craved forgiveness."[82] Rebecca Hamlett confessed to lying with Jack Negro "many times," but as his denial was accepted by the court, her claim is hardly compelling.[83] William Healey, caught in the act, admitted that "this was not the first time he had had her."[84] Doubts about the girls who confessed to only one or two sexual encounters are reinforced by Sarah Vinton's statement of 20 June 1681: "I desiar too be deeply humbled in that I sayed he had no moar to doo with me but once when he had divers times." Given the unlikelihood of conception occurring from occasional acts of coition, we must conclude that many girls were lying in their confessions about the extent of their sexual experience.[85]

Conclusion

The examples of perjured or absconding suspects and other types of evasiveness might lead us to believe that the actual level of sexual experience among the unmarried was a good deal higher than the court records suggest. It could be argued that only when a girl was unlucky enough to become obviously pregnant was her sexual activity in danger of being investigated, and that even then, the chances of her partner being truly named and forced to shoulder his financial responsibilities were modest, at least after 1663.

Before accepting that the fornication on record was only a small indication of the activity, however, we should consider evidence to the contrary about the efficiency of law enforcement within the county. The sheer number of people in each town who were officially responsible for law and order is impressive. Lay officers included any resident magistrate or associate or commissioner for small causes; the constable (larger towns like Cambridge and Charlestown had two); the town selectmen, who might number seven leading citizens; the grand juryman; the watch, who patrolled the town after the 9 P.M. curfew; and the tythingmen, responsible by the act of 1679 for the moral oversight of ten families. Among church members, the one or two ministers, the lay ruling elders, deacons, occasional deaconesses and catechisers frequently kept the whole community in their oversight.

All of these officials were elected or nominated by their constituents.[86] Constables were generally chosen from among responsible artisans or yeomen. Thus Thomas Danforth began his long career of distinguished public service as constable of Cambridge in 1645, in company with "Mr" Joseph Cooke.[87] Most of the rare complaints about constables in seventeenth-century Massachusetts cited their over-zealousness, and the evidence of the Middlesex files endorses their general efficiency and commitment.[88] In the 1690s when so many adolescents tried to abscond from justice, the constables usually caught the culprits eventually.[89] There is similarly considerable evidence that watchmen were active and alert after curfew, particularly in the Charles River towns. It is reasonable to assume that they were as efficient in inland towns in the last quarter of the century when Indian attacks were feared. Since lay and church officials customarily worked together in the maintenance of discipline—indeed they might well be the same individual wearing different hats, like Thomas Danforth who was simultaneously a magistrate, a ruling elder, and a catechist—they could be said to provide "a finely meshed net that trapped most erring citizens."[90] Certainly the detailed investigations mounted when infanticide was suspected endorses such a view of the effectiveness of the authorities.

Quite apart from law enforcement officials, however, all citizens, and especially church members, had a duty to maintain a holy watchfulness over their neighbors.[91] As we have seen and shall see again in subsequent chapters, many people took this obligation seriously, sometimes overzealously. If there was frequently an element of sheer nosiness about their prying, they had two vested interests in preventing sexual activity among the unmarried. People understood that condoning breaches of the moral code would invite God's wrath on the whole community; the person who turned a blind eye to sin was as bad as the sinner. Moreover, if a bastard was born in a community, there was always the possibility that the citizens would be called upon to support it and its mother, especially if the father remained undiscovered or absconded or failed to keep up maintenance payments.[92] Young people suspected of sexual misdemeanors had to provide two sureties for their appearance at court. The people of Middlesex therefore had compelling spiritual and material reasons for vigilance.

On the other hand, there might be equally powerful reasons for families of sexually active youngsters to preserve their reputations by a variety of stratagems such as marrying the couple quickly, separating the partners before conception occurred, or spiriting pregnant girls away. Thus the Bloods evaded justice if not publicity. We shall have occasion to multiply such examples later. It is possible too that many more private arrangements, like those attempted by Needham, Coller, and Cheney, successfully eluded the "laish of the law" and the eyes of neighbors. It is conceivable that communities dedicated in town covenants to "brotherly love" may have stepped in to prevent or resolve problems caused by illicit sexual activity with informal, extralegal solutions. Several such attempts are mentioned in testimony, though none of those reported actually resulted in an evasion of conviction.

Against these possibilities and the temptation voiced by some unmarried mothers to name falsely rich young men as the fathers of their bastards must be set the fact that only three of the ninety-six men involved in fornication cases actually appealed to the Court of Assistants, and only one of these was successful.[93] If these men were really innocent of paternity, as they often claimed, it seems likely more would have appealed their cases to restore their reputations and to save a considerable amount of money.

In the light of these conflicting possibilities, we may venture three preliminary conclusions. There may have been more breaches of the laws against fornication than is noted in the court records, but, given the watchfulness of both the authorities and the communities at large, it seems unlikely that the ninety-six cases appearing in court were only the unlucky few who were detected among a majority who escaped. Second, there was a sharp decline, starting in the 1660s, in the truthfulness and sense of responsibility of those accused of fornication. This drop in standards began before the new law about reputed fatherhood was passed in 1668; nonetheless the new procedures may have unwittingly encouraged dishonesty and evasion. The candor, acceptance of moral consequences, and healing penitence that we should expect to find are notably missing. Third, women both as midwives and as unmarried mothers commanded considerable influence in their communities especially after 1668. This does not jibe with the picture of unchecked patriarchal authority.

Before these tentative suggestions can be more fully tested, we need to examine in greater detail the personnel involved and the circumstances surrounding adolescent sexual activity. To these topics we now turn.

2 / Courtship and Patriarchal Authority

I N A SOCIETY dominated by property-owning and property-conscious patriarchs courtship should be strictly supervised. Where adolescents, many of them servants, "were in a sense all waiting to marry each other,"[1] their elders, either fathers or masters *in loco parentis,* must control the queue so that matches suitable to *their* economic requirements and aspirations be concluded at the right time for the family. Such considerations should outweigh the fickle romantic attractions of the young. While puritans required that couples should only marry if they could come to love each other, they accepted the old English proverb that there was more to marriage than four bare legs in a bed. Indeed, they often warned about the dangers of love at first sight, of succumbing to mere physical attractions. Marriage in haste for such reasons could too easily lead to repentance at leisure. Wisdom, experience, and prudence all required that "friends," as parents and kinfolk were termed, should take a leading part in the establishment of a new household.

Little is known about the courtship practices of "the plain and sturdy folk of colonial life." They rarely left love letters or diaries. Certain pieces of evidence have been advanced to support the idea of strict paternal control. The demographers have demonstrated that marriages were delayed until the middle or late twenties, and that children tended to marry—or be married off—according to their birth order.[2] The laws of the colony penalized as a crime "the drawing away the affections of a maid" without her parents' permission. Three cases in the Middlesex records suggest that ardent wooers had met with some encouragement from the wooed, despite being warned off by outraged fathers. Deacon

Upham of Malden complained in June 1658 about Paul Wilson's "violent solliciting his daughter against *his* will." The court supported parental authority by admonishing Wilson and taking a ten pound bond for his good behavior.[3] In April 1662, Marmaduke Johnson was fined five pounds for a similar offense against Samuel Greene.[4] One deceived father declared that serious suitors required parental "leave to frequent, discorse and keep company with their daughter."[5]

When his daughter rebelled against his authority, Richard Dexter invoked financial penalties against her new husband saying, "As you married her without my consent, you shal keepe her without my help." His disinherited daughter wrote "Pray father excuse my undutyfullness."[6] She had to write because her mother had "beaten her out of dores." In eleven fornication cases, family patriarchs initiated action either by complaints to the court or by bringing suits. Thus on 8 April 1680 Robert Procter brought a civil action against Thomas Marrable "for defiling his daughter Elizabeth to *his* [i.e., Procter's] great damage shee having by him a bastard child."[7] Sergeant Parmenter of Sudbury sued Christopher Bannister of neighboring Marlborough on 26 February 1665 for "trespass for defilling his daughter and getting her with child."[8] All this evidence would support the contention that in courtship the parents called the tune, or as one father put it, his daughter "was at his disposing."[9]

Before accepting this impression, however, it will be useful to glean what we can about courtship both from the ninety-six fornication cases as a whole and from four richly documented cases of disputed paternity. Any information thus uncovered will be an invaluable addition to our pitifully meager knowledge of the psychology of young unmarried plebeians.

Although the files are often highly revealing about courtship practices and personal motivations, forty-seven of the ninety-six cases are known to us only by the names of the couples in the order books. Even in several of the remaining forty-nine cases the supporting documentation is very slight. In forty-six cases the status of the unmarried mother had been established. Forty-one of them were servants, three were widows, and two were daughters of the household seduced by male servants. Twenty-seven of the men involved were definitely servants. It would be surprising if many of the "mystery cases" did not also involve servants.

From this count it is obvious that in Middlesex County, the group most vulnerable to sexual exploitation were young women in their late teens or early twenties living away from home.[10] In their study of seventeenth-century Maryland, Lois Carr and Lorena Walsh argue that the absence of parental or kin supervision was the crucial factor in deciding whether unmarried girls became pregnant.[11] On the face of it, this appears to be the case in Middlesex too. Though masters and dames took over quasi-parental roles for their dependents, they could not be expected to bring to bear the same commitment as natural parents to the control and oversight of their charges. The rarity of convictions of daughters living at home would seem to underline the argument for patriarchal power.

All was not quite as it seemed in many of the cases cited above, however. A closer examination of the eleven cases in which injured patriarchs took action on behalf of deflowered womenfolk suggests that they were untypical. In three cases seducers seem to have reneged on an undertaking to marry;[12] in one, force was suspected in the seduction;[13] in another, the daughter referred to her "childish condition";[14] in yet another, the girl seems to have been "sure" to another man.[15] One reputed father had smuggled his lover out of the colony to have her baby without her parents' knowledge, let alone consent.[16] Seven of the eleven cases occurred shortly after King Philip's War when the supply of eligible husbands had been suddenly and severely limited by male casualties.[17] The laws of Massachusetts formally checked patriarchalism by laying it down that parents should not put obstacles in the way of young couples wishing to marry.[18] Finally, there was one crucial difference between the maids of Massachusetts and the single women of Maryland. Most Middlesex women had parents in the vicinity, not 3,000 miles away in England. Sheer inaccessibility could not explain lack of patriarchal control, as it could further south. The case for parental domination, then, remains unproven.

Survey of Evidence

For a young woman to have intercourse with a man was an act of profound rebellion not only against her parents but also against the deeply-held mores of the community and the church. It was a sin which besmirched the soul; it was frequently described as uncleanness or defilement. The Middlesex bench would undoubtedly have endorsed the diatribe of a New Haven magistrate, delivered to a suspected couple, that fornication was "a sin which shutts [them] out of the kingdome of heaven, without repentance, and a sinn which layes them open to shame and punishment in this court. It is that which the Holy Ghost brands with the name of folly, it is that wherein men show their brutishness, therfore as the whip is for the horse and asse so a rod is for the fooles back."[19] So great was the "incivilitie" or lack of civic virtue involved in the crime that a Massachusetts law of 1665 prescribed disfranchisement of freemen convicted of fornication. Masses of testimony in the court files leave no doubt that the seriousness of this "shameful sinn" was universally known.[20]

Why then did young people, allegedly so "resolutely unerotic" due to their upbringing and culture, take such appalling risks? Why was courtship allowed to breach the bounds of propriety?

One potential means of lowering inhibitions can be quickly eliminated. Drink was cited in only a few cases as the reason for girls' succumbing. Thus in 1666 Rachel Smith was given strong waters at the end of an exhausting day before she agreed to have sex in goodman Hall's fields.[21] Similarly Ann Mark had imbibed from "a bowl of milk punch" before she was caught in bed with John Holloway by the watch in September 1687.[22] Strong liquor is mentioned on three occasions as an ingredient of rowdy parties, but it is rarely given as a cause of serious breaches of the moral code.[23]

What seems to have overcome resistance most frequently was either an offer of marriage and/or a declaration of love on the part of the man or infatuation on the part of the young woman. Male promises were occasionally conditional upon pregnancy but usually they were not.[24] Thus Daniel Smith spent "many nights inticing [Mary Grant] into his company by saying he intended to make her his wife." Having lured her into her father's leanto, "he used her as if she was his wife." The story in this case, and in her sister Abigail's, ended with promises kept, but often they were not.[25] Sarah Ward wrote of Zechariah Maynard that "he often showed much love to me and promised to marye me. I did not think he would have Runawaye and leave me in this condition."[26] While questioning a pregnant girl, Elizabeth Paine assumed that some such inducement would have to have been offered to persuade her to agree.[27]

Love was mentioned several times as a potent factor either in maids' surrendering to the importunities of their swains or in their naming men once they were pregnant. A witness in the 1696 Varnum and Coburn case thought Susannah "had some love for him by her designs [but] he did not take notice of her." Her naming of John Varnum was her revenge for unrequited passion.[28] Elizabeth Wells had brought home a nosegay, hurtleberries, wild grapes, and pears given her by Andrew Robinson as an indication of his affections.[29] A once ardent but now reluctant youth admitted that he had given Mary Linfield "a silver bodkin and hath sat up with her and kept her company by night and by day sundry times." The examining magistrate, Gookin, noted that "the maid . . . is so gone in her affections as that shee may grow either melancholy or mad whereby prejudice may ensue."[30] When Benjamin Knowlton overtook his sometime girlfriend Mary Pike who was walking with Edward Hodsman, "Mary ran after sd. Knowlton and held his sleeve but he minded her not."[31] Another jilting lover, John Row, was reported to have said to his still infatuated girl, "You flung nutts at me and enticed me. Then he hasted to go out of the roome and shee layed hold on his coate saying that shee must speake with him, he sayed looke looke see Josephs Mistris."[32] Elizabeth Wells claimed to have said to James Tufts during lovemaking, "You will take many a blow now but you will not be toucht at other times." Mary Ball's letter to Michael Bacon reminded him, "You onely on earth knowe how things were at first with us." Edward Hodsman boasted of Mary Pike's infatuation for him that "hee could doe what he would with her."[33] Similarly Paul Wilson flaunted his way with women. "If he could get the affections of a maid and he could affect the maid he would have her, doe al her friends and the men of New England what they could."[34]

Other men were less cynically manipulative. John Coller described Elizabeth Ross as "a garl that he had a great love for" and Marmaduke Johnson told Elizabeth Green that he loved her as his own life, that his love was undying. When she was moved out of his reach, he tore his hair in the best romantic tradition.[35] In two rare love letters, a sailor addressed his girlfriend as "My harts delight," and Jane Bowen wrote to David Dunster, in a barely decipherable scrawl:

> My love I remember my love to you hoping your welfare and I hope to imbras thee . . . I received a letter from you July 1 maks me love you the more because of your expression therein. If you can love me bestow me word or tel me so far wel My Love and dear Esa.[36]

Sarah Dexter obviously fell head over heels in love with Edward Pinson and eloped with him, although she was promised to someone else.[37] Even the austere Wigglesworth became infatuated with his maid. "Your affections are too far gone in this matter," he was warned. "Put the object out of your sight."[38]

Some restraint of ardor might be advisable until love was obviously reciprocated. Thus, one girl was asked "if she was so symple to send to her sweete hart and to woo him," and Pinson claimed, "It is not necessary for him to say that he was in love before he knew whether he was beloved."[39] Such precautions were essentially romantic, however. In the dusk of a September evening, Sarah Crouch, sitting on a bank beside the road from Charlestown to Watertown, mistook John Grant for his brother. According to John she called out "Christopher Christopher . . . Christopher I love you above all men . . . I am overcome in my love . . . ready to make away with my selfe . . . exceeding joyfull when I see you." John Grant was hardly an impartial witness, but it seems reasonable to presume that he would not report behavior that was completely implausible, especially when there were two witnesses present.[40] In fact evidence of affection, love, or infatuation among young couples is never described as though it were exceptional or abnormal.

There are other indications that love and affection played an important part in adolescent relationships. In a minimum of fourteen cases the lovers lived under the same roof. Thomas Hooker, sometime minister of Cambridge, described from personal experience how "it is with parties that live in the same family, and their affections are drawn one towards another in marriage; they will cast their occasions so, that if it be possible, they will be together and have one another's company and they will talk together and work together and the time goeth merrily suddenly, all the while their affections are drawing on."[41] Most couples lived in the same or a neighboring town. There is abundant evidence that intimacy was the culmination of long-term relationships in many cases. Elizabeth Frost, for example, said "John Needham frequented her company two or three years" before they lay together, and Anne Williamson admitted to having been intimate with Thomas Abbott "a good space since."[42]

This suggests that the nature of sexuality among many of the unmarried was, in Edward Shorter's terms, "expressive" rather than merely "manipulative" or "instrumental." Sexual intercourse was an expression of affection, part of a "normalisation of romance" rather than a weapon used "for such external objectives as obtaining a marriage partner or avoiding trouble with a superior" or an occasional solution to physical frustrations when inhibitions were lowered.[43]

Support for this view might also be adduced from the seasonality of conceptions. If conceptions are clumped in certain months, this may be a sign that sexual activity is still in the manipulative stage, something young people engage in at bucolic holiday seasons, for instance, whereas a more even spread of conceptions across the year is seen as the result of expressive sexuality between couples "making love" to each other.

In 56 of the total 161 cases of pre- and extramarital fornication in our

Table 4 / Months of conception of pre- and extramarital fornication cases, 1649–1699

	Jan.	Feb.	Mar.	Apr.	May	June	July	Aug.	Sept.	Oct.	Nov.	Dec.	Periodic Totals
RECORDS													
1649–63			2	2						3		1	8
1663–71	1		2	1		1			1			1	7
1671–80		1	1		5	1	1		1		1		11
1680–86		2				1	1		1	2			7
1686–89				1			1						2
1689–92			2					2	1	1	1		7
1692–99	1		3		1		2	1	2		2	2	14
MONTHLY TOTALS	2	3	10	4	6	3	5	3	6	6	4	4	56

study, it has been possible to discover the month of conception. The findings are set out in table 4.

These figures do not reflect the seasonality of illegitimate conceptions that has been noted in some English statistics—namely high rates in midsummer and December and a low in October. Puritan Middlesex had purged itself of those traditional revels which were the occasion of sexual expression in the old country. The high in March may have been connected with militia training days, while seductions in September and October are often associated with harvesting crops.[44] Otherwise, with the exception of the midwinter months of January and February, conceptions are spread pretty evenly across the calendar year with warm light months coming out almost equal to cold dark ones. This "decline in the amplitude of seasonality" should be treated with great caution, especially as the sample of cases is so small, but it may be further support for the contention that love often played an important role in the relationships of the unmarried.[45]

Finally, in a dozen cases it has been possible to trace the later lives of unmarried mothers. One woman lived out her life unmarried, but the remaining eleven found husbands other than the reputed fathers of their bastards.[46] Perhaps community mores were more flexible and forgiving, and the damage of lost virginity less irremediable than they are often depicted.

So far the evidence from our survey of the fornication cases in the records is neatly balanced. In the one scale are the cases where fathers actively censored courtships they felt unsuitable, or intervened in court when they had been circumvented, or strictly controlled daughters living at home. In the other, however, we have seen examples of young people resolutely following the dictates of their own hearts, falling in love with each other and expressing that love through intimacy, thereby affronting popular mores and revolting against parental considerations.

For help in unraveling the problem of whether courtship among ordinary young couples was autonomous or parentally monitored, we turn to four well-documented cases of disputed paternity. The details of these relationships between adolescents and with their parents and other adults may lead us to less ambivalent conclusions.

Case Studies: Courtship

On 3 January 1669 Sarah Crouch of Charlestown gave birth to a bastard; on 26 March she was questioned by Thomas Danforth and Daniel

Gookin. She confessed to committing fornication and named Christopher Grant of Watertown, aged twenty, as the father. He had had "the use of her body" three times. The first, when the child was begotten, was on the evening of 30 March 1668, Trooping Day at Cambridge. Grant came to her master, John Knight, a cooper, for a three gallon runlett. He asked to speak with her and led her toward an empty house on a wharf. When she demurred at entering "to be naught with him," he told her, "A bigger sin than that might be pardoned" and "promised her no hurt should come of it: if there did he would marry her or else he were a Rogue in his heart. . . . Any man was a rogue who knew a maid carnally without promising marriage. If she was not good enough to make his wife she was not good enough to make his whore. It would not be known if he married her soon after."[47] They stayed in the house about an hour.

The second time was the Saturday before Election, 25 April 1668, when Grant came to "her fathers house in the bedroom the sun about two hours high her father and mother from home . . . he found her ironing he took her by the hand and said what have any body against it why I should not make use of my owne and took the iron from her hand . . . He said he had cured me of the green sickness.[48] He asked me how long afore [i.e., since] I had the sines of a maid [menstruation] and I told him three days afore the first time he had to doe with me and then he said O Lord my hart akes." She appeared to have missed her period.

The third time was during pease harvest in June when Grant and his elder stepbrother Joshua visited the Crouches at dusk. Sarah's mother sent her to fetch in the servant Thomas Jones to supper; Christopher "asked leave of her mother if he might go forth with her." Permission was granted "they not going out of hearing." Grant said as they walked on the highway toward Crosswell's, "I must have a small bout and did haul her under the fence." Thomas Jones, who had been going steady with Sarah, had seen this performance from a hiding place in the barn and now emerged. "Sary tak note hencefurrard I will have nothing to say to you any more." Grant asked, "Thomas shel I kiss your garle," to which he replied, "Take her and if you will." Grant said "he could maintain her as well as a dirt dauber . . . a crouch back rogue."

In September Sarah broke the news of her pregnancy to Grant, as "we did sit on the stile on the causeway . . . he said he would marry me if I would make away with the child which I did refuse to do for which I bless my God." At the end of her examination Sarah insisted, "He promised marriage or I never would have yeelded." All of this "Christopher Grant denied with great protestations of inocency . . . If his denial were false God would punish his enormity with severe judgment." However, since Sarah had maintained throughout her delivery that the "child was Christopher Grants and no one elses," and that he had offered to marry her only three days before, something more persuasive than simple denial was needed to escape a maintenance order.

Fortunately counterevidence was at hand. John Knight, a widower, did not think highly of his sometime maidservant.

> Severall times she sett up verie late. I told her of it and that I would tell her parents of her late hours but she gave me a very short answer . . . A few nights later my child that lay with her cryed out. I called to her severall times but she gave no answer. . . . [She was not in bed] I went downstairs and found the door locked which I forced her to open. I found both her and Sarah Largin both undressed . . . Sarah Largin ran off undressed shedding clothes . . . I asked her what men were these. At length she said Peeter Brigs. I asked if the other were Thomas Jones but she gave me no answer. I warned her that I would turne her out of doors if [it happened again].

He seems to have decided to carry out his threat. On the day that Goody Mirricke came to do his washing, he went "out of towne to get another maid. Returning between 3 and 4 o'clock I found the child crying but Sarah Crouch from home. Goody Mirricke believed she was at her house. I sent for her twice, then I went my self for her and found the latch in. I threatened to break the door down and found there Sarah Crouch and Sarah Largin with . . . Peter Briggs and Michell Tandy."

Joseph Bacheler and Paul Wilson had both seen Sarah and Thomas Jones "on a bed together at Theophilus Marches last election day at Boston [late April 1668]." John Cutler attested that "at the beginning of September last, I saw Sarah Crouch and a man over the fields. I asked her father if he knew, he said he had given his leave." Grant produced alibis and further evidence of Sarah's untrustworthiness, notably from Sarah Largin.[49]

The Crouch camp was not without countercharges. Mary Crouch, Sarah's seventeen-year-old sister, reported a contretemps with Grant in early June 1668.

> He asked me whether I was sure [engaged] to another man. I said whats that to you. Have you been drinking. He answered No he would tell me how much he had drunk. I said it was nothing to me what he had drunk. Then he begonn to meddell with me then he went to take my coats up. I told him I would call my father. He said he would marry me if I would yeeld to him but because I would not he give me a box one the eare and said get yee gon you durty slot now I will go to your sister . . . [Later] I followed them and he haled her away and I could not catch up with them.

I told my mother who sent me to fetch Sarah and I met them coming home.

The exact nature of Sarah's relationship with Thomas Jones was a matter of considerable interest. The deformed Jones, a bricklayer aged twenty-four, corroborated her account of "the small bout" in June. Paul Wilson witnessed Grant asking Goodman Crouch in March 1668 whether Sarah was promised to Jones; the father replied, "Not as far as he knew" and Grant boasted that "he would have her before Thomas Jones would."[50] Ursula Cole repeated a conversation with Jones: "He told Sarah Crouch she looked as though she was bigg with child, to which she answered If I am with child you shall provide blanketts for it." Sarah told Goody Cole that "Thomas Jones and she were sure together but afterwards I heard they were broken off. Sarah said it was because Thomas was jealous of Christopher Grant but he hath no cause." The court disagreed and adjudged Grant the father.

There is however a further twist to the story. In a subsequent file is a petition from Sarah Crouch, Sr.; it is undated but was probably presented in June 1670.[51]

Thomas Jones and Sarah Crouch [Jr.] were lawfully published & firmly promised with the consent of their parents three months before this act was done . . . Thomas Jones his sister was very angry and set his father against him, and turned him out of doore and would not owne him no more to be his child. Hereupon they were concluded to be married the next week. His parents persuaded them to rest a while to see if he could get his fathers consent & he waited the best part of three months but in vain. Thomas was very much troubled and came to our house & noboddy at home but shee, *did overcome her to* committ this act and after he had don it was so troubled in his mind & with his Sister persuading of him went away to sea to Barbados; when he returned he maried and is now gon to sea again.[52]

The church records of Charlestown confirm that this petition refers to a *second* case of (premarital) fornication.

13 March 1670: Sarai Crouch fornication with Thomas Jones excommunicated for persisting so impenitently incorrigibly in that sin while under censure for that committed March 21 1669 [date of previous censure]

Sarah Crouch was thus a "repeater" in conceiving two children out of wedlock. The opposition of the Jones family to the match is understandable, given her first bastard and her family's reputation. Yet Thomas Jones seems to have been eager to marry her despite being jilted earlier. The offspring of this union of disabled and discarded was another Sarah, who was convicted of lascivious behavior in 1695.[53]

Simultaneously with Charlestown's problems, the town of Malden was riven by scandal in the late winter of 1669. The trouble centered on the household of Peter Tufts, a leading citizen, and later tythingman and representative.[54] The source of conflict was the pregnancy of Elizabeth Wells, a servant who had arrived some time the preceding year from England. Wells accused Peter Tufts's son James of taking his will of her twice, once unloading wheat, once "at Indian Harvest when my master bargained with Mr Greenleafe for an ox . . . Another time when I was milking he asked me if I were with childe. I told him I could not tell but if I were with child the child was his." James Tufts made his "solemn profession before this honoured court that I never had anything to doe with her in that kind." The Tufts family had another candidate to propose; this was Andrew Robinson, originally of Charlestown but lately a Malden servant of low repute. In their view he was a fitting partner in crime for the loudmouthed and discreditable Wells. Robinson, when examined by Thomas Danforth, denied the accusation.

The evidence the Tuftses assembled against Wells and Robinson was mainly from their own ranks; the two commonest deponents were Mary Tufts, "aged fourteen next June," and her friend Mary Jefts, aged fifteen. These two recounted much of the boasting bawdy of the recent immigrant: her desertion of her two-year-old son, her burying bastards, her procuring abortions, her intention of hoodwinking midwife and magistrates about paternity if she were ever pregnant. Some of her stories could easily have come straight from jest books or ballads, and she seems to have had a wide and retentive audience. Samuel Blunt, aged twenty-two, testified:

> Elizabeth Wells said that in England she and another maid had gotten three young men into their bedchamber, after which her father had locked the [outside] door and carried the key up to his chamber . . . She therefore cut the bedcord and let the young men down by it [out of the chamber window.] This making a great noise her father asked whats the matter. Elizabeth Wells answered the base rotten Bedcord was broaken and almost broke their necks, and he said Peace Bette hold thy Tongue Ile buy another tomorrow and said Wells and the other maid lay and laught.

She also told the two girls that she had "held the doore till a man was naught with three or four maids in England and if her father had not called her away she had been the fifth."

Whenever Robinson was around the house, she tried to obtain some privacy. One summer sabbath when her master and dame were at meeting, he and she went up to the chamber. She told the seven-year-old Elizabeth Tufts, who followed them to the stairs, to "Go away! She could go nowhere but I would follow her." She told a visiting youth "the pigeons would be on his pease & hastned him away. Shee so said because Andrew Robinson was there." Jonathan Tufts, aged ten, remembered that when he was watching cattle Wells and Robinson relieved him and told him to go home and watch the children instead. She admitted Robinson's "offering to medle with her" and was almost caught in a midnight tryst.

The Tufts' witnesses showed Wells to be a congenital liar. The grandmother, Elizabeth Peirce, described the maid servant as "addicted to lying with conviction. One time she knew her to be lying but Elizabeth Wells said as she had a soul it was not so." She had even lied about being pregnant, though Mary Tufts, Jr. had seen her "drink something and go out of the house and vomit. She asked what it was and sd. Wells replied savin boiled in beer and she drank some more. She told this dept. not to tell Elizabeth Jefts."

What was left of Robinson's character was undermined by the sixteen- or seventeen-year-old Martha Faulkner.

> When I dwelt with John Pratt two year since my master and dame being out one night and I abed with the children, Andrew Robinson came down to me having no clothes on but his shirt & he began to pull the bed clothes off from me and thereby he wakened me. I asked him what do you here He said I come to lie down upon the bed by you. I said Get you gon and he said Arise out this bed from the children and go into the other bed that I may lie with you & often thus he urged me. I told him I will not I will dye first to which he replied Why you will not be with child you foole if you keep your own counsell it will not be known. [His enticements were twice repeated.] I would not have spoken of this evil cariadg of his but heard some saying he was not given to such vice.

What of James Tufts? Despite his constant denials, general good character, and an alibi from his mother, there was one blot on his reputation. Eighteen-year-old Mary Mudge reported how "two years ago at my fathers house James Tufts being present I gave him some cherries. He said Huzzy you have given me worm eaten cherries but I will pay you for it & came and took hold on me & I held by the bar of the window & then by a great tubb & he dragged me from that & laid me on the bed & violently held me & lay on me kissing me . . . I pulled his hair and cryed out and my brothers Thomas and John coming he left me." This admittedly uncorroborated account sounded dangerously like Wells's.

The weight of evidence, however, suggests that Robinson was the father, and that James Tufts was unlucky "to be rich enough able to maintain it [the child] whether it were his or no." Unfortunately most of the testimony pointing to Robinson comes from members of the Tufts family or their dependents, and the new mother clung to her accusation of James Tufts throughout her labor. Although the order book has not survived, the Malden records speak of "James the child of James Tufts and Elizabeth Wells."[55]

Benjamin Knowlton and Mary Pike, both of Reading, appeared in court, charged with fornication on 6 October 1674, three weeks before Mary gave birth to a child. The justices were faced with a bafflingly contradictory array of evidence collected after the initial complaint of James Pike, Mary's father. Richard Russell had examined the pair face to face on 20 August. Mary said "Ben Knowlton had the use of her body the first week of April last & no other man whatsoever at one time or another." Knowlton responded "as in the presence of God [he] never had the use of her body in his life; he was never in her company save in the presence of her father and mother."

There was an embarrassing amount of evidence against Knowlton. Not only had the pair been "together a considerable while before her being with child came to be known in the town," but he had asked some incriminating questions: "What is the matter with you? You are not well. Are you breeding?" He demanded later "why she did not acquaint him with the crime charged on him before she published it abroad in the town." He was also alleged to have said, "If the said Mary would have told him how it was with her within a month after the fact committed, he would have married her and the world should have been never the wiser." A neighbor of the Pikes, Sarah Thompson, gave Mary an excellent character; she was "helpful, diligent and no carriage in her justly offensive." William Symmes, minister's son and leading selectman of Reading, and Jonathan Poole, the town's representative, described a meeting between the two parties on 3 August at Deacon Cowdrey's with Mary's father present.[56] Mary charged that "Knollton . . . did it once & no more . . . about day light shutting in on the first fift day [Thursday] in Aprill last." Knowlton, duly "cautioned to remember that god & his conscience did know how far he was guilty," again denied any guilt. He sluffed off one question about some incriminating comments. He was then asked "what made him to say to a credible person (being urged to owne wherein he was guilty) that he had denied the fact so often & to so many that now he knew not how to owne it." He admitted the words, "adding that if he were guilty he would have owned it; that that was his meaning." This was not particularly persuasive. To a neighbor's challenge, he admitted "throwing her [Mary] on the cabin bed . . . on [militia] company trayning day at night."

Knowlton had an alternative candidate for fatherhood and several witnesses to support his case. One had "seen Mary Pike and Edward Hodsman aloan in the Bushis two or three our within the nit and Richard Beats and Mary Pike likewise both of them severall times." Another "heard Edward Hodsman say Mary Pike was such an one as hee could doe what hee would with her." Several testified that "Edward Hodsman said that Goodman Pike would not let him have his daughter hee [Pike] would be glad ere long for to come with his cap in his hand and entreat him for to have his daughter." Hodsman then departed for Rhode Island.

Why should he want to marry a pregnant Mary unless he had himself made her so? Since she charged Knowlton with one offense only six-and-a-half months before she gave birth, perhaps Hodsman had been with her beforehand. Although Mary quickly changed the date to early February and two witnesses deposed that Hodsman had planned the Rhode Island trip long before Mary conceived, the evidence seems nicely balanced.

Someone was plainly lying, and Reading residents thought it was Knowlton. The court shared this view; "Benjamin Knowlton is to stand as the reputed father of the said child & is sentenced to make provision for the maintenance thereof & to give security."[57] It sentenced Mary Pike to twenty stripes or a fine of ten pounds, later abated to five pounds.

Susannah Coburn or Colburn, who gave birth in January 1696 to a bastard in Dracut, a frontier settlement near Chelmsford, was a maid-servant in the household of Samuel and Sarah Varnum. At her confinement, as we have seen, she refused to name the father, but in her confession to the court she charged her master's son John with paternity. The two families, who had been neighbors in Ipswich and had pioneered the settlement north of the Merrimack River in the 1660s, were related by the marriage of Hannah Varnum to Ezra Coburn, Susannah's uncle. John Varnum, aged twenty-seven, denied the charge, and the failure to name him during travail denied the court acceptable legal proof of paternity and opened the floodgates to a torrent of circumstantial evidence.

Several witnesses supported Susannah's contention that she dared not name Varnum because his mother was her midwife and his brother had threatened her. Susannah, the daughter of Edward Coburn, Jr.,

who had died aged thirty-three in 1675, sought sympathy by reminding the court that she was an orphan and "few of my friends were
with me." She also had few friends to testify on her behalf at the June
1696 court in answer to the battery of depositions marshaled by the
Varnums. Their defense took two lines: Susannah's subsequent regret
at naming John, and the nomination of alternative candidates for
maintenance payments. Hannah Coburn described a conversation with
Susannah about ten days after her delivery.

> I asked her why she did not rise and she replied O aunt, I have no hart to
> rise. . . . I am a great sinner, nobody will endure me. . . . Asked who is
> the father . . . she answered if it would save my life I can not tell who is the
> father of my child and wept bitterly.

To her seventy-eight-year-old master she admitted "that she had belied
[his] son John . . . and did weep bitterly." Four witnesses suggested
that her motive for naming him had been his failure to respond to her
advances. "She would sware that she would be revenged of him. This
was not long before she was brate to bede."

The alternative nominees for paternity were numerous. One was
Samuel Fuller. John Varnum's brothers testified:

> Sam Fuller was very intamet with Susannah Colburn in the spring of [1695]
> in the night . . . they were much absent both of them in prayer time from
> the family . . . their master reproved them both much. We heard Sam
> Fuller tell Susannah Colburn that he had fucket hur many a time & she
> replied you cant doe me any hurt or no hurt for you arent above half a man
> and he, being rebuked, replied let her be damed un she well, she has set in
> my lap & kist me forty times.

Five weeks after delivery she told a witness "she would give me twenty
shillings if I would fetch this rogue Fuller to her for she would make
him to maintain her child."

Richard Graves was another possibility canvassed. The two Varnum
brothers reported that in early May 1695 Susannah "was gone from hur
master's house a considerable time to the other garrison." They pointed
out to her when she returned that there was no bed for her there and
asked her where she had slept. She answered "with Graves. We told her
we would kepe account or reckoning for her, and told Richard Graves,
who replied If you have her word for it that is sufficient ent it?" Two
women remembered "Susannah Colburn receiving blows on her belly,
then she said Have a care, you will kill a young graves." The third
prospective parent was more vaguely described: "Susannah Colburn
went away with the soldiers [ten of whom were garrisoned at Dracut]

one night though her master forbade it [and] reprooved her when she returned." No one would have any doubt about what that evidence implied.

In the event, the court, sitting on 23 June 1696, "considering the circumstances and pleas then made dismissed John Varnum with costs." Susannah Coburn was convicted of fornication and sentenced to the standard penalty of a forty shilling fine or ten stripes.[58]

These four highly detailed cases—there are thirty-four depositions in the Tufts-Wells case alone—provide us with an extraordinarily vivid account of courtship psychology and of family dynamics. We can almost hear the persuasive hypocrisy of Grant and his subsequent arrogance of sexual possession and disdain for the "dirt dauber" he had temporarily supplanted; the similar self-satisfaction of Hodsman, whom the Pikes obviously felt their daughter was far too good for (much as the Joneses seem to have regarded the Crouches); the shock expressed by Grant when he realized that Sarah had missed her period and the argument at the stile about what to do. We can share the sense of Knowlton's entrapment in the moral snare of his initial denial; Susannah Coburn's angry frustration at Varnum's lack of interest, her accepting of Sam Fuller as a second-best substitute, and her subsequent postpartum depression and guilt; or Elizabeth Wells's child-clogged life which could both provide an uncritical audience for her tales but also deprive her of any privacy.

Conclusion

Beyond recapturing these feelings from the past, however, we are mainly concerned here with what these little dramas tell us about the individual autonomy and attitudes of adolescents. All the young women showed signs of love for the men they claimed had fathered their children. We have already recounted Sarah Crouch's profession to Christopher Grant's brother and Elizabeth Pike's running after Knowlton; both Elizabeth Wells and Susannah Coburn were alleged to have been infatuated with their masters' sons. Three of the alternative candidates for fatherhood—Hodsman, Jones, and Robinson—had all expressed their keenness for women who preferred other men. On the other hand, Grant and Hodsman were said to have used proprietorial, manipulative expressions about their sexual control of Crouch and Pike. Tufts's "taking his will of her" and Knowlton's "throwing her on the cabin bed" hardly strike us as the seductions of sophisticated, expressive lovemakers. All these accounts, however, come from patently hostile witnesses.

Grant's initial persuasion of Crouch, according to her account, not only minimized the sin but reassured her that she would not become pregnant, and if she did he would marry her. When the worst happened he wanted her to abort her five-month fetus, presumably so that both of them could masquerade as unspotted virgins at the wedding. Robinson, who was only fourteen or fifteen in 1667, tried similar, vain, assurances with Martha Faulkner. Grant too got a dusty answer from Mary Crouch, despite his offer of marriage to her. By then she probably knew about her sister's pregnancy. Knowlton was said to have been agreeable to a shotgun wedding if only Elizabeth had told him that she had missed her period. There never seemed to have been any question of James Tufts marrying Elizabeth Wells, but he was apparently concerned that she might be pregnant. Grant, Graves, and Robinson come across from this and other evidence as rustic Casanovas eager to have to do with any girls they could persuade into bed with them; perhaps that was why suspicion rested on them as candidates for paternity.

All four women were reputed, admittedly by partial witnesses, to have had romantic or sexual experience with other men; three of them hardly resemble models of submissive, indoctrinated chastity. To Crouch, Wells, and possibly Pike pregnancy rather than loss of virginity was the danger to be feared; only Faulkner unequivocally expressed sentiments about her virginity—"I will dye first"—which would have won the applause of puritan moralists. I have not been able to discover what happened to Pike or Coburn, but Wells as well as Crouch later married.

As so often happens, the evidence here is not clear-cut. Yet it is undeniable that there are plenty of signs of personal affection and of these young people taking the law into their hands by their individual initiatives. They do not come across as the puppets of puritan morality. Their behavior supports the contentions of such scholars of early modern Europe as Jean-Louis Flandrin, Natalie Davis, or Peter Burke that "love has a place in peasant society . . . ordinary people are not passive slaves of authority, routine or economic determinism . . . they can make choices, rebel against constraints or manoeuvre within them."[59]

Was family government then a paper tiger? Not entirely, from the evidence here. Both Coburn and Wells were exceptional in being parentless; Sarah Crouch's father was an alcoholic who seems to have remarried after Sarah's mother died. In the Pike case where a genuine patriarch was involved, James Pike prosecuted his daughter's lover. But he had been unable to prevent his daughter consorting after dark with either Hodsman or Richard Betts. Masters such as Tufts were told of nocturnal movements but they were "weary and careless," and their control of their servants seems largely ineffective.

Yet, paradoxically, in the Crouch case there is plenty of material about adult supervision. Grant requested permission from both Knight to speak with his servant Sarah and her stepmother to walk out with her; he was not allowed to go beyond earshot. Similarly she had had to get her father's permission to walk across the field with a man. On the occasion when Grant hauled her away without leave, she was hauled back again on her stepmother's orders. When Knight caught Sarah merely sitting up late he threatened to tell her parents, and Mary Crouch quickly dissuaded Grant from meddling with her by the same means. Sarah had not told her father that she was pregnant out of fear that "he would knock her on the head." Yet when Goodman Crouch was asked if Sarah were engaged, his answer, "Not as far as he knew," betrays a certain lack of parental control.

In the Pike testimony Edward Hodsman had formally asked James Pike's leave to court Mary and had been refused. On the other hand, his boast that "hee could doe what hee would with her" may suggest that he went ahead anyway. It could just have been adolescent bravado. When Mary became pregnant, her father orchestrated community pressure on Knowlton both by individuals and by confrontation with selectman, deacon, and deputy. The ostensible purpose of this meeting, three months before the court case, was to bring Knowlton to confess. If he had, would he not then have been further pressured into marriage? Probably unable to bear the odium of public reproach, Knowlton "lit out for the territories" soon after the case. In Springfield, with poetic justice, he married a woman with an illegitimate child.

Thomas Jones's ancient father furiously threw him out and disowned him when he sought to marry Sarah Crouch. The couple reacted by arranging a quick wedding, but Thomas's psychological need for his father's approval (and perhaps his financial need for an inheritance) persuaded them to delay. Even after he had impregnated Sarah, family pressure sent him on the long voyage to the West Indies. The Grant family did all they could to extract Christopher from the case; they provided alibis, defense testimony, supported his appeal, and twice petitioned the court. The testimony in the Coburn case shows that the Varnum family—still in the 1690s, a "little church" with family prayers and Christian conventions of forgiveness—used both threats, sympathy, and persuasion with Susannah in their campaign to clear John's name. Female members of the Tufts family from the ages of seventy-three to seven swore a total of twelve depositions in court. In fact the clearest feature of these cases is the way in which extended family loyalties manifested themselves in defense both of an individual kinsman and of the notion of family honor within the community. Joseph Varnum's chilling threat to Susannah that "if anybody laid a bastard child to any of them they would hand their house blood" smacks more of a Sicilian vendetta than of the "peaceable kingdoms" of New England. Yet threatened settlements way out on the frontier of Middlesex, like Dracut or Lancaster or Dunstable or Groton, were no strangers to violence in the last quarter of the seventeenth century. Susannah's father had been killed by Indians in 1675 and his house burnt, and two of Joseph's brothers had been killed before their father's eyes the following year.

Despite this evidence of parental and family power, the fact remains that these four girls, however closely watched in their households and communities, however superficially the rules of courtship were observed, still became pregnant, one of them twice. The Grants, Crouches, Tuftses, Pikes, Varnums, and Coburns were all church members, their children all "born within the Covenant of Grace," so they cannot simply be written off as an atypical antipuritan subculture. The conventional wisdom about patriarchal power and suppressed dependents emerges somewhat dented at the end of this survey. The younger generation, sometimes ostensibly deferential, sometimes ready with very short answers, seem to have been adept at circumventing or bending the strict rules of courtship so as to follow their hearts' desires. The supposedly all-powerful patriarchs seem to have been left with the far from glorious task of picking up the pieces caused by their children's autonomous initiatives. We shall meet others in this role as we turn to the analogous problem of prenuptial fornication.

3 / Pregnant Brides and Broken Promises

HE occurrence of pre-marital illicit sex was primarily a breach of and failure in household discipline."[1] This is the conclusion of a recent study of an English county, and our task here is to discover whether the same held true for a Massachusetts county. The number of brides who went to their weddings already pregnant has been widely investigated by demographers. Since both marriages and births are recorded in English parish or American town or county records, it is (in theory at least) a relatively straightforward task to count them.[2] For early modern England most investigators agree that one in five brides was pregnant.[3] A similar proportion has been found in early Maryland.[4] Whether the other four nonexpectant brides had also had sexual experience, it is, of course, impossible to discover from such sources.

Bridal pregnancy has also fascinated social historians. Couples who married in traditional western society had had to wait up to ten or more years from the time they became sexually mature to the time they could, at betrothal or engagement, look forward to legitimate sexual activity. Why could they not wait the few more weeks until marriage? Was it because of a popular acceptance of "betrothal license" that couples once "sure" could indulge their long-controlled sexual appetites?[5] Or were more varied motives at work? For instance, was the pregnancy a way to force acceptance of marriage from parents reluctant to break up family assets or approve their offsprings' choice?[6] Was it to force foot-dragging males to propose?[7] Were most expectant couples entering shotgun marriages? Or were they the victims of unpredictable economic, social, or political crises which somehow wrecked their plans?[8] All of these explanations for bridal pregnancy have been offered

by various researchers. Whichever proves to have been the most probable cause for the sixty-six cases in Middlesex will obviously have considerable bearing on our investigation of patriarchal power in relation
to adolescent autonomy. If the most plausible motive were to prove to
be a desperate means of forcing parents to agree to the marriage, then
parental control would emerge as a potent force. If, however, most
pregnant marriages proved to be hasty arrangements to conceal an unexpected expectancy, then it would follow that adolescents exercised
considerable individual initiative.

Along with these embarrassments we shall also look at three cases of
breach of promise. These actions represent the obverse side to bridal
pregnancy, where usually a young man who had impregnated his
fiancée or his girlfriend had the moral responsibility to marry her. In
breaches of promise one or other of the partners who were "agreed"
reneged on their undertakings. The testimony in these cases will give us
valuable information about roles, motivations, and mores.

In Middlesex any married couple whose first child arrived less than
seven months after marriage was automatically under suspicion legally
for committing fornication.[9] Great care was taken to identify cases of
genuine prematurity, and sentences reflected the belief that "if the man
mought marry the woman the sin would not be so great in the sight of
God as it would be if he did not."[10] To reduce the temptation to jump
the gun, matrimony was expected to follow within a month of betrothal, which must take place before witnesses. Betrothal was a contract; by Massachusetts law intercourse with a third party thereafter
was adultery. Intention to marry must be published by the posting of
banns; the marriage must be regularly performed in the hometown
before witnesses and it must be recorded. These regulations and precautions were of well-tried English origin. There were two major differences in Massachusetts, however. Matrimony there was considered
a civil contract and was therefore performed by a magistrate.[11] Since
fornication was considered both crime and sin, "covenanted" couples
were liable to double punishment by church and state. Without confession, their offspring were denied baptism.[12]

Survey of Evidence

The great majority of couples charged with premarital fornication confessed. Having married, they usually had no alternative. Most of the
statements of penitence surviving are from members of elect families.
Indeed, they had probably already been delivered before church mem-

bers prior to being filed in the court records. The confessions were generally fulsomely self-flagellating. Thus Jacob Farrer and his wife bewailed

> our great and crying sin which cries aloud in the ears of God for vengeance and in the ears of man for Justice to be executed . . . [from] the deep impression on our spirits we desire to fear and tremble before the Lord . . . [and are] deeply and truly humbled before his people . . . yet, notwithstanding [we draw the court's attention to] our low and mean condition in respect of outward things.[13]

Susannah Lawrence, finally married to a mariner then at sea, admitted she had been "justly left of God" and had been "trusting of my own strength laying myself exposed and liable to many, and at last, too strong temptations." This "miserable wretch" bemoaned "my great and horrid wickedness hainously provoking to God and man by this my great folly committed in this our Israel" and sought abatement of her five pound fine.[14]

Sometimes a note of calculation appears amid the wailing and gnashing of teeth. In April 1686 Ebenezer Austin, who had tested the court's patience by first absconding, then demanding a jury, and needlessly disputing the clerk's records, finally abased himself. "But, [being] a young-beginner in the world, [with] only what his industry (with the blessing of God) doth bring in, and the difficulty of maintaining a family in these hard times," he sought a remission of all or part of the fine. The court in its mercy abated it by twenty shillings.[15]

John and Mary Cummins of Woburn were more specific about their hard times in June 1691. They fully accepted the humbling providences that their premarital fornication had brought down. However, they sought to persuade the bench that they had suffered enough with a four pound fine. John had been "imprest under Andros" and had to borrow nine pounds for a substitute. Then he had been sent on the disastrous expedition to Canada in 1690 where he both needed expensive nursing for a fever and also lost his weapons (his gun cost thirty-five shillings to replace). "In the time of childbirth the hand of God was against us still which was accompanied with great charge, sorrow and misery . . . all hopes of life failed." In August their fine was halved.[16] Samuel Fowl, a carpenter of Charlestown, ended the confession of his fornication with: "None the less he never denied it but so far complyd with the law of God as to marry with the woman [Susanna Blany] with whom he committed that sin."[17] At least he was not a Grant or a Knowlton.

None of the confessions mentions disobedience to parents; the penitents speak as autonomous individuals. They almost always set their instinctual willfulness against the injunctions of the Lord who abandoned the disobedient to their fate. Hephzibah Tailer confessed to "the natural inclination which I find in me to breach Gods commands . . . this Beast he tare them in pieces."[18] Bethia Hide explained that "God permitted me to fall into the vile sin of uncleaness."[19] "God withdrew his protection from me and permitted me to committ that great sin against him" bewailed Mary Parmenter.[20] Daniel and Mary Smith "born within the Covenant of Grace the many privileges whereof we have been made partakers of" cited "Sathans temptations in persuading to deny it" for their "horrible and abominable sin of uncleannes."[21] Joshua and Grizell Fletcher "desire to be ashamed and hope that God will give them wisdom to walk circumspectly" in the future.[22] Mary Ball blamed "my owne harte [for] the grossness of my abominable sin and the insupportable displeasure of God."[23] Samuel and Lydea Wright claimed to "abhor ourselves and repent in dust and ashes, loath both the sin and ourselves for it, the corruptions of our own sinful hearts and the temtations of the devil."[24]

Any assumption that penitents were morally brainwashed adolescents also needs qualification. Many petitions are in scriveners' hands, and the similarity of formulae suggests that heartfelt cries of sorrow might be bought by the yard. The pleas may have been what was known to influence churches or justices. Some confessions defy credulity. Would the Elizabeth Wells who had boasted so blatantly about her sexual escapades really thenceforward "walk humbly before God all my days"? Was the foul-mouthed Susannah Coburn, alleged to have coupled with at least three men, "humbled before the Lord and sensable of evil"?[25] Finally, the petitioners had little to lose by a show of self-flagellation and often an abatement of fine and their children's baptism to gain.

On several occasions, the court even intervened to check unreasonable obduracy.[26] In December 1679 the sentence on George Parmenter and his wife was respited until their parents had appeared "to answer why they denied them the consumation of their marriage for so many months after they were in order thereto."[27] The ill-starred Joneses, as we have seen, similarly pled three months' wait in a vain attempt to win his father's consent.[28]

Some parents actively helped their children to challenge presentments or even evade the law. Thus, Abigail Hastings's assertion that she "went a true virgin to the marriage bed" and that her twenty-six week pregnancy was prematurely terminated by a fall down a trapdoor was endorsed by Deacon Hastings and his wife.[29] The baby born to Samuel and Lydia Wright was also undoubtedly premature. The wet-nurse "attempted to give the child her breast opening its mouth but could not cause any refreshment to be taken." Yet Danforth, the examining magistrate, wanted to know why Lydia's mother "caried it so privatly that the neighbours were unacquainted with the birth before the death." Because, she answered, "further reproaches [of abortion] should follow thereon." Such doubts were put to rest by witnesses who saw the child's corpse, but the Wrights were convicted of premarital fornication.[30] Elizabeth, wife of John Barnard "was delivered of a child within 3 months after her marriage which lived 2 daies. John Barnard [denied] that the child was begotten before theire marriage." His mother and the midwife testified that it was an "auntimely burth . . . i cant sai that the woman had gon halfe hur time." Nevertheless another suspicious private burial led to conviction.[31]

John and Susannah Wiggins of Medford had gotten married out of township and county at Lynn in Essex. There, the resident magistrate, Captain Marshall, "strictly examined them if they were published [i.e., banns posted] according to the Laws. A. Yes. Did Susannahs father so swear. A. Yea. Goodman Marble did intreat Capt Marshall to mary them . . . it was an honest bisnes. . . . Marble would bear him harmless . . . the bride was at his Desposing." The severe ten pound fine *and* corporal punishment inflicted on the couple, suggest that the bench took grave exception to an attempt to evade the law covering premarital fornication.[32] They may have even ordered that John and Susannah remarry in Medford.[33]

Most parents in this survey were either, like Goodman Marble, accessories after the fact or else disregarded. The only exceptions were the few parents who broke the law by delaying weddings. Newlyweds, though not above self-justification in their confessions, took full responsibility for their actions. This is vividly illustrated in the bizarre case of Joseph and Elizabeth Bent.

Early in 1667 Elizabeth Bent gave birth to a full-term child twenty-seven weeks after her marriage to Joseph Bent of Sudbury.[34] Although Joseph had previously "owned the childe to be his," he now averred "that he had no knowledge of his wife until after marriage."[35] Elizabeth subsequently admitted to the midwife and selectmen that the father was James Taylor, with whom she had "had to doe severall times: & . . . James Taylor said to her that *she should be silent*[36] & he would begett a boy for Joseph who had spoken to her once . . . & Joseph would not mind [i.e., know about] it & that James Taylor told her that he would speake to Joseph to come & he would tell him that she would have him: & that he told her that she should not tell but she said she resolved she would not be silent for she would not damme her soule." Joseph solemnly assured his parents that he was innocent and asked John Stone to write a letter for Elizabeth to her father. Stone agreed "only he told her he would write nothing for her but what she should her selfe present." She repeated her story.

Stone, and others, were plainly suspicious. They had good reason. On 30 March 1667 "divers in our church" heard the following confession:

> I Joseph Bent do from the bottom of my hart acknowledge and confesse that through the temptation of Satan and the provocation of my owne lust that I did fall into the sin of uncleanes before marriage with Elizabeth my wife, and thereby dishonoured my body and the estate of mariage which God as a bed undefiled hath apointed . . . And I have sadly fallen into another sin, of denying contrary to my conscience that the childe borne by my wife was not mine . . . and was well pleased that it was layd unto an other, and he somtyme of such a family whose honour and good name I should not have . . . violated.[37]

Whatever the motivations at work here,[38] one conclusion is clear. In both the fantasy and the factual accounts, the parents were left in complete ignorance of what was going on. They were not consulted about the engagement; they were deceived about paternity. The show of deference to their authority was a cynical formality. In this case, at least, we can rule out patriarchal oppression as a cause of sin; the parents, like James Taylor, were far more sinned against than sinning.

The midwife had been careful to ask Goody Bent whether she was espoused when she had to do with James Taylor, and Elizabeth was equally careful to deny it. Had she not, it would have become "a hanging matter" as adultery within contract.[39] Breach of contract, on the other hand, was a civil action. It might lead to criminal proceedings later if fornication had taken place. While marriage lessened the guilt of premarital sex, breach of promise would increase it. Damages awarded reflected this.

Case Studies: Breach of Promise

In 1661 the case of John Whitticus or Whittaker, husbandman of Cambridge, came up, and with it, a confusion of names.[40] He and Mary Linfield had been courting for some time. "He gave her a silver bodkin and hath sat up with her and kept her company by night and by day sundry times."[41] Mary, an orphan, was a chaste girl: "Beeing demanded whether he could charge any dishonesty upon her hee said nay he knew nothing against her in that kind." There was no excuse for honorable escape there. She was devoted to him to the point of distraction, even though he had twice promised to marry her and twice let her down. His justification for his jilting of her at his examination was simply that "his affection for her is less than formerly." He may have been subjected to pressure from the authorities or fellow townspeople. After his examination "he solemnly promises forthwith to take to his wife the sd. Elizabeth [sic] Linfield & caused the publication of the said marriage to be affixed upon the meeting house door . . . but now he refuseth to performe this contract."

He was summoned to court on 2 April 1661 having "confessed he had promised marriage to Mary Linfield before sundry witnesses and afterwards refused the same." When he was called, he did not appear. Eventually he arrived, to be told by the court that "he had behaved towards Mary Linfield with much unfaythfulness and fraud." Bond of fifty pounds was taken from him and from each of his two sureties for his appearance at the next court, for recompense to Mary Linfield and for the town to be secured from charge. There are no entries referring to this case in the records of the next or subsequent courts. The confusion of names by the recorder in this case may be a clue to this silence, for shortly afterward Whittaker did marry an Elizabeth. It is possible that he jilted Mary Linfield in favor of her sister Elizabeth. It would not be the first or the last time that such a transfer of affections had happened.[42]

The 1666 action of Richard Dexter of Malden against Edward Pinson of London reads more like a Restoration rogue tale or a French fabliau than life in rural New England. There are twelve long documents on file, but the events can be quickly summarized. Sarah Dexter was either promised to Obadiah Bridges[43] or engagement was imminent when Edward Pinson arrived on the scene. He was recently from London—a seaman or merchant probably—and with his ready ways and ready cash and promises of London life and London riches he appears to have swept Sarah off her feet. Her father was less infatuated and warned Pinson (who had only recently buried his first wife) to cease keeping company with his daughter. The pair nailed up banns on the meeting-house door, but they were pulled down. Then, while the parents were at meeting, they eloped from Malden only to return four days later claiming to have been married by Captain Marshall of Lynn. They wanted to sail off to England. It was probably at this point that Dexter addressed Pinson as "rogue, bastard dogg and son of a whore" and that Bridget Dexter beat her daughter out of the house.

It emerged later that the young Lothario had presented a forged letter of parental consent to the Lynn magistrate; the witness was Andrew Robinson, a notorious lecher already encountered. In a calmer statement Dexter bewailed the "taking from me a daughter of Israel & bestowing on me a daughter of Ishmael," but the last laugh was on Pinson. He discovered that his rustic bride had already been pregnant when he met her. She had "lost her virginitie being overcome in Boston by a man who promiseth her marriage but afterwards went off to sea and since she heard he had a wife in England."[44] The court would not have been satisfied with this poetic justice, but what their judgment was has not survived.[45]

When Elizabeth Mancer and her daughter were espied merrily seducing a sailor in their naked bed in Charlestown in 1689, it was John Row, a twenty-seven-year-old shipwright who burst in on the scene and later denounced the trio in high-minded terms. He was the son of Elias Row, a successful mariner, who paid £130 for twenty-eight acres of land in Charlestown in 1678 and was often on the grand jury of the Court of Assistants in the 1670s and 1680s. In the summer of 1685 Martha Beale, daughter of William Beale of Marblehead, was maidservant to Elias Row.

> The testimony of William Beale aged upward of fivety six yeares testifieth and sayeth that upon the eleventh day of September last [1685] by my ackcount upon the Allmnack,[46] then Elias Row of Charlestowne told mee that my daughter Martha Beale . . . cryed & made bitter complaint to him that his son had defilld her body by carnall copulation. John Row came in instantly into the Roome & owned the fackt aforementioned. Elias Row & John Row desired not to noise the fackt aforesaid abroade but to ioyne the parties aforesaid in marriage; & this was the very first time that I heard of the aforesayd. Then instantly Martha Beale came into the roome. I did then reprove her. What she sayd I doe not remember but we all agreed to marry the parties aforesayd uppon the next second day [Monday] followinge & my daughter Martha went out of the roome weeping, & then instantly I found my daughter Martha allon weepings & then shee sayed to mee pray you ffather bee not soe much troubled for hee forced mee by violence in this house hee hath torne and hauled mee & strove to gett his will uppon my body in as violent a manner as a woolfe uppon a sheepe & once in the day time hee over mastered mee & then I cryed oute & then hee left off & begged of mee to forgive him very ernestly & many times after hee begged of mee to forgive him, sayinge hee would never offer mee such

an abuse any more but I was minded since to see how hee would behave himselfe but a certaine time afterwards at bed time I wente to bed in the darke and locked the door unto mee but Row was hidden in the bed roome secretly unknowne unto mee & beeing in bed he then came uppon mee at unawares to mee, at first I was loath to cry oute or to raise a tumult in my masters house & his son alsoe, but strove against him to prevent him in his intents untill I was quite tired & my breath spent & allmost dead so that I could not cry out when I tryed to doe it, & all the time hee held mee downe & kept his hand on my face I thoughte to stop my mouth & soe he gott his will uppon my body by violence, & then he went away, and my selfe not being able to rest I rose oute of my bed & wept in a mournefull condition all the nighte longe afterwards, but durst not goe downe into the neither roome nor out of the house for feare of my master who used to carry very cross to mee & I dreaded to ackquaint him with it, but the next *mourninge*[47] day I sayed unto Elias Row aforesayd Sir I have receaved an abuse in your house the wch. I must ackquaint you with all but shee sayed hee sayed to her, dam you the devill take you doe not tell mee of it.[48] Then she sayed that shee told gooddy Kelly of it; that John Row had abused her boddy & that shee pittyed her but could not helpe her; then shee sayed that shee put on corrage & tould her master Elias Row, that his son John Row had forcibly abused & ravished her body against her will; & that then hee sayed that hee would aske his son aboute it & shee sayed that shee heared Elias Row & his son John Row taulkinge together, & that John Row sayed its tru, what shall I doe aboute it & that Elias Row sayed you must marry her & soone afterward Elias Row owned unto her that his son John Row owned to him all that shee told him concerninge the abuse aforesayed & denyed non of it.

Beale's three large pages of spidery handwriting continued the narrative. The following evening he came to Charlestown "expecting the publication of marriage . . . had been set up accordinge to agreement" but John was reluctant and

seemingly wept, it was in the darke I could not see his face. Hee then sayed to me If Martha bee not with childe I am loath to marry with her for I love another better I am very sorry for what I have don if it were to doe againe I would never doe it, but I then replyed unto him John Shee came not into your bed chamber but you came into hers . . . at unawares to her . . . if you break the agreement of marriage there is another course to be taken with you . . . then he wrote their publishmente & nayled it uppon Charlestowne Meetinge house. September thirteene . . . in the evening Elias Row said to mee your daughter is not with child John is bound to sea we will not marry them untill he returneth back because it will raise a suspicion in peoples breasts & people will taulk much of them.

Row offered various safeguards against his son's desertion (no pay until return, the ship's master forewarned) and the couple were formally betrothed before the two fathers the next day. Old Elias informed William that although John "took a pet in his head" that his father was "about to marry a young woman and disinherit him, hee is mistaken." He would inherit all unmoveables entailed on his children; if he broke his engagement, Elias would cut him off. William Beale returned to Marblehead no doubt reassured.

Two days later, September 16

> in the morning soone after it was light my daughter Martha Beale came into my house having as she sayed travelled all the night from Charlestown to Marblehead. She then wept lamentably complaineinge that she was utterly undon . . . John and his ffather denyed all that was agreed upon.

Beale went to the governor, a relative, who counseled one final attempt at agreement in the presence of Captain Hunting. Martha, at first, "fell into a most sore languishing condition shee beinge overwhelmed with the troobles . . . but afterwards being somthinge better" confronted jilting John. She solemnly charged him with ravishing her against her will, "a thinge that I allways hated from my childhood . . . her cry reached to heaven against him." He replied:

> Doe doe now you make a bluster aboute towne and country of it & see what youle gett by it you flunge nuts at mee & entised mee then he hasted to goe out of the roome & she layed hold on his coate saying that shee must speake with him, he sayed Looke looke see Josephs Mistris.[49]

When Beale reminded him of his engagement, he said:

> he was forced soe to doe. . . . What the pox what the plague will you have me to marry your daughter against my will. What if I should beate her twoo or three or half a dozen times a weeke. Help youre self if you can, I did not promise to marry her except shee bee with child & Elias Row came into the same roome and bid us all get out of the house saying you must not thinke that you can beat Elias Row with a faggot stick.

Samuel Hunting corroborated this account, adding some telling details. Row asked Martha why she did not cry out when the alleged ravishment was taking place; she said "she was not willing to hang him." She admitted that "she held on to him severall times and would hardly lett him go, but it was after he had defiled her & unfitted her for another man against her will and it was to persuade him to marry her."

On 6 April 1686 the court received a petition from William Beale complaining that John Row had violated his daughter. Some witnesses testified that Martha herself seemed unaware of any complaint and simply wanted John Row to marry her. Hannah Perkins, Row's aunt, quoted her as saying that "the Governor[50] was her cousin & if John Row would marry with her the governor would forgive him and not bring him to court. Goody Perkins, I am as sure with child by him as ever any maid was."[51] The elders of Charlestown Church signed a testimonial dated 21 September 1685 as to the christian and sober character of Martha Beale and her desire for church membership which the pastor's death had delayed.

On 6 April 1686 the court fined Row five pounds and "sentenced" him to marry Martha within fourteen days. If he refused, he was "to pay William Beale . . . one hundred pound in money." He "openly declared his Resolution never to marry with Martha" and appealed to the superior court.[52] The case was settled out of court by the payment of fifteen pounds to the Beales. In 1687 Elias Row died, leaving £764 in personal estate. The same year John married. His bride was not Martha Beale, however, but seventeen-year-old Ruth Knil of Boston. Their son Elias, aged sixteen months, drowned in a tub of water in 1696. Already a sick man by 1697, Row was dead by 30 January 1699.[53]

These domestic tragedies confirm in detail some of our previous suggestions: the vulnerability both physical and psychological of servant maids, the long-term nature of many adolescent relationships, the ability of the young to find opportunities for their affairs, and the force of public opinion. They also give two rare examples of patriarchal financial sanctions being employed. The attitudes toward virginity reveal an unattractive but conventional double standard. To Pinson, discovery of Sarah's previous sexual experience is a blow to his self-esteem; to the Beales loss of virginity is a disaster; to the Rows this is regrettable and worth fifteen pounds in compensation, but it is not sufficient grounds to require marriage. The court certainly endorsed the Beales' view and so did public opinion if the Rows' fears of publicity are anything to go by. In this connection, the later records of "deflowered" women are pertinent. Though, as we saw, quite a few of them eventually found husbands, none made good matches. They had to make do with widowers, cripples, men of tarnished reputation or of a lower class.[54] The persistence of suits against "defilers" to the end of the century suggests that chastity continued to be highly valued. These cases enrich our understanding of adolescent psychology, family dynamics, and popular mores; we must now integrate them into our broader consideration of bridal pregnancy.

Conclusion

The most remarkable feature of the sixty-six cases of bridal pregnancy in the court records is the fact that at least two out of three cases involved at least one member of a church family.[55] It was quite common for culprits to be the offspring of leading church members, ministers, or deacons.[56] The Beale, Row, and Dexter families were also "within the Covenant of Grace," and Pinson in a letter to Michael Wigglesworth claimed to be a personal friend of leading ministers. His first wife had been a deacon's daughter. In church disciplines, baptism of premaritally conceived children must be prefaced by parental confession. This requirement had no bearing on criminal proceedings, however. Why then did "children of the church" predominate in this way? It seems inconceivable that the nonelect would be more law-abiding in this area. It is equally incredible that the authorities would turn a blind eye to nonregenerate families' bridal pregnancies. Would they tacitly tolerate betrothal license among the "goats"? This brings us back to the various explanations for premarital pregnancy sketched earlier.

We can quickly rule out the idea that betrothal license was officially condoned. Many influential puritan dogmatists were on record as condemning any premarital sexual experience. Philip Stubbes, the great Elizabethan anatomist of abuses, described such misbehavior as "vomits and quagmires";[57] William Gouge thought the fact that "many take liberty after a contract [betrothal] to know their spouse, as if they were married: an unwarrantable and dishonest practice."[58] William Perkins urged men not to marry "a woman as hath beene formerly defloured" and asserted that marriage contracts between nonvirgins were illegal.[59] When a group of puritan laymen took control in Terling, Essex, one of their first targets for reformation of manners was betrothal license, which significantly was never prosecuted in nonpuritan Maryland.[60] In 1665 the Massachusetts General Court complained that many persons were unwilling to save their virginity until marriage,[61] but the tone of confessions demonstrates that sex among the engaged was still generally held to be a serious crime. Massachusetts law made it an offense for parents to delay a marriage once the young couple was "sure" and in five cases such obstruction was pled as a mitigating factor.[62] Yet in no case did they claim that delay excused them. Thomas Jones was "trobled in his mind" by what he had done, and John Roy spoke of being "overcome by temptation."

The persistence of official condemnation does not rule out the possibility that nonelect families accepted betrothal license as part of the old English popular culture. Where other sources than prosecutions have been used to compute premarital fornication, however, the incidence is similar. Thus the eight couples of Watertown detected by genealogical research are matched by eight convictions in the court records.[63] There is only one ambivalent hint in any of the often candid testimony that betrothal license was ever regarded as acceptable. When Thomas Goble discovered Joseph Groves and Esther Nicholls under a blanket together in his bedroom, he asked Groves "What they might have done if both parties had been agreed?" To Nicholls he said, "If they had been both agreed I would not tell what they might have done." Groves's response was that "he had never sought her, and knew not whether she was a maid or a wife." Nicholls answered that "she was never counted a whore in her life." It is possible to interpret Goble's remarks to his maidservant as "If you two had been engaged I would keep quiet about this," but a more likely reading seems to me to be "If you two had been engaged, your petting might have led you into sexual intercourse if I had not caught you in time." Whatever Goble meant—and he was fined five pounds for entertaining Groves in his house—it is a slender thread on which to hang a theory of widespread popular betrothal license.[64]

Did adolescents use pregnancy as a means to force parents to agree to marriage?[65] Was this especially the case where a child of the church wished to marry into an unregenerate family, a practice frowned on by the godly? We do have some evidence to support such a possibility. Thus Edward Hodsman, a nonchurch member, stated that though initially "Goodman Pike would not let him have his daughter hee [Pike] would be glad ere long to come with his cap in his hand and entreat him for to have his daughter." Thomas Jones may have "overcome" Sarah Crouch, an unmarried mother under church admonition, in order to persuade his father. Edward Pinson stole a march on Sarah Dexter's unwilling parents by eloping and entering a clandestine marriage. Yet these are the only cases where such motives are voiced and in each one the evidence is ambivalent. Furthermore, many convictions concerned couples who both came from godly families.

There is similarly little evidence to support the suggestion that young women deliberately got themselves pregnant to hook their man. It is possible that Martha Beale may have done so. Mary Atherton slept with her husband before marriage and then told her master, who forced Thomas Atherton to marry her. She, however, was already pregnant by a Negro at the time.[66] On the other hand, no young woman who had been promised marriage by her seducer ever sought to put pressure on him by sueing him, and two expectant mothers adamantly refused to marry the fathers of their children when enjoined to do so by the court.[67]

We are thrown back on the last two possibilities mooted: external circumstances or shotgun weddings. Historians were alerted to the first explanation by both the coincidence of premarital fornication increases with unstable economic conditions, and by the way in which fornication trends parallel those for bridal pregnancy. Economic—or political or social—shocks to the system could interfere with marriage plans and, by causing delays, reveal or induce prenuptial mistakes. A period of "courtship intensity" encouraged by prosperous conditions could, if suddenly interrupted, produce a rise of both extra- and premarital fornication cases. In the Middlesex Files, two couples do cite "these hard times" in their confessions.[68] Both cases occur during periods of instability: 1686, shortly after the loss of the first charter, and 1691 in the wake of the Glorious Revolution. Similarly, in one or two fornication cases, reputed fathers, who might in other circumstances have married their bastard bearers immediately, refer to war service or having to go to sea as reasons for irresponsibility.[69] The figures also give some support here. Cases of bridal pregnancy, previously extremely rare, begin to rise in the years after 1666, following the devastating wheat blight in Massachusetts.[70] After King Philip's War, the number of convicted fornicators from church families rose steeply between 1676 and 1680—ten out of sixteen for the period 1671–1680—while those children of the church convicted of bridal pregnancy fell to only two for the whole period. In the 1680s and early 1690s—politically the most insecure period in the second half of the century—the incidence of premarital fornication cases is relatively high. There were more of these than fornication convictions between 1681 and 1686, and five cases in both 1691 and 1692, the highest annual totals.

The apparent connection should be treated with great caution however. There are other possible explanations for some of the statistics. For instance the General Court's campaign against immorality may have netted more suspects in the late 1660s; the institution of tything-men in the 1670s and the Reform Synod of 1679 may have had similar results.[71] Those who cited hard times sought reduction in fines rather than justification for their crimes, and it is usually not clear whether military or sea service provided excuses or possible escapes.[72] Finally the small numbers involved make it arguable that correlations were purely fortuitous. What does emerge, however, is the close relationship between bastardy trends and bridal pregnancy. With the authority of the court behind her, the unmarried mother was able to compel the reputed father to provide maintenance. Somehow or other, the pregnant bride had managed to compel the father to go one crucial step further: to marry her.

By this process of elimination, shotgun marriages emerge as the most likely explanation of bridal pregnancy. The pressures that could be brought to bear on a young man "to make an honest woman"[73] (a seventeenth-century usage) of the girl he had impregnated were intense. The very fact that the law of 1648 included injunction to marry as a penalty for fornication and that the Middlesex bench in 1657 could order James Ross to marry Mary Goodenow "unless she and her friends shall give just reason for her deniall" gives some sense of official attitudes,[74] as do the reduced penalties meted out to fornicators who subsequently married.

The front rank of shotgunners were the parents, however, especially the girl's parents. William Beale held one at John Row's head when he hesitated about nailing up the banns; he recruited his gubernatorial relative to lend him firepower; finally he brought in the court who offered Row the alternatives of marriage or massive damage payments. Elias Row, an erstwhile ally, proposed first a quick concealing marriage and then, when the need for urgency had ebbed, disinheritance of his son as a guarantee of a future match. James Pike likewise summoned the leading citizens of Reading to put the screws on Benjamin Knowlton, who, if he had been told "within a month after the fact committed would have married her and the world should never have been the wiser." In the fantasy fornication concocted by the Bents, James Taylor was alleged to have told Elizabeth to agree to the proposed espousals with Joseph immediately after the imagined intercourse. Both Joseph and Elizabeth contacted their parents to assure them, respectively, of innocence and penitence. When they finally confessed their fraud, they specifically apologized for slurring someone "of such a family whose honour and good name I should not have suffered so to have been violated." Goodman Marble not only shepherded his pregnant daughter and her lover across the county line to Lynn, but also belied himself to get them married there. Major Thomas Savage, whose own daughter Dionysia bore a bastard in 1678, forced two of his servants to marry when his maid became pregnant.[75] Daniel Gookin, the Cambridge magistrate, acted in loco parentis in behalf of Mary Linfield to try to force John Whittaker to keep his word.

Community pressure was another means of shaming young men into marriage. Knowlton's crime was "published abroad in the town."

He was finally forced to decamp. There were "sundry witnesses" when John Whittaker "promised marriage to Mary Linfield." The Bents had to tell their tale over and over again to disbelieving townspeople. The Rows "desired not to noise the fackt aforesaid abroad"; they worried that a rushed wedding "will raise a suspicion in peoples breasts and people will talk much of them." Writing to Michael Wigglesworth, Pinson complained, "My name, my fame and my credit is blemisht here by a Crew of Rusticks," no doubt Malden neighbors of the Dexters. In the face of these serried ranks of moral marksmen, it is not difficult to imagine errant and hesitant young men deciding that discretion was the better part of valor.

Yet some adolescents resisted the moral suasion and blackmail of parents, the power of hostile public opinion, and the rulings of the bench. Why? The reason given by Whittaker and Row and Dexter and implied by Knowlton's behavior was that their affections had cooled. Love mattered; not some potential love once they were married, but love now. What John Row was saying to the man eager to be his father-in-law was "Marry for love, or repent at leisure." Knowlton would rather leave Reading than settle for married life there with a woman he no longer cared for. Sarah Dexter's preference for Pinson over Obadiah Bridges was based on strong personal attraction for a dashing young beau.

What enlightenment does our survey of the possible reasons for bridal pregnancy cast on the problem of high involvement on the part of children of the godly? It does not seem to have been a means of blackmail to force elect parents to allow "mixed" marriages into unregenerate families, and there is little evidence of widespread betrothal license among the latter. We must conclude then that church families were more successful in constraining their errant children into marriage, or that the offenders themselves were more responsible individuals. The higher percentage of nonregenerate children convicted of fornication seems to bear this out.[76]

So far as our inquiry into family dynamics is concerned, the pressuring by the patriarchs only occurs *after* their children have asserted themselves. Most of the evidence presented here shows the adolescents involved taking the first initiatives, sometimes in the teeth of their parents' wishes: the wealthy Elias Row could hardly have welcomed alliance with the undistinguished Beales, and the rage of the Dexters at the thwarting of the Bridges match is tangible. Once again romantic predilections play a large part, and once again the parents are left to try to clear up the mess, to save family honor, to persuade young men to do the decent thing. This at least is the impression that we draw from the sixty-six cases in the records. Yet we should remember that on average only one birth in every two hundred was punished as premaritally conceived, and that the ratio for Middlesex was minuscule in comparison with England or the southern colonies, and below that of other Massachusetts counties. The very rarity of cases may be a potent argument for the continuing patriarchal authority in family government.

4 / Sexual Deviance and Abuse

ARLY modern Western societies were unique in the long delay they imposed on marriage after the onset of puberty.[1] What happened to youthful sexual drives during this frustrating decade or more has been the source of considerable contention among historians. One school argues that, thanks to patriarchal indoctrination and especially to the puritan variety with its taboos against filthiness and pollution, adolescents repressed their sexual urges and lived chastely until marriage. Scholars such as Stone and Shorter cite the low level of fornication convictions as evidence that "the lives of most young people were resolutely unerotic."[2] This view has not gone unchallenged. There are various other means available to adolescents to satisfy their sexual needs short of heterosexual intercourse resulting in an illegitimate or prenuptially conceived child. The most obvious is masturbation, solitary or mutual, but there is also homosexuality, bestiality, petting, coitus interruptus, anal or oral sex,[3] or intercourse by unmarried men with either married women or prostitutes or prepubescent girls.[4] All of these forms of sexual activity could be common among groups or individuals; if so, the historical indicators of sexual continence would present a totally misleading appearance.

If such a youthful conspiracy against chastity existed, we should expect some of the subverters to be caught. Further we could anticipate some of the unsuppressed to lose their self-control and attempt to gratify their lusts by force if necessary. In this chapter we analyze the evidence in Middlesex for such deviant activities as masturbation, homosexuality, and bestiality, and for examples of sexual abuse. In the next we shall turn to the question of whether such a phenomenon as adolescent culture existed there.

Survey of Evidence

In strictly controlled and structured single-sex societies in modern times, such as boarding schools, masturbation is common and a certain amount of homosexuality also occurs. Although there are scattered references to solitary or group masturbation in other New England court records, including one case of a father with a son,[5] there is no mention of this particular "depravity" in the Middlesex Records. That puritan dogma held self-abuse to be a depravity cannot be doubted. Though Onan had, in fact, been struck dead by God for coitus interruptus, preachers like Thomas Cobbett, Samuel Danforth, the Mathers, and Michael Wigglesworth all cited his fate and regarded "self-pollution" as a fatal step along the primrose path to perdition, with sodomy as a likely stop along the way.[6] New Haven law went so far as to ordain a maximum punishment of death for mutual masturbation, since it "tends to the sin of sodomy if it be not one kind of it."[7] Charles Morton, briefly resident in Charlestown, was reproducing received wisdom when he wrote, "The seed itself . . . is made out of the purest blood . . . whence follows that the Abuse of it in any wicked way is consecrating the best of our bodyes to the divell." There were medical grounds for condemning the wanton ejaculation of semen. If this vital fluid were wasted, growth would be stunted, the brain weakened, and "many filthy loathsome diseases" might be generated.[8]

May we then conclude from the absence of court cases and these draconian warnings that masturbation was a rare vice in Middlesex? Perhaps. While a tutor at Harvard, Michael Wigglesworth went through interminable agonies of remorse over wet dreams and a seminal discharge.[9] Cotton Mather, who publicly warned against the vice several times, admitted in his diary that he was sorely tempted, but never used the contemplated solution, to "cut off my right hand."[10] These future ministers certainly seem to have internalized the guilt attached to self-pollution. However, they may have been untypical. In his letter of advice to his son about to enter Harvard in 1672, Thomas Shepard, Jr., minister of Charlestown, warned him against "youthful lusts, speculative wantonness and secret filthiness, which God sees in the dark and for which God hardens and blinds young men's hearts . . . there are and will be such in every scholastic society, for the most part, as will teach you how to be filthy."[11] As a Harvard graduate himself, he presumably wrote from experience. In 1690 Cotton Mather wrote, "Beware of having light thoughts about some sorts of uncleanness wherein many young people have been so infatuated as to excuse themselves. These are abominable self-pollutions which many, that would loath to commit other kinds of uncleanness, look upon as little, venial, easy Peccadillos." Mather took a close interest in the doings of young folks at this time and was still only twenty-seven himself. He later stated that "many, many are guilty . . . so many that if stoning were the punishment a mountain could not afford stones enough."[12] If he and Shepard are to be believed, then, masturbation did not occur in the court records because people turned a blind eye to a mere "trick of youth."

Sodomy and bestiality were capital crimes in both England and Massachusetts; as felonies they came under the jurisdiction of the Court of Assistants, though the county court sometimes held a preliminary hearing. Thus, on 28 December 1658 Abraham Howell was presented by the Middlesex grand jury for "sodomiticall uncleanes." There is no record of the Court of Assistants having heard the case remanded to them.[13] Two presentments of Middlesex men for bestiality were made in the 1670s. On 6 October 1674 John Barrett of Chelmsford was dismissed with an admonition after no legal evidence appeared against him. There survive in the Prince Collection of the Boston Public Library two depositions recorded by Thomas Danforth on 9 September 1676 which were subsequently sworn in the Court of Assistants at the trial of John Lawrence on 8 March 1677. Between seven and eight in the morning on 5 September Thomas Michelson of Cambridge, aged about twenty, was in the marshes on the south side of Cambridge Bridge. He claimed to have seen Lawrence

> standing on a tree that lay along on the ground having his face towards his
> mares tail and his hand clasped about her Buttock and after a while he saw
> him with draw himselfe a little from the body of the mare and as he thought
> he turned the mares tayle on the one side and then he again clasped his
> hands about her Buttocks as before and wrought with his body against her,
> at the sight whereof he was so amazed that he knew not what to do whether
> to speake to him or be silent but turning his face towards the bridge he
> saw Isaac Amsden coming along the highway . . . they both charged
> Lawrence with the said wicked and abominable act but he peremptorily
> denied the same, and when asked whether he had not attempted it: he burst
> out crying and said he would say no more to them . . . he was within three
> or four rod [16 or 22 yards] of John Lawrence.

Amsden, another Cambridge man, aged about twenty-one, deposed that

> Thomas Michelson came to him . . . and was greatly affrighted and as a man amazed and said to him he had seen that that morning that he had rather given £100 than to have sene it. . . . He [Amsden] was too far away to witness the act.

In the absence of two witnesses Lawrence was acquitted.[14]

Only two men were executed for bestiality in seventeenth-century Massachusetts, none for sodomy. Unlike masturbation, these were probably extremely rare practices. The reactions of the discoverer, the discovered, and of other courts to these crimes "not to be named" were of shocked horror at such depravity. Even jokes about these topics were severely punished. Edmund Dorman was overheard praying for marriage: "Lord thou knowest my necessity and canst supply it, Lord bend and bow her will and make her sensible of my condition." When a disreputable wag opined that "it may be his mare that God would make servisable," he quickly incurred the wrath of the authorities.[15]

Cases of men seeking sex with prepubescent girls are similarly rare. Three of the four single males so convicted were Indians or Negroes. In the case of Thomas Dublet, Indian, in 1660, his victim Elizabeth Stow, aged only seven or eight, apparently gave him some encouragement. The main prosecution witness was Mary How, aged forty, who had been baby-sitting at the time.

> Elizabeth Stow says Here comes my man & the Indian says Here is my squa. [While How was getting the baby to sleep] the Indian and Elizabeth went out to the corn field out of her hearing. He laid her down upon her backe & turned up her coats on her face & then put his finger in at the bottom of her belly and then lying upon her did with some other thing hurt her at the bottom of her belly which made her cry Oh Oh but afterward hee let her goe. . . . She [How] hath often seen & observed wanton & uncivill carridges by the aforesaid Elizabeth Stow and hath told her father who corrected her. She found signes of seed upon the childs wombe & some attempt of breaches in entering her body but not very farr.

Sexual intercourse with a girl under ten, even with her consent, was a capital offense, but penetration had to be proved.[16] Dublet's sentence of paying a twenty pound fine or being sold out of the colony reflects the court's indignation.[17]

All the evidence from English and New England court records in the seventeenth century suggests that apart from masturbation, deviant sexual activity was exceedingly rare. Men and women of the middle and lower orders took their pleasures straight, without complications, though often with a boisterous lack of finesse. Cases of homosexuality, bestiality, or paedophilia in the published records are so uncommon as to be statistically insignificant. What we know of the seventeenth-century English suggests that sexual experimentation and libertinism were the outcome of sophisticated, leisured, privileged, and urbanized groups, such as court or literary coteries;[18] these prerequisites would effectively exclude the population of Middlesex County, Massachusetts.

The extreme rarity of convictions for deviant sexuality is, of course, no proof that Middlesex adolescents were resolute in living unerotic lives. There are ten cases, seven of them between 1672 and 1686, in which young men felt so resolutely erotic that they attempted to force women to do their will. In six of these cases, their victims were married women, and in another the woman involved was living with another man. There is no hint in the surviving depositions, however, that wives had been consciously chosen so as to avoid the consequences of the bastardy laws, a stratagem notorious in English popular tales of cuckoldry.[19] Nor do the wives conform to the chapbook model of complaisance; they all resist importunities vigorously. Thus Sarah Smith, attacked in a swamp by Robert Bartlett in October 1655, explained, "I was very earnest with him to lett mee goe. . . . I told him I would not . . . and it pleased God to keep in mee a resolution not to yeeld and he did at length lett me goe . . . he told mee he could have done it whether I would or noe."[20] When William Mahoone flung down Jane Allen, violently turned up her clothes, "and with his hand did immodestly touch her . . . she caught his hair and screamed for her husband and at length escaped."[21] The recently married Elizabeth Glasier had been importuned by Timothy Brooks "unto wanton dalliance" for a month in the summer of 1662 and had finally been lured into a room, "but this examinant denies hee had the use of her but only attempted it and had loosed his breeches with examinant resisting what she could."[22] Middlesex wives were not pushovers.

Case Studies: Sexual Abuse

When Andrew Robinson called at the house of Joseph Wilson, blacksmith of Malden, he found he had gone out. Robinson and Sarah, the smith's wife, waited up for him till near midnight when she, being unwell, went to bed, leaving Robinson, who was twenty, with the fifteen-year-old apprentice. Within half an hour, Robinson, "having mad the dor so fast with the padhooks that 100 could not open it," appeared by her bedside.

> [He] told her that he would come to bed to her but she tould him that he should not but he said he would come to bed and would lie in her husbands place. She askt him if he was not ashamed to come to a womans bed and he tould her he would put out the light she askt him if he was ashamed to be so uncivil and bad him go to bed where he might or els go out Adors but he begin to lean over the bed She tould him he would hurt the child. He bad her lay the child on the other side and he would come in that side and keep her warm for she would be a cold now her husband was not at home & when she spak to him he stel urged her to speak sofly that the youth might not hear, & then he got his hand into har bosom & she shufd it out again. And then he began to pull up the bed clothes but when she saw that he was
> ———,[23] she was much afraid.

In the last lines of her testimony she told how she threatened to cry out and call the youth, and then Robinson went away. Under examination by Daniel Gookin, Robinson confessed. He was sentenced to a forty shilling fine and a ten pound bond for good behavior.[24]

George Newby of Lancaster, indicted in April 1686 for "vitious and unclean deboyst carriages" against two sisters-in-law, had similarly caught them when their husbands were out. With Experience, the wife of Isaac Wheeler, he

> then offered abuse to the woman & laid out his nakedness and rubbed his sackrit members on her hand as also used many arguments to draw her to uncleannes with him.

Tabitha, the wife of Abraham Wheeler, was likewise

> alone in the house with a sucking child. Newby offered abuse to the woman using many arguments with her to commit adultery with him & told her it was no great matter so to do for it was a small sin & might be repented of: with other speeches as she saith he urged her.[25]

Like Sarah Wilson, Tabitha Wheeler used her baby to inhibit the urges of her attacker.

Apart from harvest time, men and women usually worked separately: women in house or farmyard, men in barn or field. The main exceptions to this were various craftsmen with opportunities to mix with women, such as housewrights or millers, who had a particularly unsavory reputation. In traditional society, "trouble at mill" described relations other than the industrial.

Robert Montgomery, apprentice miller in Charlestown[26] in 1676, ran true to professional form, according to Goodwife Sarah Stretcher, aged twenty-six.

> At the end of April last Robert Mungomery pulled her down in his lap and would have been naught with her and told her if she would he would give her stuff enof to make her a gown or else money, which[ever] she would, and had not a man come in he would a forced me, done what I could for my Lief . . . he would have had me gon to forging[27] with him and leve my children with the ould woman & she should not want for money if she would go along with him.

This solicitor of "sundry women that brought grist to his mill," a blatant menace to Charlestown chastity, was sentenced to twenty stripes and dismissed.[28]

Most of the wives involved in these cases of sexual abuse and harassment emerge as models of married morality. Since they or their husbands initiated prosecution by complaints, this is hardly surprising. In the case of Elizabeth Glasier, she had failed to tell her husband about the incident with Brooks for two weeks because "she feared his displeasure." The court seems to have been suspicious of her evidence and found the complaint not legally proven. We shall later encounter married women who were far less straitlaced and single women who were free and easy with their favors. These were exceptional, however. Unlike the young bucks and bravoes of Jacobean or Restoration London, young men overcome by lust in Middlesex could not expect the jaunty wives of citizens to assuage their fires.

In three of the four cases of sexual abuse involving young males and single women, the evidence that emerged under examination transformed what had initially appeared to be rapes or attempted rapes into more complex encounters. The complaint of Mary Davis aged twenty-four, sometime servant of her uncle Henry Spring, seemed straightforward. On 3 September 1666 she accused Jonathan Phillips,[29] aged thirty-three, of "often attempting after a wicked and dissolute manner to have carnal copulation with her . . . [and other] lewd and wicked practises." Her specific allegation referred to a Saturday in July at the house of John Chadwick or Shattuck, where, after

striving with her by the chimney, he tooke her up in his Armes and caryed
her from that place to another room where was a bed & layd her uppon it &
there begged her to yield to him in fulfilling his lustfull desiers on her & she
denied him with many expressions of her unwillingness but he still
persisted uncovering himselfe in a shamefull manner for such an act & she
gatt hold of his throat & nipping him soare gat of the bed from him & ran
away & after that he ran away also. Also in the bedroom he begged her to
consent to him by saying he had to doe with sundry young women whom
he named & he could have his desier and not get her with child and could
give them steele powder. She said she would cry out but cannot say if she
did.

He had striven "to have his will and lust with her for more than a
yeere." Her uncle and aunt, Henry and Mehitabel Spring, had seen
Phillips "lurking about his yards and once saw him take hold of Mary
Davis. Sundry times she would run in from milking because John
Phillips doth haunt her so. . . . Eleven weeks since about 10 at night
when we were a bed she came to our bed asking us to warn sd. Phillips
from the house."

Despite this persuasive circumstantial evidence, corroboration of the
attempted rape was needed. This was where John Chadwick came in,
and with him came suspicion and doubt. In almost identical evidence,
this convicted thief claimed to have witnessed the assault from outside
his house.[30] He did not convince. Why had he not intervened? Witnesses described the solid wall through which he said he had seen the
attack, his spiteful jealousy of Phillips, and attempts to suborn a witness. Examination revealed that Chadwick and Davis were living
together "with no relation of master and servant between them and that
their lodging room is one and the same." Phillips's ardor had lured him
into a malicious and collusive trap.[31]

The examination of the twenty-one-year-old Hannah Gardiner about
the behavior of her father's servant Richard Nevers seemed likewise
damning. Five or six days before election day in May 1674:

She having watched with her Aunt & Mrs Syms two nights & but one day
between & having much washing to doe . . . about the fore part of the
day, she being weary with washing & drousy & sleepy sitting asleping by
the fire, on a suddaine unknown & unheard of to hir, a man comes in &
taking her up by the middle to her amazement, throwing her downe
& haling her by the heels about the Roome, she striving what she could &
crying out he would kill her & undoe her; now knowing it was Richard
Nevers; when he had tyred her with haling her in that manner fell on her,

clapt his hands violently and hard on her stomach And throughing hir apron on her mouth Cryed out she was a fooll, & being oppressed with & tired by him he forced his will on her, & when he left her crying (he had undon her) he sayd she was a prateing and lying fool & went his wayes.

Nevers's account of events four nights later on election day eve was given to John and Sarah Green. He claimed that

being crowded in bed because Goodman Whitemore was lodging he went down to sleepe uppon the forme. He said he found Anna Gardiner leaning against the mantel a washing of hir selfe. We asked him What, her hands and her face? He replied he thought the most part of her which, said he, was a temptation unto me & I have had to doe with her.

Even if Hannah was not consciously tempting him by the fireside, it seems unlikely that he could "have had to doe with her" in a crowded house without her acquiescence. In February 1675, after giving birth, Hannah crucially amended her account: Nevers "did the act which was altogether against her will *at first*."[32] On 1 April 1675 she admitted the truth of Nevers's statement. Five days later, the court severely punished both of them for "committing folly together."

This verdict obviously did not please Richard Gardiner, a church member and considerable landowner. In June 1675 he brought a civil action against Nevers for "deflouring his daughter, Anna Gardiner, with all just and due damages." His specific reasons for pursuing the case emerged later.

When first accused of fathering Hannah Gardiners child Richard Nevers denied he had anithing to do with Hannah Gardiner in such a way. Richard Gardiner said that if Richard Nevers would confesse he would not hinder him from marrying his daughter in case his daughter was willing to have him. Whereupon Richard Nevers did confess the next day to the constable and this deponent . . . that he mought mary the woman & the sin would not be so great in the sight of God as it would be if he did not.

What outraged the father was the fact that Nevers had reneged on his implied promise to marry and had brought disrepute to the family name. The civil case dragged on for two years. Twice the apparently baffled Middlesex jury found against Nevers with twenty pound damages, but he won his appeal to the Court of Assistants on 4 September 1677. Despite this, Hannah did eventually find a husband in John Coddington of Boston.[33]

An analogous case occupied the attention of the court in April 1680. At the previous Court of Assistants in Boston Thomas Waters, a tinker, late of Woburn, had been charged with the rape of Bethya, daughter of John Johnson.[34] The jury found him not guilty, mainly because Bethya "publicly owned her whordom" with him in court.

> She was asked why she had not gone home. She said she was afraid the tinker would knock her on the head. She was asked Did the tinker haul her? She answered No, he took her by the hands and led her into the room . . . she drank of his beer and went abroad with him . . . Her father did not give the tinker his consent but in jest . . . [but her father] greeted the tinker saying he was glad to see him and if it was Gods will he should have his child and drank a pot of cider with him. Her father took the tinker by the hand and bid him goodnight.

What had initially appeared to be a capital case of rape had become simple fornication, with some suggestion of parental condonation. Waters was banished. Bethya Johnson was sentenced to the higher than normal punishment of fifteen stripes or a five pound fine.[35]

Absence of documentation in the case of Benjamin Simons of Woburn prevents our being certain that the same process occurred, but it looks very much like it. In September 1676 Simons was indicted before the Court of Assistants for raping Elizabeth Pierce near the garrison house the previous July while King Philip's War was raging. The jury found him not guilty of rape but guilty of attempted rape. The case then seems to have been referred to the Middlesex County Court, but in a different form. In December the charge was "wanton dallying with Elizabeth Pierce tending to uncleanness." Simons elected a jury trial; after two jurors had been objected to, he was found guilty. Despite the fact that Robert Pierce deposed about Simons's ill-behavior with another girl in the garrison in the spring, and Elizabeth's claim that she had told Simons to "lett mee alone for it will bee both sin and a shame to you and me as long as we live," she too was fined two pounds along with Simons. Somewhere along the line, evidence, now lost, probably came out that she was a less unwilling victim than she appeared.[36]

Conclusion

Should we conclude from these cases of sexual abuse and harassment that the libido of unmarried males in Middlesex was rampant and unrepressed? Hardly. There were on average only two cases per decade, and even at their most frequent in the 1670s and 1680s they were still comparatively rare.[37] In most of the cases the men involved were either untypical or had already earned distinctly unsavory reputations.

Mahoone came from an Irish family,[38] and Waters, the tinker, was a lawless vagabond in trouble for lying, cheating, theft, and swearing.[39] Montgomery was a Scot, lacking the normal supervision of a master. Jonathan Phillips, though the son of the first minister of Watertown, had a bad record in the town. Ten years earlier he had been hauled before the selectmen "to give answere of his loosse living." His mother was to place him under "government, or otherwise to dispose of him to some such place or way that may in able the towne to give answer to the law." He had also been convicted that year in the county court of consorting with known criminals, particularly the notorious Knaps.[40]

Richard Nevers had also been in trouble. In 1667 he had been convicted of turning his back on the ordinance of baptism. He had also been involved in sexual experiments at Dedham which culminated in court proceedings at the Suffolk County Court in July 1674. On the evening of Thanksgiving Day in November 1674, according to Elizabeth Knight, the seventeen-year-old servant of Captain Carter of Woburn,

> Richard Nevers offered me abuse in putting his hands under my coates, but I turning aside with much adoe saved my selfe & when I was settled to milking he againe tooke me by the shoulders and pulled me backwards allmost but I clapt one hand on the ground & hold fast the cows teat with the other hand & cried out & John Abbot came.[41]

Andrew Robinson had already attempted to seduce Martha Faulkner and been involved with Elizabeth Wells.[42] Joseph Grant came from a thoroughly disreputable family and had one bastard to his credit already.[43] Robert Montgomery had offered "lascivious and wanton carraiges towards *sundry* women." The Lancaster selectmen reported of George Newby that "since he came to our town he has attempted to pervert all thats good and has been a leader to all manner of Evill." He was again convicted in April 1691 for "horrid wickedness & profaneness." Not only had he slandered ministers, calling them "Liars, Drones and Whoremasters," but he had boasted that

> he lay with a whore seven times in one night . . . his manner was not to persuade them lest they should repent but to lay violent hands on them & down with them to wrights & commit the act & then let them repent after ward . . . he claimed he had had the pox seven times.[44]

Finally, Simons was alleged to have carried on lewdly with a girl in his mother's house.[45] In short, these vulpine rogues could hardly be depicted as typical of the young men of the county. Whatever their family backgrounds, they represented a criminally inclined group.[46]

Apart, then, from impressionistic assertions by divines that masturbation was common and commonly excused, the evidence on sexual deviance, abuse, and harassment would seem to support the contention that in these areas of potential sexual release the typical youth of the county exercised exemplary self-control. The testimony suggests that people had internalized the taboos against homosexuality and bestiality and regarded them with horror; the fact that married women appealed to the shame of their attackers, none of whom was successful, implies that inhibitions were pretty near the surface here too. There were no reported rapes in the legal definition of that term. Most of the offenses we have discussed in this chapter—the exception is masturbation—were extremely serious; rape, sodomy, and bestiality were all "hanging matters." Before coming to any final conclusion about the general eroticism of the youth of Middlesex we must turn to other aspects of sexual expression and to the question of whether there was a detectable youth culture in the county. Only then can we strike a balance between patriarchal power and adolescent autonomy.

5 / Adolescent Culture

HE unquestioned dominance of the patriarch within the restricted nucleated patriarchal family required, according to Stone, the removal of any external agencies of subversion. For the father or master to command the undivided loyalties and uncritical obedience of adolescents, there must be no alternative reference groups, with alternative values and alternative authority. Among such groups whose decline has been seen as a prerequisite for the making of the modern family, one of the most important was youth groups. Considerable research has been done on such groups in traditional society as the French Abbeys of Misrule, German and Swiss *Bruderschaften,* and English apprentice organizations, but very little for seventeenth-century American groups. [1] If it could be shown that such groups existed in Middlesex County, and if their values were subversive of adult, puritan standards, then a severe blow would be dealt to the thesis that New England was the acme of patriarchalism. The existence of a generation gap would argue that the authority of Middlesex fathers was far less absolute than has been claimed.

The ideology of Massachusetts law and of countless sermons and conduct books, much of it imported from England, was unequivocally patriarchal. Thus, all single persons were required to "live under family government." [2] A model contract required that an apprentice "his master faithfully shall serve, his secrets keep, his lawful commandments every where obey." A long list of prohibitions included fornication, marriage, cards, dice, haunting alehouses or taverns. "He shall not absent himself day or night from his masters service without his leave." [3] Such authoritarian training should produce an obedient, reverent, continent young man like Robert Williams of Marlborough: "he desired to live under family government and has done so since his time was out [with his master]. He has committed himself into mens houses of good report . . . and [has striven] to walk inoffensive to all men." An attached testimonial described him as one having "Christian conversation, pliable to the orders of my family . . . he mindeth the best things and opposeth all vice and vanity."[4] Sons and daughters were expected to show respect for their parents, who owned their labor until majority, to remain close to them, and to care for them in their old age.[5] Incorrigible disobedience on the part of a son was a capital offense.[6] Youngsters who got out of hand were regularly removed from their families and placed in more strictly disciplined households.[7] The court customarily appointed guardians for orphans. In theory, then, the adolescents of Middlesex should have been under strict and relentless control until the time came in their mid or late twenties to marry and set up their own households.

The court records reveal that there was an embarrassing gap between theory and practice. Apart from a number of insubordinate individuals, like Susannah Coburn,[8] who invited her venerable master to "kiss her arse," or John Long, whose richly profane cursing was witnessed by the worthies of Cambridge and Charlestown,[9] there is considerable evidence of group activities by adolescents. In this chapter we shall concentrate on those involving some kind of sexual activity and, having reviewed eleven documented cases, will assess the evidence from these and sixteen other groups to see whether they add up to a plausible argument for a distinct youth culture.

Case Studies: Adolescent Group Activities

The first case, heard in 1658, involved a disreputable servant Paul Wilson, aged nineteen. It was alleged that early on May Morning, the Malden deacon's son, Phineas Upham, and his wife of two weeks had been subjected to unwelcome attentions orchestrated by Wilson.

> Upon the last day of April in the night at too of the cloke after midnight [i.e., May Morning] there was a noise heard by Phinehas Upham and his Wife at the side of the house, by which they were awakned out of their sleepe; his wife being awakned first was strucke with a great feare: Wee heard musicke and dansing which was no smal disturbance to us: And they came harkeing unto our window where wee lay, which they did three times, between which times they danced and played with their musicke, with much laughter.

The English folk festival of May Morning had strong sexual connotations, as did the prurient interest in the bedroom activities of newly-weds. Wilson was convicted at the same court of "violently soliciting" Upham's sister against her father's will.[10]

On 22 July 1660 after a general militia training at Cambridge two men, Samuel Stearns aged twenty-two and John Fleming aged eighteen, and nine girls were charged with "suspicion of uncivill cariages and disorderly conduct at Andrew Belcher's ordinary and the College," though witnesses claimed twenty were involved in all. Stearns "had Sarah Boatson in his lapp and did kiss her . . . at a chamber of one of the scholars shee knew not." She admitted being "in a room in the New College . . . and saw some of the young men kissing the maids and in particular John Fleming did kiss & daly with the daughter of Evan Thomas his wife of Boston called Mary." Others had noticed this couple earlier in the day "in a very uncivill manner walking up and down among the company at the general trayning and saw . . . Fleming in the open field salute the said wench by kissing her sundry times the which was matter of great offence to them & sundry others." Fleming was subsequently "put to seafaring employment" by his guardian with the court's approval.[11]

A year later Thomas Danforth recorded the complaint of Elizabeth Holmes of Cambridge, aged nineteen, about the sexual advances and titillating talk of her father's contemporary and neighbor, Thomas Langhorn. He responded by painting Elizabeth—an innocent victim in her account—in her true colors. He claimed that she was "a slanderer of divers persons . . . as a young woman in this towne [said] to be with childe before maradge which was not soe." When her father (who later died) had been told, he had answered, "If he would buy her from the whipping post he would not give it for she had been a lyinge tatelinge girle & that she would not leave it [until] she had some smarte for it." When a brother of the congregation had complained, her father had directed him to the governor "for she was paste his government" with her lying and tale-telling. "When she was reproved for some imodest speeches about the nature of womene & was asked whear she learned them she answered that some girles in the towne had boukes that learned them prity thinges." Another source of her dirty talk was "one Smith that wronged Mr. Jonathan Hayne & that was often in her company." It is probable that "the girles in the towne" would meet together to discuss the revelations of some gynecological–cum–bawdy manual like *Aristotle's Problems* or *Aristotle's Master-Piece* rather than individually imbibing—even if they all could read—in complete isolation.[12]

The literary equivalent of the charivari, the lampoon, was the subject of a letter dated 18 March 1664 to the court from the Commissioners for Small Causes of Concord. Two libels, both obscene in subject matter and language, had been nailed up on the meeting house. One culprit, John Slater, a young man in his early twenties, claimed on examination that "some others did join him" in this ridicule planned for St. Valentine's Day. He took all the blame rather than reveal the names of his fellow conspirators.[13]

At 10 P.M. on 29 April 1668, an hour after curfew, the watch heard the sounds of carousing coming from the house of the disreputable Henry Salter of Charlestown. They saw three men in the chamber, but when they knocked at the bolted front door, there was a general exodus from the back, in which they recognized Joseph Batchelor and Sylvester Hayes, a noted sexual troublemaker. Once admitted grudgingly, they found Nicholas Bartlett, a seaman, sitting at a table and a woman in the chamber in bed. They returned an hour later to be assured through a locked door by Deborah Hadlock that no visitors were there, but found Samuel Sibino, an Indian, and Matthew Brooke, a servant. They later came upon three more men on the streets who refused to say where they had been and threw stones at them.[14]

We have already encountered the evidence of John Knight in the disputed paternity case involving the bastard born to Sarah Crouch in 1669. She and Sarah Largin, who also bore a bastard, had been regularly engaging in group sex with at least three men, both in the sleeping Knight household and in a neighbor's empty house for a considerable period of 1668.[15] Deacon Samuel Fletcher had similar problems that year in his household at Chelmsford. His scapegrace son Joshua, aged twenty-four, had already been convicted of window-breaking and had been to Rhode Island where he continued his disobedience among the Quakers. He was a devotee of horse-coursing and racing and had followed "idle and expensive courses at Groton, Concord, etc." He failed to attend church meetings when in Chelmsford. It was his nocturnal escapades, however, which brought him before the court and the church. He acknowledged

> that three several nights, after bedtime, he went into Mr. Fiskes [the minister] Dwelling house at Chelmsford, at an open window by a ladder that

he brought with him; the said window opening into a chamber, where was
the lodging place of Gresill Juell servant to Mr. Fiske.

Fiske's notebook adds the information that Joshua and Grizel, who
was only fifteen, spent whole nights together, though on one occasion
John Waldo was also present. Fiske was particularly scandalized that
Joshua "boasted of his exploits to the younger ones to corrupt them and
make them like himself in shameless wickedness." He had obviously
attracted to himself a group of acolytes unhealthily impressed with his
sexual adventures. Perhaps Waldo was taken along in order to validate
his account. Grizel Fletcher later gave birth to a premaritally conceived
child.[16]

When the Gardiner family was seeking to restore its daughter Hannah's
reputation with a civil action in 1675, her brother John bore witness to
Richard Nevers's boasting about previous nocturnal escapades.

> He and his company had sat up many a time a great part of the night at
> Dedham sawmill to heare a booke read wherein he said he learned to give
> maides such thinges as would make them follow him about so that he could
> do with them what he would and further said he once saw it made use of
> . . . he said these were but tricks of youth.

Nevers's reference to "his company" implies an organized gathering,
rather than simply an ad hoc flocking when news of the titillating reading matter spread.[17] A court case in Suffolk proved that he was not
exaggerating. On 28 July 1674 Edward Pigge had been convicted of
"useing indirect meanes by powders and other wayes unlawfull to engage the affections or desires of women kinde and for begetting Ruth
Henningway of Roxbury with Childe . . . and making suite to and
drawing away the affections of the daughter of Robert Sanford without
first obtaining theire parents consent."[18]

The fullest account of adolescent company keeping has survived in
records at Harvard rather than in the county court records. Thomas
Danforth, acting as a single magistrate in a petty sessional capacity,
investigated events in Cambridge during the winter of 1676–77, following the end of King Philip's War. As he examined twenty people
between 4 and 8 January 1677 about a disturbance at Jonathan Cane's
house on 3 January, it gradually emerged that a large company of young
men (including Harvard students and Negroes) and maids had for four
months been organizing regular nocturnal meetings. Quarts of rum
and gallons of cider had been drunk, some of the young men admitted
to having sung and danced, and at Cane's a supper of pork, beef,

turnips, and an apple pie had been cooked. These parties started at curfew time, 9 P.M., and went on till 1 or 2 A.M., on one occasion to near dawn. Only one of the group had once been prevented from attending by her master. On 9 January four girls in their teens and early twenties and nine youths were admonished with costs for "being from out of the house of their parents and meeting at unseasonable times, and of night walking, and companying together contrary to civility and good nurture to vitiate one another." Two others with unsavory reputations were fined or whipped.

One of the most interesting aspects of this well-organized company, whose parties culminated during the traditional English holiday season of the Twelve Days of Christmas, was that some adults of the town condoned the assemblies. Indeed, at Aaron Boardman's shop during the investigations, Abraham Arrington, aged fifty-five, was dissatisfied and expressed the opinion that

> it was a sad thing young persons could not meet together w[hen] they were come home from the warr but they must be thus requited, and he did beleuiv if the young men of watertown should be dealt with in the manner they would go negh to burne the towne over their eares that should so serve them. and it was a pitfull thing that a young man and mayd could not be together but such reports must come of it, and he did beleuiv ere long the young men must pass by the mayds like quakers and take no notice of them, lest they shoud . . . be taken notice of: and if there were any Service to be done for the Country it must be the young men that must do it, and let them do all they could a young man could neuer be made an old man and if a man were but in a by corner and heard the confession the young persons made before mr Danforth he aloues it would be a parcell of such blind stuffe as was not worth the hearkening unto, or words to the purpose.

For his pains Arrington was bound to appear before the next county court "to answer for uttering seditious and naughty words . . . tending to breaking down the pales of government."[19]

In the highly detailed slander action brought by members of the Martin family against Hannah Long of Charlestown, evidence was presented about adolescent get-togethers before and at Thanksgiving 1681. The last party went on till 2 A.M. with cakes and liquor and the singing of dirty songs by a girl and a youth. A maid reported that John Long, a neighbor, kept pleading with her to come to him "for he said he had had a boute with the other three and I must have a bout with him too." Another girl said "that base rogue John Long he want to play the rogue with me." Several other young men were alleged to have been involved in these nefarious assemblies which went back two-and-a-half years.[20]

The last example to concern us in detail comes from the disputed paternity case over the bastard born to Susannah Coburn at Dracut in 1696. According to Dorothy Hildrich, herself later convicted of fornication, "a company of men and maids had a brisk froehlic sundry nights in November at the mill of her uncle Hildrich" where rum and cider were drunk and sexual matters discussed. Other depositions pointed to adolescent high jinks at one of the garrison houses in the frontier settlement.[21]

The estimated one hundred adolescents involved in these cases were hardly the repressed neurotics depicted by some historians. They gathered in defiance of parents, masters, and authority. They were resolutely interested in the opposite sex and in sex itself. They refused to conform to the model constructed by their elders and betters.

There are sixteen other examples of group activity by adolescents in the records, including a celebration of Guy Fawkes Night in Charlestown in 1662 with "bonefires" made from fences and "sundry guns shot of"[22] and a gang of townsmen and gownsmen led by Samuel Gibson of Cambridge who specialized in banquets of stolen poultry during the winter of 1684–85. Both Danforth and Gookin figured among their victims.[23] Other companies were convicted of tavern-haunting, drunkenness after militia training, robbery, practical joking during the Lord's Supper, fighting and swearing, window-breaking, and breaches of the peace.[24] In 1668 the General Court instituted a purge of young people "living from under family government" and the eight out of fourteen constables' returns of names which survive on the Middlesex files listed a total of twenty-nine individuals, including several miscreants like Paul Wilson, already well known to the authorities.[25] The appointment of officials by several towns during the late 1660s and 1670s to maintain decorum during church services specified that it was the youth among the congregations whose disturbances and inattention had precipitated such needs.[26]

The dates in twenty-five out of these twenty-seven examples of group activity have been recovered. Twenty-three occurred during the winter months between October and April. In many of the incidents the precise number of young people taking part is not given. The largest group recorded was twenty, the smallest four, but from the contexts and activities involved in many of the examples it is reasonable to assume that between ten and twenty young people usually took part.

Does the evidence presented here add up to proof of the existence of a distinct youth culture? If so, what was its nature and its role?

Survey of Evidence

We must concede first that nothing so highly organized as the French Abbeys of Misrule existed. Second, the companies of young people in Middlesex do not appear from the evidence in the court records to have had any long-term cohesion or any institutional permanence. The longest periods for which regular adolescent get-togethers are recorded are for one winter or for the indeterminate "sundry nights" or "many a time." Again, it has only been possible in one or two cases to establish any permanence of membership; Paul Wilson was active for over a decade in ordering youthful amusements, and the Gibson brothers of Cambridge plagued the town with their pranks, or "reaks" as Danforth described them, for over eight years.[27] Moreover, there is no sign even in the busy port of Charlestown of the kind of apprentice organization of contemporary London.

Should we then conclude that adolescent groupings were so sporadic and haphazard that they can hardly be represented as evidence of a distinct culture? I think not. Four pointers suggest that the data offered deserve further consideration.

Most of the meetings chronicled here come down to us only by casual allusion in depositions relating to other matters. Many gatherings were plainly clandestine, in deserted mills or at night after older people were safely in bed. It is significant that almost all the reported cases occurred during wintertime when get-togethers had to take place indoors. In the warm summer months companies could gather in woods or fields undetected. It was only when gatherings got out of hand that they came to the direct attention of the authorities. Comments by Abraham Arrington on the bumptiousness of the young men of Watertown find virtually no echoes in the records. Arrington's naughty words would themselves be unknown to us but for the chance survival of Danforth's notes in the Harvard archives. Since adolescent gatherings came under the cognizance of single justices it is quite possible that if other magistrates' records had survived we should know of many more such companies.

It is notoriously dangerous to argue from silence in the records, but in this case justification for our conjectures that the adolescent companying may be far from uncommon appears from an unexpected source. In a 1655 letter to Governor John Endicott from Peter Bulkeley, first minister of Concord, we read of servants and children who "yet take liberty to be abroad in the nights and run into their sinful miscarriages not to be suffered under a Christian government."[28] This was an early example of a whole flood of clerical attacks on the rising generation and the decay of family government, which began in the 1650s, reached a crescendo in the 1670s, and was still rumbling on in the 1690s.

Many of the criticisms of the young by such Jeremiahs as the Mathers singled out just the kind of activities appearing in the Middlesex records: "chambering and wantonness," "wickedness on the night of the sabbath," "folly and lewdness at harvest time," "drinking and vain company," or "going far from their fathers houses." Young people were monotonously warned against "the snares of evil company" to which they were known to be particularly prone. Ceaseless vigilance over potentially subversive servants was recommended.[29] A general weakness of youth was often described as "an inordinate affection for liberty" or "a fondness for freedom." The tone of such attacks is aptly epitomized in Benjamin Wadsworth's condemnation of adolescent sins.

> They must have their liberty . . . to give or receive visits of their own accord, and when they will; liberty to keep what company they please; liberty to be out late on nights, to come and go almost when they will, without telling why or wherefore; such liberty they contend for, they wont be ruled, governed or restrained.[30]

When recording their conversions, individuals often confessed to the past folly of associating with wicked companions.[31]

This repeated emphasis on the passion of the young for each other's company and their secrecy about it was reflected too in acts of the General Court. The law of 1668 against single-living attacked those who "did not serve their parents or masters as children, apprentices, hired servants or journey men ought to do and usually did in our native country being subject to their commands and discipline." The presence of masterless men and women "doth occasion much sin and prophanes to encrease among us to the dishonour of God, and the ensnaring of many children and servants, by the dissolute lives and practices of such as do live from under family government and is a great discouragement to those family governours who conscientiously endeavour to bring up their youth in all Christian nurture." A law of 1672 forbade "youth, maids and other persons uncivilly walking in the streets and fields of Saturday and Sunday nights." "Single persons that live from under family government, stubborn and disorderly children and servants, nightwalkers, typlers, sabbath breakers by night or by day" were a major target of the tythingmen in 1679.[32] Official pronouncements, clerical or lay, then, go a long way to support the idea that the courts only heard a minority of cases of adolescent association.

The dates of the cases in the court records are also illuminating. Seventeen of the twenty-six examples come from the period 1657 to 1669; thirteen were presented by the grand jury. During the same period, the General Court instituted its purge on masterless persons, pulpit attacks on adolescents began and the Half-Way Covenant bringing "children of the church" under church discipline was introduced. Thereafter, despite attacks on lax family government growing shriller and more frequent, presentments for single-living appear only spasmodically in the court or town records and prosecutions for youthful consorting become markedly rarer. It could be that it declined in actuality, but the increasing clerical and lay complaints militate against such an explanation. The chief men of Groton did not feel that the young had relapsed into quietness and obedience. On 9 October 1695 they wrote of a youth who was civil, sober, and blameless as though he were an exception. He was given "to no vice or extravigancy as too many yonksters are and the generality of our inhabitants do much fear."[33] It is far more likely that after a campaign of suppression in the later 1650s and the 1660s, gatherings came to be tolerated and/or that the gatherers became more artful in evading detection. If this were so, the argument that adolescent meetings were common would gain further credibility.

Studies of adolescence in England during the seventeenth century have made much of the mobility of the servant population and the resultant freedom from family control which frequent changes of town and employer afforded. Servants undoubtedly used this freedom to form associations of their own choice and to create an adolescent subculture.[34] There is considerable evidence in New England records that geographical mobility increased markedly in the last two decades of the century. It would be surprising if this were not mirrored by an increase in adolescent association.

Two towns, Cambridge and Charlestown, with four and ten cases respectively, account for the majority of our twenty-six examples. This is predictable. Harvard not only swelled the number of adolescents in Cambridge, but also attracted young apprentices to service trades in the town. Charlestown was an important harbor and ship-building center with a large population of young seamen, dockworkers, and apprentice artisans. Nevertheless the remaining twelve examples occurred in eight widely-spaced townships, suggesting that the two early foundations on the Charles River did not have a monopoly of adolescent culture.

Two other questions still require examination. Were the youth groups advocating an alternative set of values or merely reinforcing the mores and attitudes of their elders? Was there an institutional substratum to provide permanence and stability to adolescent societies? Without satisfactory answers to these, the existence of a distinct youth culture would still be doubtful.

The subjects of action and discussion of the Middlesex sample could hardly be said to reinforce the dominant mores of Massachusetts society. The traditional celebrations of Guy Fawkes Night, the Twelve Days of Christmas, St. Valentine's Day, or Mayday were hated symbols of a popular culture which puritans emigrated from old England to escape.[35]

One of the commonest topics discussed, and even experimented with, at secret trysts of the young, was sexuality. Though puritans may not have been unduly squeamish about sex in theory, they appear from the court records to have had a highly developed sense of modesty about the topic. They certainly appear to have omitted the subject of sex education from the upbringing of their children. Why else would titillating manuals have made such fascinating reading material? Why else would a sophomoric relish for dirty words and obscene acts have so delighted the young of Concord?

By law and by individual indentures, servants were forbidden to frequent taverns and eating houses. No doubt the prospect of profit induced some publicans to turn a blind eye to infractions, but the several instances of illicit adolescent drunkenness were nonetheless blatant contraventions of a social code requiring moderation and sobriety. The nailing up of filthy verses could, just conceivably, have had normative aims, but the wish to shock was surely paramount. Finally, the turkey suppers in Cambridge, culminating in the purloining of worshipful poultry on a fast day, were an affront to authority and to a day of solemn communal humiliation as well as to the eighth commandment. None of the activities of young people could be reasonably interpreted as reinforcing adult norms and values. "Misrule" rather than conformity was the name of the game. It was only in the 1680s that authority, in the person of Cotton Mather, sought to harness youthful sociability to the side of godliness and the morality of the establishment through "Associations of Young Folks."[36]

It could, of course, be objected that drinking to excess, "chambering and wantonness," petty theft, sporadic violence and mayhem, sexual boasting and prurient curiosity—"bunches of kids sowing their wild oats"—have been the types of behavior expected of the young any time anywhere. Yet Massachusetts in the seventeenth century was emphatically not any time anywhere. It was an idealistic bible commonwealth, a holy experiment with extraordinary expectations of its inhabitants. What might have been shrugged off as mere "tricks of youth" in more conventional societies were regarded there as subversive and God-provoking. Tolerance of adolescent sins invited divine retribution on all, and there was plenty of scope for the Almighty in such a marginal society.

That ordinary adults, not just clergy and magistrates, felt a sense of generational conflict is suggested by the seditious statement by Abraham Arrington. There *was* antipathy between young men and older men, and in the case of Elizabeth Holmes or Sarah Crouch or Susannah Coburn, between young women and older men too. It was a two-way business. As well as the constant official bewailing of the disobedience, pride, and stubbornness of the rising generation, ordinary elders articulated it too. In 1650 William Knap, in his seventies, paid five shillings for a kiss with Phoebe Page, "and old Knap said that young men would only give a touch but he would give her a cleaveing kiss."[37] As we shall see, William Healey derided his young wife's relatively easy admission to church membership compared to his own in the good old days.[38] We shall encounter several other examples in subsequent chapters.

On a broader scale, Sumner Chilton Powell has demonstrated how conflict between younger men and established patriarchs in Sudbury led to the breakaway foundation of Marlborough in the 1650s[39] and Philip Greven has suggested similar antagonisms in Andover over the transmission of family wealth.[40] The fact that seventeenth-century New Englanders thought habitually in the quite artificial terms of generations, and equated the second and third generations with declension may be symbolic of this continuing conflict.

We still need evidence of some kind of institutional backbone if we are to convert into a distinct culture what might otherwise be interpreted as haphazard outbursts of youthful escape from adult control or occasional fortuitous curiosity about forbidden fruit. Perhaps the fact that three of our incidents occurred after militia training days, a fourth after a year-long war, and a fifth in a garrisoned frontier region in constant danger of attack is a clue worth following, as too might be the penchant for gregariousness on religious holidays.

The militia was numerically dominated by young unmarried men;

most of those associated with the peer group activities discussed here have been identified as militiamen. Training days took place eight times a year, including general trainings of the whole county regiment. Though training was meant to be a serious business, it was a welcome break from the steady routine of work. The tradition imported from England was that musters resembled a "Maygame," which implies a holiday spirit and uninhibited frolics with the opposite sex. In 1645 an abortive attempt to found three private militia companies is thought to have had "a social function as well."[41]

That the events in the Middlesex records were not isolated incidents is suggested by Urian Oakes's criticism of Middlesex artillery parades on 10 September 1677, "as if they were days to meet on, to smoke, to carouse, to swagger and dishonor God with the great bravery [bravado]. O make a business of it," he implored, "and not a play."[42] The diary of Hetty Shepard paints a colorful picture of accompanying antics and merry entertainment of training days in the same decade.[43] So serious had the problem become by 1679 that Daniel Gookin, Cambridge magistrate and senior militia officer, felt constrained to issue an order condemning drinking on muster days. "Wine strong liquors and cider brought to the field [where are] great conventions of peoples [lead to] many people both English and Indian that come to such meetings as well as souldiers commit[ting] many disorders, as drunkenness, fighting, neglect of duty etc."[44]

The militia companies of individual towns often developed strong esprit de corps and camaraderie, especially among the younger members. When, for instance, the householders of Cambridge petitioned the General Court against any concessions to the crown on 17 October 1664, an appendix was added with thirty-five signatories.

> We whose names are subscribed being of the traine band [militia company] and singell men in the above sayd town, doe also desire to manifest our selves to be of the same mind with our parents, masters and the aged men and householders of the place.[45]

Sometimes, however, as in the elections of captains in Roxbury in 1647 and Reading in 1677, there would be divisions between the younger and older generations, providing both an education in practical politics and partisan cohesion.[46] Either way it is not difficult to see how the militia could serve as an institution which bound young men (and the young women spectators who usually attended the exercises) into long-term groups through their sharing in regular training sessions and the dangers of war. Nor is it hard to imagine that, after the formal business was concluded, informal gatherings of both sexes would regularly take place in a relaxed holiday atmosphere.

The other occasion when young people would be corralled in close proximity away from parental eyes would be the frequent church services in the meeting house. Might not some of the disorder reported from that age group be put down to whispered plans for group assignations on sabbath nights, whose desecration caused Increase Mather so much pain? Once a month on sacrament days, the uncovenanted youth might be largely unsupervised while the saints took communion. There are several recorded instances of youthful horseplay during this break.[47] Alternatively, skipping church would give adolescents a chance for nefarious activities together. There were other opportunities in the year for youth to get together—like the long drawn-out survival campaigns of summer to get in the harvests from hay in July to corn and fruit in October, or annual election days, or quarterly court days—but military training and church probably provided the best institutional encouragement for the development of an adolescent culture.

Conclusion

Though we have had to argue from inference and from documentary silence, there does appear to be sufficient evidence in the Middlesex records, supported by incessant official pronouncements, to argue that after the late 1650s patriarchal power was in retreat. The confession of Robert Holmes that his daughter was "paste his government" is echoed in the jeremiads and orders of the General Court thundering against the decline of family control. In Massachusetts, as in England, "youthe will have its swinge."[48]

There is, however, one loose end, which applies to other chapters in this section as well. What if the young people who appeared before the court presented for fornication, bridal pregnancy, breach of promise, sexual deviancy, and illicit group activities were completely untypical of young people in the county as a whole? If, like the sexual abusers, they turned out to be markedly different from the normal cross section of the community, a deviant, criminally-inclined subculture or even a counterculture, then we should know no more about the silent majority than we did at the beginning. To this problem we must briefly turn.

6 / Typical Adolescents

THE term "puritan" is, by general concurrence, notoriously difficult to define. There is, however, some agreement about its literal sense: puritans were deeply concerned about purity. This sense is at the heart of Thomas Gataker's famous description of 1623.

> If a man live somewhat more strictly than the looser sort doe, though not so strictly neither as his Christian profession requireth of him, (for even the best and the forwardest have their failings and come farre short of what they should) he shall not scape to have those opprobious tearmes and titles fastened on him, of a Precisian, a Puritane and the like. . . . If he be conversant in Gods word, and diligent in frequenting the ministry of it; he is a Bible-bearer, and a gadder up and downe after Sermons. If he make conscience of an oath, and will reprove others when they sweare, he is a superstitious fellow, too straitlaced, more nice than wise. If hee will not swill and swagger, drinke healths and play the goodfellow, goe for company to a Brothel-house, or to a Playhouse, little better, the very seminaries and nurseries of all filthinesse and prophanenesse; he is a man altogether unsociable, of a melancholy disposition, little better than a lunaticke, as they said sometimes of John the Baptist.[1]

It was also central to Thomas Hooker's advice to the godly in Chelmsford, England, that they should "avoid private contact with the vulgar or even with those of the godly who persisted in some sort of serious error." His farewell sermon in 1631, *The Danger of Destruction*, described exile as "a refuge for his Noahs and his Lots, a rock and a shelter for his righteous ones to run unto; and those that were vexed to see the ungodly lives of the people in this wicked land, shall there be safe."[2]

Despite the immense amount of research on New England puritanism, there is still little agreement as to whether it produced divided or homogeneous societies, two cultures, the elect sheep against the unregenerate goats, or one, with all subscribing to godly ideals, the unregenerate as eager for conversion as the elect were relieved to have experienced it. Were the saints "winnowed out of a mixt multitude . . . gathered out of the world" in New England, or had most of those who had come to the wilderness already been "choice grain," self-selected by their commitment?[3]

Some persuasive evidence and arguments have been advanced for the exclusivity of the godly. Thomas Hutchinson recorded the fear as early as the 1630s that as the great migration swelled "worldly men might [make up] the major part."[4] Building on Increase Mather's truism that "the lines of election for the most part run through the loins of godly parents," Edmund S. Morgan has postulated a growing puritan tribalism.[5] Further support for the idea of such self-limiting sectarianism has been adduced from widespread lay and vocal clerical opposition to the Half-Way Covenant. "A corrupt masse of unbelievers . . . children of strangers, uncircumcised in heart, shall be brought into God's sanctuary to pollute it."[6] The Cambridge Platform had already laid down that excommunicants be deprived of "all familiar communion" with their former brethren.[7] They had reverted to "the world's people" as Hetty Shepard termed the nongodly.[8] The concept of declension centered on the losing struggle of goodness between the eternal magnetic fields of the Word against the World, God against Gold, Salvation against Selfishness. A recent analyst of conversion has argued that early New England "lay culture was a web of interactions between sinners and saints as each group sought to win converts."[9]

Other scholars, however, have stressed the social cohesiveness of all New England society as evidenced by town covenants,[10] the reclamatory or cathartic aims of the law or the reintegration of penitent sinners into communities.[11] Puritanism was an evangelizing religion, they argue. The Half-Way Covenant should be seen as a lifeline to the uncertain, opposition to it not necessarily a sign of exclusivity. The rituals of the church, the plain style of sermons, covenant revivals, days of thanksgiving and humiliation provided ideological foci for all the congregation.[12] They point to the sophisticated understanding of Calvinism and the New England Way by quite humble people and the marked lack of confidence and self-assurance of converts.[13] Others instance the strikingly low crime rates as a sign that the great majority of New Englanders, whether church members or not, had internalized the dominant values of the culture.[14]

Where were alternative foci for a counterculture? The second and third generation merchants have been identified as standard-bearers of competing values, but they were a small isolated group lacking wide influence among ordinary people; many of them seem to have remained staunchly calvinist.[15] The alleged existence of commercialist values among groups in Salem Village and Springfield are largely based on inference and their subversiveness has been overemphasized.[16] If there was a battle for the souls of New Englanders between saints and sinners, it has proved hard to find the crusading forces of sin.

We have suggested that youth culture may have provided a focus for the rising generation of the second half of the century, but we need to address the crucial question of whether the adolescents who fornicated and associated were an untypical, isolated subculture, or whether they transcended the dregs of society and embraced a wider range of backgrounds and classes. We need too to gauge the long-term importance of such a culture. Did its values change people's lives permanently or was its influence only transitory? Finally, in an appendix to this chapter, we must briefly examine various groups which because of either heterodox beliefs or racial origins were outside the relatively homogeneous culture of the majority of the county. How did their mores interact with those of the puritans and how was their behavior reflected in the overall counts of sexual misdemeanors?

Survey of Evidence

It is now widely acknowledged by British demographers and social historians that there was a tendency for sexual misdemeanors to run in families over several generations. Not only did "every village have its problem family" but there is also persuasive evidence for the "existence of a sub-society of the bastardy-prone."[17] This early aspect of what has been termed, not wholly appropriately in this particular area, "the cycle of deprivation," has not surprisingly been the monopoly in early modern England of the very poor, the landless, the unsettled, the vagabonds, and "masterless men." Was it representatives of comparable groups in Middlesex who dominated the lists of sexually incontinent or inquisitive youth? Even a cursory examination of the court records reveals the same surnames recurring time and again. Thus, for instance, we find Mary, the daughter of Thomas Goodenow of Sudbury, convicted in April 1657 of fornication with James Ross, a Scottish servant, whom she adamantly refused to marry. In 1672 her sister Jane married Christopher Bannister of neighboring Marlborough, who had been convicted of fornication with Mary Parmenter in 1665, both of whose brothers John and George were to be similarly guilty in 1668 and 1679. One of Ross's daughters was punished for fornication in 1692. Returning to the Goodenow clan, Mary's first cousin Hannah was convicted of fornication in 1678, and Hannah's father, Captain John, was forced to resign all offices because of his adultery in 1697.[18] Thus from tracing family connections with one case, we have uncovered three families with multiple offenders.

Another example is the Edes family. Twelve months after widow Mary Tufts Edes was convicted of fornication in December 1697, her son John confessed to premarital fornication with "his now wife" Grace Lawrence Edes. In 1669 Mary's brother had been convicted of fornication with the serving maid Elizabeth Wells. Grace Edes's elder sister Martha Lawrence Dix was convicted of the same crime in 1698, committed with an unknown man six months before her marriage to John Dix. Another sister, Susannah, had confessed to carnal copulation in June 1679 and escaped from Watertown gaol two years later. The John Lawrence charged with bestiality in 1679 was probably a cousin.[19] Once again we have uncovered a web of three families all particularly prone to sexual misadventures.

A search of town records adds to the impression given by the court records. Watertown, for instance, was plagued by the misdeeds of two families. In 1657 Christopher Grant, senior, who lived near the Cambridge line and glazed the first building at Harvard, was fined 3s. 4d. for "inordinate and loose practises in expenditure at Thomas Smiths" alehouse. Two years later his daughter Abigail, aged twenty-four, confessed to fornication with Roger Rose, whom she later married. Her father was again fined 3s. 4d. in December 1661 for coming into court "disordered through excessive drinking." He and her mother were involved in a slander suit in 1665. Three years later a second daughter Mary, after initial denial, was persuaded to confess her premarital fornication with Daniel Smith in the Grants' lean-to barn. Her brother, Christopher junior, aged twenty, was named in 1669 by Sarah Crouch as the father of her bastard. Other girls testified to his attempts to seduce them. On 2 April 1678 Joseph Grant, aged thirty-two, who had followed his father into the glazing trade, was convicted of fathering a bastard on Sarah Fiske and of harassing her sister Mary. The following year Christopher junior was again in trouble; this time before the Court of Assistants for concealing the murder of a bastard begotten on the body of Cardin Drabston, a servant of his father's. One generation of Grants had among them produced five babies conceived out of wedlock.[20]

The Knaps were rivals in delinquency. The patriarch William has already appeared boasting of his kisses. A carpenter by trade, he was fined in October 1651 for "undecent words" and in 1656 the town was forced to support him because of his age and poverty. The same year his recently married son James was convicted of adultery with Mary Davis. He and his brother John were convicted in 1657 for thieving from at least seven people and for "inordinate life." Another brother, William, was in trouble with the Watertown selectmen in 1671 over the neglect of his daughter's education. Is it any wonder that John Knap, Jr., coming from such a family background committed premarital fornication in 1686? Several of the families with whom the Grant and Knap families had to do were also guilty of multiple sexual crimes.[21] In fact by delving into the sexual liaisons of four families we have unearthed seven other families with a total of twenty sexual offenses between them. Other examples, noted elsewhere, could easily be multiplied.[22] It begins to look as though the English pattern may have been transplanted.

"Repeaters" or women convicted of having extramarital relations with more than one man or bearing more than one bastard also occur. Sarah Dawes was convicted of bastard-bearing in 1656 and again in 1659. Widow Seaborne Cromwell, who became the belated wife of Robert Parris, was sentenced to fifteen stripes in 1663 for fornication before marriage, "being a second offence of this kind." We have already met Sarah Crouch, bastard-bearer and then pregnant bride. Ruth Sawtle's first baby was attributed to Zechariah Smith who died before its birth in 1672; two years later she was charged with fornication with Thomas Loverun. Esther Nicholls, involved in wanton and lascivious carriages with Joseph Groves in 1673 was convicted of bastardy in Suffolk in 1675. Mary Mitchelson, implicated in the turkey suppers at Cambridge, died in 1685 giving birth to her second bastard. Sarah Pore bore two bastards to the same man in 1682 and 1685; Abigail Lilly named two different fathers in 1691 and 1697. Jane Bowen and Elizabeth Wells admitted giving birth to "many" and to two bastards respectively. Mary Bartlett had had at least two bastards when convicted in 1699 and had probably concealed the birth of another. In 1695 Richard Graves admitted "he had had to do with Johannah Perry but doth not own that he is the father" of her offspring. Three years later John Spring "would not deny what Bethia Hide accuses him of provided she accuses the other person in this matter." As well as these thirteen bastardy-prone or promiscuous girls, another nine were vehemently suspected, often with good reason.[23]

The evidence offered here of problem families and bastardy-prone and promiscuous women seems to suggest that indeed there was a counterculture of untypical adolescents who rejected puritan ideals of chastity and contributed disproportionately to the sexual activity of the unmarried. Some we have noted came from poverty-stricken households whose patriarchs notably failed to govern their dependents according to puritan requirements. Should we conclude then that the adolescent majority, properly raised in well-ordered households, conformed to the model and obediently waited until marriage before satisfying their sexual drives?

Such a conclusion would be highly misleading. A review of all the cases of sexual misdemeanors and group activities, embracing at a minimum some six hundred adolescents, shows quite clearly that bastardy-prone girls or problem families at the bottom of the social scale only contributed a tiny proportion to the total of adolescent offenders. The relative rarity of repeaters in Middlesex supports the parallel contention for England that "most illegitimate children in traditional times were brought to baptism by mothers who appear on that occasion, and on that occasion only, in the registers. These evanescent women are like the famous sparrow in the Nordic story, which flies through the one door out of the dark, traverses the tiny area of light, and passes out of the other door into the dark again."[24]

Similarly I have only been able to trace a mere thirteen families where evidence of either parental neglect, poverty, or incompatibility could possibly have accounted for immorality by offspring.[25] Only four of these families have been identified as poverty-stricken. In only nine more cases had fathers—or in the case of girls, mothers—died before the subsequent offender reached the age of fourteen when they would, in any case, have been put out to another family.[26] An additional nineteen families had records of either two sexual offenders in one generation or sexual offenders in both parent and child generations.[27] All of these categories together produce only seventy-two offenders out of a minimum of six hundred, or one in eight.

A closer look at some of the families we have examined provides a further contrary finding. While the Knaps, with the patriarch on poor relief, fit in with the model of problem families as pauperized, the Parmenters and the Goodenows were leading citizens of Sudbury, providing deacons for the church, officers for the militia, members of the boards of selectmen, and representatives at the General Court. Indeed, the main complaint against Captain Goodenow in 1697 had been that he monopolized all the town offices.[28] The Grants, the Tuftses, the

Crouches, and the Pages were all solid middle-class artisans or yeomen, all members of the church.[29]

I have elsewhere drawn attention to the offspring of puritan divines and lay leaders in seventeenth-century Massachusetts who failed to live up to the rigorous requirements of their parents: Mathers, Cottons, Sewalls, Dudleys, Winthrops, Welds, Wards, Savages, Keaynes, or Willoughbies.[30] The Middlesex records add considerably to this list. We encounter, for instance, both the daughter and the granddaughter of Captain Edward Johnson, author of *The Wonder-working Providence of Sion's Saviour,* both guilty of fornication,[31] as were two sons of President Henry Dunster of Harvard.[32] The abandoned baby Major Daniel Gookin found on his porch one morning in 1677 had been sired by his son Samuel; five years earlier his slave Sylvanus had been convicted of fornication; in 1685 his maid Hannah Brackett named John Eliot (Gookin's grandson as well as the son and grandson of ministers) as her seducer.[33] Gookin's predecessor in command of the colonial militia, Edward Mitchelson, also had a daughter convicted of fornication.[34] Other ministerial families whose reputations were besmirched by their offspring were the Phillipses, Shermans, Welds, Graveses, and Frosts.[35] Altogether I have counted members of thirty-five elite families convicted of sexual offenses, almost all of them extramarital fornication.[36] These reprobates were scourged by Jeremiahs in the last two decades of the century. There are, claimed William Hubbard "none more vicious in their lives than such as have had the best advantage for piety in their education."[37] Cotton Mather sympathized (from personal experience) with "families of everlasting renown whose grandchildren are become either foolish or wicked."[38]

It was not just the elite families who were thus shamed. As early as 1657 Ezekiel Rogers bemoaned the backsliding of the children of the saints.[39] We have already seen that for a minimum of sixty-five percent of those couples convicted of bridal pregnancy, at least one of the partners was either a church member or the child of one. The comparable percentages for other offenses are fornication forty-seven percent and adultery and adulterous carriages thirty-one percent.[40] Of the seventy-two named and traceable company-keepers, thirty-seven were from church, thirty-five from unregenerate families.[41] Among assemblers caught were John Fleming, son of the deacon of Watertown; Ephraim and Thomas Frost, sons of the ruling elder of Cambridge; Francis Wainwright whose father was a wealthy Ipswich merchant; and future ministers James Allen and Thomas Barnard.[42] The young people

of Middlesex did not suffer from class consciousness, elect exclusive-
ness, or color prejudice—two regular attenders of the Cambridge
meetings in the winter of 1675–76 were Negroes, both owned by
Daniel Gookin since their childhood, one of whom had fathered a bastard on a white girl.[43]

Conclusion

Despite appearances, then, adolescent sexual offenses transcended class
and church lines. Fornication and bridal pregnancy were emphatically
not the preserve of a small subculture where family government had
failed. They were lapses just as likely to bring shame to the elite or the
elect. Membership of subversive youth groups was equally diverse.
Their generational counterculture was not limited to oddballs, misfits,
or established juvenile delinquents. By the late 1650s patriarchal control
seems to have lost its vigor. Around this time we noticed a marked
change in the truthfulness and acceptance of responsibility by young
people presented for sexual offenses. The number of offenses begins to
rise in the 1660s, as do the ratios of bastardy and bridal pregnancy. Concurrently attacks on the rising generation and parental permissiveness
begin and the shelved proposals for a Half-Way Covenant are revived.
One result of its passage in 1662 was to bring a greatly augmented
number of adolescents under the jurisdiction of church discipline.

Yet, despite all this evidence of moral decay in the 1660s, which appears to have continued and even accelerated for the rest of the century,
we must remind ourselves that by such yardsticks as ratios of bastardy
or bridal pregnancy Middlesex County maintained comparatively very
high standards of morality. How can we square this with the existence
of a youth culture which took an earthy interest in sexual matters and
spurned the models of obedience, reverence, and continence advertised
by their elders? How too can we reconcile these rebellious, gregarious,
and hilarious young people with the isolated, neurotic youths like
Michael Wigglesworth and Cotton Mather who engaged in obsessive
spiritual conflict with sin, self, and sex?

The most plausible answer is that this subversiveness was just a passing phase. Contemporary commentators and surviving church records
agree that the usual age for admission for church membership was the
middle or late twenties. Philip Greven, reviewing puritan spiritual
autobiographies, describes how "over and over again the recollections
of evangelicals reveal the emergence during youth and early adulthood
of a growing sense of selfhood and self will, an increasing confidence

that they can act on their own behalf and for their own purposes apart from the expectations set for them by parents or others." This commonly experienced sense of "independence, self-worth and autonomy" was often accompanied by a period of self-assertion, wildness, and "corruption" before the onset of conviction.[44] Though the throes of conversion might be protracted, it seems probable that youthful rebelliousness often extended well into the twenties and that the beginnings of a more introspective frame of mind were precipitated by the experience of marriage, economic independence, and the prospects of parenthood which marked the individual's passage into full adulthood.[45] As Hooker noted, "Those whom God doth call it is most commonly in their middle age." His mentor, Richard Sibbes, observed that childbirth made women psychologically susceptible to religious ideas and conversion. The danger to their own lives brought them to nearer communion with God.[46] This reaction to peril may have brushed off on their husbands, or the new responsibilities of fatherhood may have concentrated male minds wonderfully. The fulsome confessions of couples convicted of premarital fornication would tend to support this thesis that the end of dependency marked a new period of spiritual awareness for the majority. Thus the psychological writhings of a Mather or a Wigglesworth, both grappling with callings to the ministry, may well have been atypical not so much in their intensity as in their prematurity. What were sometimes called "tricks of youth"—sexual curiosity and experimentation—may well have been the precursors, even essential precursors, to spiritual stocktaking and rebirth.

The effects of adolescent culture, then, were essentially transitory. They did not revolutionize values; they might make waves, but they did not produce floods. Nonetheless temporary adherence to alternative ideals meant that the New England Way was embraced voluntarily, willingly. The wide range of adolescents in the Middlesex records do not come across as brainwashed, will-broken automata. They *chose* to conform as they entered the adult world. To that world we must now turn.

Appendix: Religious and Racial Subgroups

There were two religious and three racial subgroups within the otherwise relatively homogeneous population of Middlesex: Quakers and Baptists on the one hand, Scots, Negroes, and Indians on the other.

Although Quakers were smeared by conventional Calvinists as sexual libertines—"all things are common as in the apostles tyme, mens wives allsoe"—there is little evidence that adherence to the Society of Friends led to a conscious flouting of puritan moral values.[47] Jerathmeel Bowers, stepbrother of Benanuel, a leading Quaker of Charlestown, proved an outrageously insolent servant and was convicted of premarital fornication,[48] and Elizabeth Cole, whose stepmother Ursula was a Friend and had said of Mr. Symmes and Mr. Shepard that "she had as live hear a catt meaw as them preach" bore a bastard by Samuel Eaton in 1674.[49] However Bowers was brought up in an orthodox, if contentious, household. His chronic insubordination—he called his mistress an "ordinary whore, a burnt-taile bitch and hopping toad"—was more likely to have developed from his foster parents' example.[50] Cole's natural mother and father were also conformists. There is no hint in either case that Quakerism had anything to do with their misdemeanors. Nor was Richard Nevers's early flirtation with the Gould Baptist group in Charlestown so much as referred to in the long drawn-out civil litigation with the Gardiners.[51] There is no evidence that religious heterodoxy brought sexual revolution in its baggage train, as it had in Münster or Interregnum England.[52]

The age-old antipathy between English and Scots broke out into war in 1649.[53] By 1652 over five hundred Scottish prisoners of war from Dunbar and Worcester had been transported as servants to Massachusetts Bay. By 1680 only some one hundred twenty remained.[54] During the 1650s they certainly made their presence felt, but as much for their savage violence as their sexual indiscipline. Thus James Ross, the father of Mary Goodenow's bastard, had received heavy punishment of thirty-nine stripes for "shamefull abuse and violence towards his master."[55] Others were presented for cruelty to the bastard of a fellow-countryman or for "uncomfortable carriages . . . towards his wife . . . bitter words from day to day [making it] very hazardous to live together."[56] They often had to make do with disreputable women: an Irish pilferer and slattern,[57] the whorish Jane Bowen,[58] the repeater Sarah Dawes,[59] or an unrequited wife.[60] When the impudent Daniel Elder sought "irregularly to draw away the affections" of a deacon's daughter, the court put him firmly in his place.[61]

After eleven sexual offenses between 1655 and 1665, Scottish names appear far less frequently in the records.[62] It is probable that many returned home after the Restoration in 1660; others may have migrated to the Connecticut Valley.[63] Those who remained were then New Englanders by choice and seem to have integrated into the culture. Their enforced residence during the 1650s comes through from the records as the presence of a very different culture whose violent impact was marked but extremely short-lived.

In his report of 1680, Governor Simon Bradstreet informed the committee of the Privy Council in London that "now and then, two or three negroes are brought hither from Barbados and other of his Majesty's plantations, and sold here for about twenty pounds a piece; so that there may be, within our government, about 100 or 120."[64] Fifteen of the twenty cases involving Negroes were for fornication.[65] In seven both partners were black; in the remaining eight, five involved white or mulatto men and black women, and three white women bearing bastards by black fathers.[66] Two black couples were convicted of premarital fornication, and a third, though serving different masters in Charlestown, convinced the Court that they had been married before arrival in Massachusetts. An attempted rape and a charge of ill-treatment of a black boy make up the total.

Although there are at least two cases each decade, prosecutions tend to come in bunches. There are three in June 1677, three in 1678, and two in the first half of 1679, for example, and four in April and May 1691. The court records give no clue as to the significance, if any, of these two clusters, which account for sixty percent of all cases and seventy-three percent of fornication cases. They may have been purely fortuitous, but two other explanations are feasible. The authorities may have tightened up their disciplining of black slaves in the wake of Indian attacks, either to placate an angry God or to cow potential collaborators. Alternatively, the earlier prosecutions may have been precipitated by the rape by a black of a three-year-old girl in 1674 and another attempted black rape in 1677.[67]

Certain owners—Wymans, Collinses, and Hemans—appear to have concentrated on slaves as laborers; four of these owners lived in Woburn. Although pregnant Negroes were not above false accusations of wealthy white males, they were also more vulnerable to white pressure. One case suggests the kind of pressure slave women might be subjected to.

The light complexion and straight brown hair of the child born in 1685 to Joanna Negro, servant to Francis Wyman of Woburn, lent credence to the rumors in the town that Joseph Carter, a married man, rather than Samson Negro his father's slave, was the father. William Johnson's magisterial examination of Joanna on 13 April 1686 records her changed, postpartum accusation of Joseph Carter.[68]

He gott her with child in the dyke nere the well and it was when . . . the generale trayning was at boston and . . . his wife was gon to Reading and as soone as he had dun he bid her laye it to Samson Captain Carters Negro man and about two months after . . . he brought Savin [an abortifacient] to her and said she might take that and it wold kill the child . . . and further he bid her smother the child as soone as it was borne and that she might smother it when she was in extremity . . . if she layd it to him he wold sett the divel to worke upon her and . . . she should never have a quiet life againe.

Her naming of Samson was "because [Joseph Carter's] wife was her midwife and might hurt her." Because Joseph denied paternity, the court sentenced only Joanna.[69] The Carter family, however, had bitter years ahead. Joseph died shortly after the case, and in May 1692 his widow and eldest daughter, both called Bethia, were accused during the Salem witchcraze and imprisoned in Woburn.

Were blacks less sexually inhibited than whites? The evidence of Hannah Smith, fourteen-year-old servant of Samuel Haugh, minister of Reading, suggested that they were.[70] "At the latter end of Indian[71] harvest last, in the cowhouse in the shutting in of evening" she went "to help Francis Flashego a [black] married man to fill sacks with Indian corn . . . without asking her consent he throws this examinant down upon the ground pulls up her coates and (his breeches being on) did with his privy member enter her body." She only prevented the rape by summoning Haugh's young daughter. He had often tried to bed her since and "said she was a hard harted maid to denie him."

Flashego told a subtly different tale. He admitted "sattisfying his desire uppon her soe farr as he could" and trying to buy her silence. Yet he pleaded provocation: "She would often jeere him because he had no children" and claimed that she had "called to her masters maid to stay where she was." In treating this as a case of fornication and punishing Hannah as well, the court showed its color blindness by preferring Flashego's account.[72] The "rapist-beast" stereotype was a prejudice of the future.

Considering their small numbers, the Negroes seem to have been prone to crimes of a sexual nature. While their traditional mores would inculcate very different attitudes to sexuality, some seem to have adopted the values of their masters. Cases of miscegenation are insufficiently documented to draw conclusions about race relations, though the alleged behavior of Joseph Carter suggests that he treated his black sexual partner like a mere commodity. Black offenders received punishment comparable to whites.

Indians made only rare appearances in sexual prosecutions; drink was their great weakness. Ellen, a Pequot, received a markedly lenient sentence for fornication in 1654.[73] Cicely Indian of Woburn was the ten-year-old victim in 1678 of sexual abuse by Thomas Keeny, a Negro, already convicted of fathering a bastard on Sue Negro.[74] Two Indians, as we have seen, were convicted of sexual abuse of white minors. In both cases the court seems to have accepted diminished responsibility in its sentencing.[75] The tiny number of sexual infractions by Indians in the court records argues a meager interaction with whites.

Although Scots and Negroes took up disproportionate space in the Middlesex Records, there is no evidence that they changed the sexual mores of the dominant English puritan culture. It is more probable that by their "outlandish" behavior they reinforced puritan conventions.[76]

PART TWO / MARRIED MORES

John Winthrop called his fourth wife, Margaret, "My Chiefe Joye in this World." She was a romantic joy. "I kisse and love thee with the kindest affeccion," he wrote. "The verye thought of thee affordes me many a kynde re-freshinge, what will then be·the enioyment of thy sweet societye, which I prize above all worldly comforts . . . thy love is such to me and so great is the bonde betweene us."[1] Just after penning these ardent lines, he gave vent to a paean of praise for Eve's love for Adam as the Arbella sailed across the Atlantic.

> *Now when the soule which is of a social nature findes any thing like to it selfe, it is like Adam when Eve was brought to him, shee must have it one with herselfe this is fleshe of my fleshe (saith shee) and bone of my bone shee conceives a great delighte in it, therfore shee desires nearenes and familiarity with it: shee hath a greate propensity to doe it good and receives such content in it, as feareing the miscarriage of her beloved shee bestows it in the inmost closett of her heart, shee will not endure that it shall want any good which shee can give it, if by occasion shee be withdrawne from the Company of it, shee is still lookeing towardes the place where she left her beloved, if shee heare it groane shee is with it presently, if shee finde it sadd and disconsolate shee sighs and mournes with it, shee hath noe such joy, as to see her beloved merry and thriving, if shee see it wronged, shee cannot beare it without passion, shee setts noe boundes of her affeccions, nor hath any thought of reward, shee findes recompence enough in the exercise of her love towardes it.[2]*

Yet nine years later he was berating William Hutchinson as "a man of a very mild temper and weak parts" being "wholly guided by his wife."[3] In 1640 he was present at the debate of the Boston church over the intransigent campaign of Mistress Ann Hibbins against a craftsman who she thought had overcharged her. Despite her husband's pleas for the church's mercy toward his "dear wife," the saints finally excommunicated her. One reason for the decision with which Winthrop concurred was

> your want of subjection to so wise and discreet a husband . . . whom God hath set to
> be your guide, whose council you should have followed unto whom you should have
> been obedient in the Lord; yet against the institution of God and the rule of the
> Apostle and to the evil example of diverse other wives you have against nature
> usurped authority over him, grieved his spirit and carried yourself as if he was
> a nobody, as if his wisdom were not to be compared to yours and to harden yourself in
> a way of disobedience to the evil example and unquietness of the family.[4]

In 1645, contrasting natural liberty, or license, with civil liberty, he elaborated
on the latter.

> This liberty is maintained and exercised in a way of subjection to authority; it is of
> the same kind of liberty wherewith Christ has made us free. The woman's own
> choice makes such a man her husband; yet being so chosen, he is her lord, and she is to
> be subject to him, yet in a way of liberty, not of bondage; and a true wife accounts her
> subjection her honor and freedom, and would not think her condition safe and free,
> but in her subjection to her husband's authority. Such is the liberty of the church
> under the authority of Christ, her king and husband; his yoke is so easy and sweet to
> her as a brides ornaments; and if through frowardness and wantonness, etc., she
> shake it off, at any time, she is at no rest in her spirit, until she take it up again; and
> whether her lord smiles upon her, and embraces her in his arms, or whether he
> frowns, or rebukes, or smites her, she apprehends the sweetness of his love in all, and
> is refreshed, supported, and instructed by every such dispensation of his authority
> over her.[5]

These markedly different emphases aptly sum up the divergent views of
modern scholars on puritan attitudes to marriage in the seventeenth century. On
the one hand are those who depict puritans as progressives who stressed the need
for love, mutuality, companionship, even "the duty of desire" or "sensuous
delight in the body of one's spouse" as essential to "Holy Matrimony." To the
Hallers, Johnson, or Leites, puritan dogmatists like Perkins, Ames, Gouge,
Gataker, Baxter, or Dodd and Cleaver advocated a "Puritan Art of Love"
which was practiced not only by Winthrop, but also by Shepard, Cotton
Mather, Hooker, and Taylor.[6] Migration to the new world further improved
the role and status of wives, according to this school of thought. It removed the
saints from the polluting, traditionalist ideas of marriage as "corporate merger,"
or institution to legitimize lust, or convenient cover for promiscuity. No longer
were their ears defiled with the hackneyed folk tales of the cuckolding of impotent
old husbands by ravenous young wives and their handsome male servants or
gallants, of wicked stepparents, or of hypocritical puritans who lusted after their
maids or failed to satisfy their wives' desires.[7] More positively, by creating both
a female shortage and a crying need for children and labor, migration conferred
greatly increased value on women. The gender blindness of gathered churches in
electing female saints symbolized the new equality, as did improved legal rights,

educational and employment opportunities, even a political voice in town affairs.[8] The New England marriage partnership is typified by the lives of Anne Bradstreet, wife and poetess, or Anne Hutchinson, wife and prophetess, or Ann Hibbins, wife and scourge of profiteers.

The contrary view is familiar to us. Puritanism enthroned the patriarch, "the cottage despot," who would applaud Winthrop's sentiments about wifely subjection and husbandly authority. Denying that there was anything particularly original or puritan about "wedded love,"[9] these critics insist that it did not have primacy for most dogmatists.[10] They quote puritans like Robert Cawdrey: "We would that the man when he loveth remember his superiority."[11] Some go so far as to argue that the unconditional love and devotion of the type praised in Eve was the unequal obligation of wives only. They were the victims of a gigantic confidence trick which gulled them into loving their oppressors. Puritan husbands actually became more oppressive in compensation for their helplessness in the face of a capricious, patriarchal, and predestinating God. The alleged gains of migrating to New England were illusory, it is claimed. Wives' labor was devoted to the worst chores; their frequent birth labors simply increased their chances of an early death. As the numbers of women saints grew, sainthood declined in status. Far from liberating the "weaker sex," puritan ideas on marriage constricted it.[12]

In this section we glean from the court records what ordinary people felt about marriage. Since our sample is so much smaller than cases involving adolescents, we must proceed by a more empirical approach, extracting what information we can from the few better documented cases. We look first at instances of marital breakdown or stress and then examine examples of male and female infidelity. From these sources we must attempt to decide which side of Winthrop's seemingly divergent attitudes—the uxorious or the authoritarian—held stronger sway in the minds of Middlesex men and women.

7 / Marital Problems

THOMAS DANFORTH came to Cambridge in 1635 at the age of eleven. He lived out his life there for the next sixty-four years. He married at the age of twenty and had twelve children. From his voluminous writings and from colony, court, and town records we can discover considerable information about his land-holdings, political opinions, spiritual attitudes, personal wealth, and social morality. Of his fifty-three years of married life we know absolutely nothing.[1] His was the typical marriage of Middlesex county so far as total silence is concerned. As with the majority of adolescents, then, we are thrown back on that minority of marriages whose malfunctioning by contemporary standards brought them into the limelight of the county court. From these breakdowns we must try to deduce what the working models looked like. What were people's expectations of marriage? What kind of a relationship ought it to be? What made a marriage successful?

Seventeen cases involving marital problems, other than adultery or adulterous carriages, came before the county court between 1649 and 1699. Nine of these involved domestic contention, seven, wife-beating, and three, desertion. Four additional cases of desertion emerged in other evidence. We look first at three detailed cases of domestic contention.

Case Studies: Domestic Contention

In May 1656 William Clements, Jr., of Cambridge sued for a divorce on the grounds that his wife "for severall years hath refused marriage fellowship." Since his conviction for neglect two years previously,

Martha Clements, lacking "naturale abilities to guide her selfe," had been in the custody of relatives.[2] The Clements's marriage had been no love match. Richard Wall had accompanied Martha and Richard Willis from Roxbury to the wedding. She had said, "If her husband were as handsome a man as Richard Willis Oh how she could love him. I told her she ought to love him [Clements] better than any other ———[3] & she would see him hanged before he should cum neere her to touche her."[4]

Many witnesses corroborated Martha's physical revulsion, sometimes carried to extremes: "About midnight in the first moneth [March] a year past I came with William Clements to his house from fishing . . . she was not abed but [we] found her in the stable between a couple of steers or a steer and an oxe & she did much miscall him Base rogue, damnd dogg and other ———[5] she often spoke thus without any provocation from her husband." Attempts "to persuade her to love him . . . if she had children by him she might love him" were met with such responses as "her heart died within her when her husband would have kissed her," or "she would rather see his heart blood out in the house than that he should come nigh to touch her for she did not like the breed so well as to have any by him."

Clements seems to have responded to her hatred with patience and loving kindness. "When the wife of William Clements lay sick he fetched beere and wheat bread from Boston. When they were first married they had so much venison that he was fain to sell some of it. . . . Her husband and his mother tended uppon her as if she had been a woman that had lyen in."[6] It was to no avail. Martha too desired divorce from what had been "a forced business." The county court gave no judgment for over a year. On 9 June 1657 they opined that it was "not meet to grant them a divorce at present but do order that they both [treat] each other according to their Marriage Covenant & that upon Complaint made such party as shall be found faulty shall be severely punished." There is no further reference to them in the Middlesex Records.[7] Their ordeal ended two-and-a-half years later when Martha died on 10 December 1659. On the following 3 April Clements married Ann Taylor, but this union also may have been childless.[8]

Hannah Hutchinson of Reading gave vent to a similar sense of physical revulsion in 1669. Of her husband Samuel "she said she would be hanged before she ever had a child by him." Her reason was overtly sexual: "Though he had a pen he had no ink[9] . . . it were as good to goe to bedd with a guelt dogg as with her husband . . . it was a pitty for her to be maried to such an ould rogue, shee being a prittie woman." Un-like Martha Clements, however, she had sought satisfaction elsewhere. "She said William Marshall was the father of her son and John Price was the father of her daughter."[10] Her frustration was channeled into domestic violence. "She would go to the gallows soon for she vowed she would kill old Sam. . . . She thought she could have hired a man to have killed ould Sam for a quart of liquor, yea for a pint, but she could not get it. . . . if he did not dy soon she would give him a drink."[11] When a girl asked what for, Hannah replied laconically "To spede him." Exacerbating this animosity was Hutchinson's indolence and improvidence.[12] When this offended her, "she flies at him and bloods his cheek." She told him "you dog you shant come in here and dragged Sam Hutchinson from the house but he gott away. . . . she fetched an axe crying I will split your brains, you shant live this night."[13]

Their shrill, shifting, shiftless lifestyle was already well known to the authorities and would continue to plague them for the next decade.[14] The violent scolding or "flyting" of the sex-starved, neglected young wife against the old, inadequate, cuckolded husband could have come straight out of a contemporary English ballad or chapbook. The people of Reading clearly regarded this strife-torn ménage as intolerable. They had informally counseled the Hutchinsons before presenting them to the court. Within a year they would be run out of town.

The six other cases of marital incompatibility reveal similar patterns of husbandly neglect, inadequacy, or instability and wifely outrage, dis-temper, or suffering. The frustration of Mary Mansfield of Charles-town against her drunken, "distempered," sponging husband John was turned against the outside world. This merchant's daughter was twice punished, once for breach of the peace in 1655, and for "exorbitant car-riages & reproachful speeches against authority" a year later.[15]

Similarly Elizabeth Ball of Watertown excused her "severall disorderly carriages against both her husband and her neighbours" in 1657 because "her husband neglects her in suffering her to want necessary supplies & allsoe did kick her."[16] Though the court counseled kindliness, love, and helpfulness in view of "her disturbed mind," Elizabeth and John were back eighteen months later. This time she had also scratched and punched her father's face.[17]

Rebecca Pattison seems to have been a melancholic, possibly suffering from the aftereffects of a miscarriage or stillbirth in 1663. James, her

Scottish husband of less than a year, drove her suicidal by his "uncomfortable carriages," bitter nagging, and recrimination.[18]

A husband's mental instability could be another cause of domestic breakdown. John Cutler was presented in 1653 by the Woburn selectmen for "idleness and neglect of his family . . . sundry times convicted of like misdemeanours . . . somewhat distempered in the head." The court gave Olive Cutler control over the family assets and committed John to another family.[19]

Henry Salter showed the same kinds of subversive and antisocial behavior as Hannah Hutchinson, Elizabeth Ball, and Elizabeth Mansfield. The Charlestown selectmen inveighed in 1673 against "the inordinate life of Henry Salter, neglecting his family, misspending his time and estate in a very wicked and injudicious manner." He may have been an alcoholic. His wife, a self-appointed moral monitor, described him as "of unsound mind." His behavior was certainly abnormally aggressive. In 1668 he escalated a drunken militia training day brawl at Cole's alehouse. "He swore and cursed more than I can remember, throwing off his clothes and offering to beat the constable he called him rogue whores bird and devil." The next year he was reported for cursing, as he went to court, against "such devills [the bench] that should make him pay three fines in one day. . . . The Plague of God rot them, the Devill rot them, the Devill have the heart of him that had his coat and shoes that night." He carried a pea hook. "One asked him did he go to hook peas at this time of year [November] to which he answered I am going up to the Justice to hook his Arse off."[20]

Daniel Metup of Watertown had been warned about neglecting his family as a young seaman. In August 1692, nearly thirty years later when he was fifty-six, "in the night late he forced his wife and children out of doors and threatened to kill her if she would not be gon." She had to shelter with a neighbor who deposed that "Daniel Metup would not let them mow his grain nor did he intend to. Whenas he was wont to improve his land by planting he would not let his sons [aged twenty-four to nineteen] doe it nor doe it himself more than halfe an acre."[21]

At this distance it is impossible to penetrate the causes of marital breakdown. Did husbandly neglect turn wives into shrews and busybodies, or did menfolk lose enthusiasm to provide for incompatible wives? Did husbandly rage make wives depressives or did melancholia test patience to the breaking point? The explicit sexual problems of the Clementses and the Hutchinsons may have affected other couples who had fewer than average children, but whether such problems were cause or effect of incompatibility we cannot know. The depiction of outspoken or assertive wives as early feminists seriously distorts the reality of their situation. Their outbursts were the frustrated, pathetic reactions of victims of circumstance, not the assertive ideology of conscious feminists. The casual husbandly violence or neglect which have typified these contentious marriages could be extended in either of two directions—wife-beating or desertion.

Case Studies: Wife-Beating

Wife-beating in Massachusetts, except in self-defense, was a punishable offense. This represented a divergence from English law, even though there was strong and widespread condemnation of husbandly violence in the old country, especially among puritans.[22] There are only seven cases in the Middlesex records[23] for our period, five of which occur in the first volume, from 1649 to 1663. Only two of these cases have illuminating testimony.[24]

The presentment of Thomas Dutton of Woburn in December 1661 is distinctly puzzling. The mystery begins with the order book which records that both Dutton *and* his wife Susan denied the accusation, but on other evidence he was found guilty and sentenced to a fine of five pounds and admonition. The other evidence came entirely from the household of a neighbor, Ensign John Carter.[25] According to him the trouble began on 29 September 1661, a Sunday.

> Mary Dutton dafter to Thomas Dutton was hid at our house that Lords Day from the time she ran untill we came home at night and then my wife & I did send her home and desired that her father would not beat her. . . . her mother replyed I have had it all redy that shee should have had.

Carter's two teenaged daughters claimed that they

> both saw Dutton beat his wife with a stick upon a Lords Day & shee had a child in her arms & she cried out you will kill my child & hee bad her fling it down & she said I will not.

The following morning, according to Carter's wife Elizabeth and his servant John Neale, there was a great outcry from Dutton's wife.

> Oh that I should live with such a man as this as should use a woman thus & cried as if shee had bin a killing & said oh wicked wretch what beat a woman we heard her crying out betwixt the blowes.

The same morning Carter and the Woburn grandjuryman confronted Dutton who said:

> he would not bee so abused by a woman & we found her a crying and her eies seemed to be swelled with crying whereby we did aprehend him gilty with reference to the outcry.

Some time later on that Monday, 30 September 1661

> Goodwife Dutton coming to our house my wife said How now Goody Dutton you had a sorre bout & said shee I feel his blowes still, laying her hands upon her arms . . . and farther John Neale and Mary Carter heard Thomas Dutton say that he hoped his wife would bee the better for it & that she loved him the better.

In Dutton's defense two subscriptions were presented to the court. The first from twenty-one people of Reading[26] testified to his "tender & loving treatment of his wife"; previous next-door neighbors had never heard any evidence of violence; to the best of their knowledge he was "a loveing husband to her." The second came from eleven witnesses to Dutton's "loving and tender carriage to his wife" and claimed that there had been no sound of any abuse "till John Carter had complained against him." At the same court Carter's man, John Neale, an important witness, was convicted for the second time of drunkenness and of profaning the sabbath. In the Dutton case the court plainly accepted the Carter evidence and fined Dutton relatively heavily.[27] His recent record may have swayed them; he had been a plaintiff in a slander suit in 1658 and a defendant the following year.[28] Nonetheless there was obvious popular resentment against the Carters who had turned a domestic tiff into a public matter, a resentment which Dutton's wife may well have shared. The Duttons' record suggests again that poverty and inadequacy probably further soured the father's foul temper.

The formal complaint lodged on 30 July 1666 against William Healey[29] of Cambridge for maltreating his wife came from her brother Samuel Green and her brother-in-law Thomas Langhorn.[30] However, the most damning evidence came from two servants, Samuel Reynolds and Daniel Beckley.

> On the 13th of Aprill William Healey sent us to Boston, but as before our departure he was chiding his wife we therefor went back to the house and saw sd. Healey beating and kicking her. On the 7th of May after all were a bed the child[31] begann to crie and Healey told her to quiet the child but it continuing he bid her to lye further off or else he would stick his teeth

down her throat and he struck her with his hand and she cried out; then he took her by the wrists and twisted her to pieces (as she afterwards said) so that she wore a plaister for two weeks and cried with the pain of it for two hours. Healey hearing us talking in bed made a bemoaning of himself as though she had beaten him and listening again he did not hear us and said to her Ah Wicked roan hast thou not done houling yet & bid her cry aloud her God was asleep and bid her gett all her lyes in a bag together and present them to her God he would not hear her else. On 27th of May there was a falling out in bed and Daniel Beckley counted three blowes and she said Will you kill me then five blows then eight. Next morning William Healey owned to Sam Reynolds that he had struck her four or five times. When Daniel Beckley was setting him over to Boston he admitted that he struck her but told him to say nothing, let her prove it. On the last of June a Saturday we were returning with Arthur from Boston when we heard a great noise from the house; we held still our oars and heard three blows and shee looking out at the window cryed for Gods sake help me he will kill me. William Healey said some of us had given her tobacco & now she was mad. His wife came from the chamber and vexed him and he caried her to the chamber and beat her. She spoke without any distemper. His constant dayly course was to curse att her & revile her & her friends, her generation as he called them beggars. He referred to her brothers Langhorn[32] and Greene to their disgrace & all her generation were thieves and whore-masters. Concerning her he would say God had burnt out one of her eyes & drawn up one side of her mouth & he would quickly do the like to the other & make her a spectacle of his wrath. He oft twitt her in the teeth of her being a [church] member,[33] saying the church saw nothing in her where-fore they received her in but that she made two or three fine kerchies[34] . . . he would oft tell her of her being nailed to the door and threshold . . . she remonstrated with him saying he must answer for them [his sins] one day before God to which he replyed do you take Gods name in your mouth; you might as well take my arse in your mouth you prophane woman . . . he said he was never whipt at the post yett . . . if there was any iniquity in him let him be brought forth and he would strip in the street . . . [they were] damned rogues and whores that know any evill by him and do not bring him forth.[35]

Daniel Gookin and Thomas Danforth examined the couple together. The wife (whose first name we never discover from the records)[36] sub-stantiated the servants' testimony, adding some further details. Her husband had also called her "lying slutt" and had used "a wand the size of a good riding rod" to beat her. Healey admitted reproachful words and some violence, but it was "not to hurt her" or was merely "acci-dental blowes in riseing from the bed." The incident heard from the boat on the last Saturday in June arose when "she put out her neck and said Come old Healey cutt off my head and he gave her a chuck under the chin & that was all. The wife says she desires she may never have a like chuck for it was to be seen many days after."

In a written statement to the court, Healey pointed out that the servants' evidence was "their apprehensions, not what they saw" and that noise and a clamorous woman tend to go together. He cited a statement by Beckley to "my mother Ives,[37] that if his dame had nobody to scould at she would scould at the wall. . . . If any words have passed from him in his passion, which are not according to godlinesse, he desires to be deeply humbled for them in the sight of God and men." Healey's final counterthrust was to question the motives of his two servants. Reynolds, "a loose and scandalous person," had been refused permission to marry Healey's daughter. Beckley, "a refractory servant," sought to "recompense his master for his correcting him for his miscarriages."

Support for Healey's defense came from two sources. Reynolds was committed on 12 August 1667 for fathering a bastard on Healey's daughter and for going to his house "in a violent manner causing William Healey to cry out murther." John Guy, aged twenty-two, who had often worked at Healey's, recounted verbal provocations.

> We won morning were att brekfast and she having the child in her armes he cutt her a peece of cheese and asked her if she would have itt and she apon no other ocagion tooke it and threw it at him and bid him eate it himselfe for she did believe that he did gruge it her and apon no other ocagion cald him Tom Tinker and ould Heiley and ould roge and said he was a murderer and had murdered three wifes allready and would murder her; then his answere was to her was this: poor woman I am sory to see thee thus discomposed and desired the lord to give her grase and many times I have heard him say to her that if that she would but be quiet with him he would let her have any thing that she wanted and she should do nothing.

Not surprisingly the aged Elizabeth Green,[38] the wife's mother, painted a rather different picture. "When her face was burnt he tooke upon him to dres her face, when her face was sore, and spoild it." She described "his carage and his childrens to her how she was slited and if anything was wasted or amis . . . she had done it. . . . She hath not so much authority as to give her children any victuals but what she must ask his daughters for."[39] If he was reproved, he threatened "he would leave [her] and now he hath spoild her he would divers times bid her get her to her friends." Finally, in claiming the foresight of mothers-in-law through the ages, she referred to her unwillingness to give consent to the match and the promises the ardent Healey had made to quiet her apprehensions of her daughter's likely "discouragments in the family from himself or children."

Although, tantalizingly, the court's judgment on this case has not survived, the testimony gives us a remarkably vivid insight into family dynamics: generational conflict between an old husband of fifty-three and a wife twenty years younger; the mythic wicked stepmother here transformed into the isolated and pilloried intruder; the jealousy of a church member of long standing for one of the recently elected saints; the reprisal powers of servants against stern masters; the baby as a source of conflict and the bed as a battlefield—one of the few places available for private warfare.[40]

This violent marriage came to an end in 1671 when the fourth Goodwife Healey seems to have died in childbirth.[41] We know from other sources that Healey held the post of keeper of the prison in Cambridge during the 1670s and early 1680s. As such he was able legally to keep his flogging arm in trim as the official executor of corporal punishment. In 1674 his services were employed by Harvard College to give a public whipping to an undergraduate who had uttered blasphemous words concerning the Holy Ghost. In 1682 when he was sixty-nine, he was caught in the prison in the act of copulation with the already heavily pregnant Mary Lovell. For this, he was dismissed from his post, evicted from his house, and sentenced with a certain poetic justice to be whipped twenty stripes in April 1683.[42] Six months later the flogged flogger flagged and died. He left an estate worth only six pounds.[43]

Case Studies: Desertion

Desertion may be the ultimate form of husbandly neglect, but it was not limited to men. Like Hannah Hutchinson, several married women ran away for spells from their husbands.[44] Mary Summers, on the other hand, typified a kind of passive desertion: "She was resolved not to come for New England" in 1665 from Biddeford in Devon, despite her husband Henry's "many invitations for . . . your presence [who are] in my eye above all women in this world." Her reluctance was stiffened by her mother and had not been an uncommon phenomenon in pioneering days.[45] It was most unlikely that Summers would have been allowed to stay in Massachusetts without his wife.[46]

There are only two cases of indigenous desertion by men in the records, though, as we shall see, Middlesex was not spared immigrant bigamists. The desertion by Thomas Boyden of his wife Martha of Woburn and their children was the subject of her pathetic petition to the court sitting at Cambridge on 7 July 1685.

> Whereas there hath hapened a most uncomfortable differance between my husband and my selfe; and I suffered so much both by words and blows from him for many years together that I was almost overwhelmed: Indeed not convenient here to express how and in what manner I was abused: I made a shift while my children were young to order them to some pore manner as I was able: but afterwards my sd. husband tought my children not to obey me nor regard what I said to them: which made me troubled to think what would becom of my childrens soules. Afterwards he left me for three or four yeers together but being threatened by authority came to me againe and stayed with me about a month: then left me with child againe and went awaye and took every thing with him that I had to subsist withall and left me five children to tak care of: besides my self with child of another [i.e., child] and now hath left me about three years more: and the charge of my lying in hath bin hard for me without mony or anything else to help my self withall but my poor hands to labour: and I having taken care of my children to put them out [i.e., with families as apprentices or servants] where they are likely to do well and now my husband threatens to take them away againe . . . they will be utterly undon and indeed I know not what to doe for I am afraid of my life to live with him . . . he is now at my uncle Holdens at freshpond in Cambridg:[47] Indeed as we now live is very unbecoming the gospell. I beseech your honers take some care of me for I am in a lonely case.

The court condemned Boyden for "his evill & unnaturall carriages," endorsed Martha's arrangements for their children, and required him to maintain his family.[48] It did not, however, order him to return. His domestic violence and undermining of maternal authority may have persuaded the bench that separation was preferable.[49]

The case of the wife and young child of William Pope[50] was brought to the attention of the court in January 1693 by the selectmen of Marlborough. Their town was a haven for dispersed settlers during the war then waging against the French and Indians. They were evidently anxious to ensure that the deserted wife and child should be formally acknowledged as the responsibility for maintenance of their legal place of settlement, Stow.[51] This business, so familiar to students of quarter sessions or municipal records of seventeenth-century England, was rare in Middlesex County until the last quarter of the century when war and resultant poverty set the indigent on the move. The court's order "to supply & provide for *as their own poor*"[52] highlighted a new and long-lasting problem for the colony.[53]

Conclusion

This parade of wretchedness gives us some valuable insights into marital relations. In only one case is a forced marriage advanced as the justification for a loveless match. In one other, parental warnings and objections had been overruled. Seven contentious spouses seem to have been mentally disturbed; Cutler, Mansfield, Salter, Martha Clements, Elizabeth Ball, Phoebe Healey, and Rebecca Pattison are described as being of distempered or discomposed minds in the records and Metup's suicidal refusal to plant or reap hardly seems sane. Nine husbands had records of improvidence and neglect of their families;[54] five husbands and three wives had also used physical violence or verbal provocation on people other than their spouses.[55] In five cases drink was an exacerbating factor.[56] Two marriages between older men and younger women added generational to personal conflict. Seven of the families had moved at least once since marrying.[57] This was probably a reflection of their poverty; all those involved were at the bottom of the social scale.

Except for the Pattisons, none of the couples was recently married. The Healeys and the Bowtells had been married for six years, but William Healey and both Bowtells had been married before. The remaining fifteen couples had all been married at least ten years, the Metups twenty-eight, the Mansfields twenty-one, and the Boydens nineteen. Dutton's battering of his wife had been directly provoked by the misbehavior of their daughter Mary. Four other families had difficult children.[58] Much of this youthful rebelliousness may have been the result of family tensions, but it is equally possible that it was a cause as well. One of Martha Boyden's complaints against her husband referred to disagreements about the upbringing of their children, and it also added to the hostility in the Healey household.

The great majority of cases of domestic violence occurred in the early part of our period. Six of the seven wife-beating cases were tried before 1670, as were presentments of six of the eight contentious marriages. This coincides with the decline in violence between masters and servants and with an apparently more relaxed attitude toward adolescent group activities. Similarly, the favored solution of desertion, with four out of the six examples after 1685, parallels the adolescent evasion of responsibility by flight in the last two decades of the century.

The lessons to be learned from the relationships of spouses are painfully obvious. If as a man you wanted a happy marriage, you should find someone your own age, avoiding any woman with a reputation as either a scold or a depressive. You should work hard at providing for your family, eschew drink, and agree on the upbringing of your children. You should stay in one place, guard your tongue, and realize that marriage does not become any easier as the years pass, particularly when children approach their teens. For a woman, many of the same guidelines would apply. Above all, you should seek a good provider who is temperamentally compatible. Otherwise as the puritan William Whately warned in 1624:

> It comes to passe, that marriage proveth to many, just as the stocks to the drunkard; into which when his head was warme with wine and Ale, he put his foot laughingly and with merriment: but a little after (having slept out his wine and cooled his head with a nap) he longs as much to get it out againe. Hence it is that divers houses are none other but even very fencing schools, wherein the two sexes seem to have met together for nothing but to try masteries.[59]

The reactions of neighbors and of the court tell us rather more than these commonsensical consumer tips about the popular expectations of marriage. More than once the bench adjured couples to treat "each other according to the Marriage Covenant" or to "live together as a man and wife ought to do." What did they intend by these phrases? The definitions harp on kindliness, love, helpfulness. "Her husband to use her kindly . . . her neighbours . . . to have a loving and helpful inspeccon toward her." A husband should have a "loving and tender carriage to his wife"; she should be to him "above all women in the world." Their relations should be "comfortable." He should not undermine her authority over their children. In sickness a model husband nursed and pampered his wife; in health he kissed and caressed her, wished to be near her. He must be physically attractive to her and able to satisfy her sexual needs. A recently bereaved widower regarded as appalling slanders "the false reports that he brock his deceased wifes hart with greife that he would be absent from her three weeks together when he was at home and would never come neare her and such like."[60] These expectations remind us of Winthrop's depiction of Eve and of the whole tenor of "The Model of Christian Charity." There is one striking difference though. These loving feelings and expressions of tenderness are expected of Adams, of husbands. Of course, a wife should reciprocate. "She ought to love him better than any other." Bearing his children should cement bonds of affection. She should "be quiet with him." This serenity and comfort should come from love.[61]

There are two notable exceptions to these idyllic popularly expressed

Ich liebe Ellen.

expectations of marriage. The first is Thomas Dutton's alleged statement "that he hoped his wife would be the better for [her beating] and that she loved him the better" for it and the fact that Susan Dutton, the victim, joined her husband in denying the accusation. These sound much more like the puritan patriarch—"What hath any man to do with it? Have not I power to correct my own wife?"—and his subjugated wife who would be "rather willing to groan than publicly discover his wicked and brutal carriage."[62] The second exception was William Healey. With his repeated violence and disdain toward his wife, depriving her of any authority within the household, he seems to fit the pattern of the cottage despot to a tee. Phoebe Healey, nameless in the records, emerges as a mere shuttlecock in a contest between male deponents for the prosecution and defense.

Where so small a sample is involved, such exceptions should give us pause. We plainly need further evidence, and for this we turn to the other sets of cases, more serious in puritan eyes, involving sexual infidelity on the parts first of men, then of women.

8 / Unfaithful Husbands

A major plank of the puritan law reform platform in England was the institution of the death penalty for adultery as prescribed in the Levitical Code.[1] Prynne, the puritan lawyer bloated with pedantic learning, gave twenty-one furious reasons for abominating breaches of the Seventh Commandment, reminding his readers that "God hath commanded [it] to be punished with death, yea and stoning to death, the most vile and shamefullest death of all others."[2] Once the English puritans came to power in 1649 they set about turning a century's advocacy into statute. Their Adultery Act became law in 1650. It comes as no surprise, then, that in October 1631, the year after the arrival of the Winthrop fleet, the Court of Assistants, "by allowance of the General Court" made adultery a capital offense. This was endorsed by the codification of 1641 and in the laws of 1648. On 21 March 1644 James Britton and Mary Latham, both married, were hanged for the crime in Boston.[3]

This evenhandedness had its limits, however. Massachusetts law, like Leviticus and the 1650 Act in England, was, in one major aspect, heavily biased against women. The Sixth Chapter of *The Laws and Liberties* reads: "If any person committ Adulterie with a married or espoused woman; the adulterer and adulteress shall surely be put to death."[4] But if any person had sexual relations with a married or espoused man, this was treated as mere fornication. Moreover the "surely" was wishful thinking. Winthrop records reprieves under the 1631 law and magisterial doubts about the Britton–Latham sentence. No other executions took place thereafter. The main reason seems to have been that juries in the Court of Assistants, as in English Assizes during the Interregnum, simply refused to convict, preferring to find couples guilty of the noncapital crime of adulterous carriages.[5] This reluctance was finally officially recognized in the 1685 drafts for a new adultery law. The Assistants demanded in their preamble that: "That odious sin of adultery too to much encreasing amongst us that due testimony be borne against that crying and land defiling sinn." They proposed that the punishment for carnal copulation with a married or espoused woman be the same as that for adulterous carriages, namely to stand on the gallows for two hours with a halter round the neck, followed by thirty-eight strokes at the carttail and committal until legal dues and security had been given. Those convicted should be barred from public office.[6] Though the sentence might be reduced the gender bias remained. Here, however, we have treated adultery as intercourse by either sex outside their marriages.

In Middlesex twenty-three married men were convicted of either attempting or actually having sexual intercourse with women other than their wives;[7] twelve succeeded, eleven were thwarted. In fifteen cases their partners/victims/rebuffers were single women, in seven they were married, and in two widows. Only one adulterous male was actually witnessed having intercourse with a married woman.[8] Three of the twenty-three were presented for adultery even though their partners were two single women and a widow; perhaps some grand jurymen were less gender-biased than the colony legislators. However, the remaining nine technical adulterers were all charged with fornication. Six of the girls involved were serving maids in the households of their seducers; four of them bore bastards. One summed up their vulnerability to the proximity, power, and prior experience of their employers: "I was not tempted by wandring abroad from the family but at home . . . and from such an one I expected good councell from."[9] A seventh single woman, already pregnant and imprisoned, was caught in the act with the gaoler. She lamented to her discoverer, "I could not help it."[10] Most of the men were accused with respect to only one woman, but four attempted the chastity of at least two, and the record holder had solicited fourteen.

The background of these men was varied. Six were church members and three more were married to church members. More than one found this opportune. The maid of John Harris, a Charlestown innkeeper, reported that when "her dame stayed at the sacrament of the Lords Day, he laid her down upon the bed . . . taking up of her clothes and putting his hand under her clothes and saying he would do her no hurt."[11] Five adulterers came from prominent families, twelve were artisans or yeomen farmers, and five, including one married Negro slave, were lower class. The great majority, fourteen out of nineteen traceable, had been married at least ten years, ten over fifteen. Two had first entered the married state over forty years previously. The frequency of cases reached a peak in the early 1680s, with seven convictions, three for adultery and four for adulterous carriages.[12] This, no doubt, helped to trigger the General Court's action in 1685.[13] During the 1690s the average dropped by more than fifty percent. In our search for further information on marital relations, we examine in this chapter six fully reported cases of male infidelity.

Case Studies

Thomas Langhorn, the town drummer of Cambridge, aged forty-six, had married into the family of Bartholomew Green, and had five children.[14] On 6 November 1663 the court considered the long and detailed complaint against him of Elizabeth Holmes, aged nineteen, the recently orphaned daughter of Robert Holmes,[15] which had been lodged with Thomas Danforth on 11 July 1663.[16]

> His mode hath bin dayly & in the evening time when he had any opportunity to come into my fathers house and trie to kisse mee; & get mee into his lap, & put his hand under my apron, & further if he could; & to tell filthy things that are too much and too troublesome to mention them. And if I had beene in a roome where a bed was he would stop me from going out, & shove mee upon the bed, & leane upon mee, & throwing himselfe upon mee, acting to me as if I had beene his wife; one time Hee gat mee agt. the house side & wd. kisse mee & I spitt in his face, & he rubbed it on mee again with his face, and one time throwing mee on the bed I striving against him Hee told mee I would not be so unwilling to ly on my backe when I had Ric Cutter[17] & he said he wd feele on my belly, & Hee wd tell mee whether it wd hurt mee when I was married. Hee said it would hurt mee 3 or 4 times; & whether I would fall with child presently, or take great pleasure in my husband. Hee said a man with a long member was most pleasure to the woman, when it went home to the womb, & if the foreskin slipt back 2 or 3 inches it would hurt her but a little at first, & hee askt mee if I had never seene his slip back, for hee said that his would often slip back, & hee would often come in & sit down & his members would hang out, & many strange words he would call them. & if any body came in Hee would cast one leg over the other & hide them; many times if I could I would run out of the house & if I could not get by him I was fain to sit still, for if I offered to goe out Hee would catch me in his lap, sundrie times hee would let his member hang out, & if at other times I tould him of it, Hee would

say Hee did know Hee would mend his breeches:[18] He told me also there was the channels in the womb of the woman, that lay in the folds, & that rubbing of them made it delightfull to Her, & a H——y[19] Bone that lyes a little above the coney & it parts the first time a man lyes with her, & that makes it painfull to her till her body be opened & that it also parts at her labor. also he asked mee if I never saw his foreskin slip back & I told him yes once I saw it, & Hee said it would doe so often: He said hee would ly with his wife 3 or 4 times in the night & when he had doen it would bee as limber as a rag & that it would bee two houres in filling & there was vessels in the mans backe that the seed emptied from vessell to vessell till the member was full again, also that his member entered 3 handfulls into his wives body, & measured a stick & showed it me as it grew bigger & longer in the acting of it. Also He told me Hee would teach mee How to ly with my Husband that it should not hurt mee & that I must pull up my legs, & Hee said that he had taught a mayd so & after she was maried shee thanked him for it, Also he told me there was a red streak in the glasse of the mans eye and that it came in by Crispin (?) Himselfe. & that it was also in the womans eye with giving up her selfe to the man. Many times hee would persuade mee to feele of his members which was his mode for two or three years together both before his sickness and after. & Hee said if I would Hee could teach mee so that a man should never force mee. also that Hee had taught a mayd that 3 days after had like to have bin forced in a cellar & that shee teld Him shee did love Him the better after &c. & that though I might make a sport of it, yet twas worth the learning. also He spake how Mr Cotton taught out of Job thou hast poured mee out like milk & curdled mee like cheese, Hee said the women blushed at it & I asked him why they blushed & he answered because of the meaning of it for said Hee the mans seed is white like milk. He said that Arristottle saith that if the seed be thin the woman will not conceive but there are many ways to thicken it and then shee may. Hee said that Mr. Rogers said that the Scripture gave more liberty to maried men than to maried women & that if a maried man committ the act with a mayde it is not death but whipping but if a maried woman with a man it is death:[20] He said that David was a good man & yet committed adultery & that a man was more suddenly taken than a woman: Also Hee came upon the Mow when I was loading Hay the last yeare & threw mee downe & gat upon mee, & said that Mr. Cooke of Boston told Him that when he was in Barbados there met him a woman that told him shee would buy a commodity of Him & pay Him al the Hole,[21] with more ill favoured storyes, & it was his common cariage to put his hands under my Apron, & would have gone further if I had not resisted him, one time Hee gat his hand to my belly, & Hee said that most of the storeys he told mee Hee had out of Arristottle & from Honest men & women.

Langhorn confessed in court in November 1663 and was sentenced to twenty-one stripes. Holmes's protestations of innocence were not entirely persuasive; she was solemnly admonished "for her bold familiarity with Langhorn in his wanton and wicked ways."[22]

What was probably most shocking about the "bold familiarity" of this pair was Langhorn's betrayal of the intimacies of the marriage bed. A witness in the Goodenow–Brooks incident reported with obvious shock, "I did hear them discorse in such a manner as was not mete for any but for a man and his wife." In 1640 a man had been prosecuted on the grounds "that he could not keepe from boyes and servantes secrete passages betwixt him and his wife about the maryage bedd." Marriage was an intimate relationship in more ways than one. Those who breached its privacy and its modesty by loose talk were guilty of shameful infidelity to their spouses.[23]

This remarkable record of sexual talk is reminiscent of both the then fashionable instructional pornography[24] and the popular sex manuals.[25] Langhorn's behavior suggests a repression similar to Pepys's. He must have concealed his sexual obsessions under a mask of discretion to be able to spend so much time alone with a young and motherless, but not altogether incurious pupil.

One of the most notorious village Lotharios was a Malden carpenter in his fifties, William Bucknam. His second wife, Sarah, had been suspected of sexual improprieties nine years previously.[26] Bucknam was convicted of "shamefull lasciviousness in his words and actions towards [fourteen] maried women" over a period of twelve years in 1662. He told Goodwife Elizabeth Webb that she "was a pretty roague and made his hart leap in his britches." He lured Rebecca Green[27] to the mill "and proferred her 2 bushells of [somebody else's] wheat to have his will there . . . he said it was no evill." The childless Elizabeth Lareby was to him an irresistible challenge: "If he had me but one halfe houre even he could get a childe by me and did proffer to put his hands under my cotes and laye hold on me . . . if I wold let him put his hand under my clothes he wold presently tell me whether I shold have children or noe." He was similarly inquisitive about the recently married Elizabeth Payne's prospects. "He said my wife was long before she was with child but after shee read Aristotles Book she was soon with child . . . he puld me into his lapp and there held me and would not lett me goe but kist me severall tymes." He told Hannah Hills:[28] "I come to see how rich your husband is"; Bridget Dexter that "he had had a mynd to me a long time"; Hannah Stowers that "he had seen women undrest before"; and another quingenarian that "he would have to do with her 2 houres together."[29]

Wifely responses lost nothing in the telling. "I detested his speeches and lustfull dalliances . . . I told him God had kept me hitherto from being a whore" (Elizabeth Webb). "I bid him leave for shame, saying will such an ould man as you be so foolish and so wicked. Are you not ashamed to doe soe" (Rebecca Greene). "I could not abide to heare a man talk soe to me" (Elizabeth Payne). "I thought it not modestie for a man to see me Half-naked" (Hannah Stowers). "I bid him goe to his owne wife" (Mary Tufts). "It was unchristian and he must mortifie the lusts of the flesh" (Elizabeth Felt) to which he responded "Come, come, yea, yea, as though [it were] a thing of no account."

Bucknam seems to have been more of a nuisance than a menace, snatching kisses, feeling legs, grabbing on to laps or round waists. His trade gave him the opportunity to catch women on their own and his tastes proved catholic: newlyweds, grandmothers, gentlewomen, church sisters, or goodwives were all fair game. Like Langhorn, however, he seems to have been strongly inhibited and easily shamed.[30] The testimony suggests that he relied on age rather than mere masculinity to lend authority to his solicitations.

For our purposes, the most intriguing aspect of the case is the leading witness for the defense: Sarah Bucknam. She smelled a plot ("this hath been a thinge searched out") and suspected

Elizabeth Payne as the chief and first instrument in accusing her husband.[31] She had pulled the chair from under him as he sat by the fire and puld meat out of his hand as he sat at meat and beat the pott to his head as he had been a drinking or his head to the pott which she could best doe and call him ould blackbeard wondering at me how I could have such a ould blackbearded man as he. . . . it was an unseemlie thing for her to behave her selfe to such a ancient man that was ould enough to be her father.

Was Sarah betraying the kind of unquestioning loyalty any patriarch would have expected from his browbeaten wife? The tone of her testimony suggests otherwise. She thought that William's wayward hands and bawdy talk were being unfairly conspired against. As we shall see, she too had been the victim of a vendetta and William had waged law in her defense.[32] She had had a "troubled spirit" after her ordeal,[33] and may have been psychologically incapable of meeting her husband's frequent and urgent sexual needs. Though her evidence did not save him from a substantial twenty-five pound fine,[34] Bucknam would describe her with more than conventional appreciation and affection when he came to write his will three years later.[35]

Thomas Wilkinson, a swineherd of Billerica, was presented for lascivious carriages just before Christmas 1680. He had been warned out of the town in 1676, the same year that he was complained of for "practise of chirurgery and physick contrary to law."[36] His neighbors found him both irresponsibly indolent and frighteningly insolent. Simon Crosby described Wilkinson's "much mispence of precious time." It took him more than a year to dig a cellar hole and then it was "so strait there was not room to set a wheel for his maid to spin in." He neglected his land and his meadow to such an extent that the selectmen reproved him. He responded in his typical surly manner: "If he did maintain his family hee might chuse whether he did work or not nor give any account to any man." When he fell out with one of his neighbors he "caryed his sword dayly in his hand for severall days." He warned another wronged neighbor "that if he spake a word of it it should cost him his whole estate." He had "dreadfully threatened" witnesses in the present case.[37]

Two married women swore particularly damaging depositions about his behavior. Mary Toothaker reported events of February 1669, nearly twelve years before.[38] Wilkinson had sat by her fire overnight on his return journey from the bay. After her husband had gone out the next morning,[39] Wilkinson

> said to her that hee would help her to a shirt cloth for her Husband; shee replyed that shee knew not how to pay him for it. The said Wilkinson answered that he would take his pay for it presently if shee were willing to it & would lay the child out of her arms; she replyed that shee would see him hang'd first. hee replyed that hee would give her a cheese also, for hee had greate neede. She againe replyed that shee would see him hang'd first, and was not he ashamed to offer such abuse to another mans wife whenas he had a wife of his owne and bid him if he were in such need to make hast home to his owne wife. The said Wilkinson replyed be hang'd to you. While the grass grow the steed starve; look you here els, & with that came walking to her with his Nakedness uncovered, in a most brutish manner. She again replyed Are you not ashamed. Then hee answered if you will neither take anything, nor give any thing then adiu to you and so departed the house.

Her husband, informed when he returned, had not reported this incident partly because of Wilkinson's threats to him, partly on advice from neighbors. "He thought he should do no good of it unless there were more witnesses." Accusations without witnesses could lead to slander actions and the further humiliation of paying both damages and costs.

Ruth, the wife of Daniel Shed, Jr., was another Wilkinson victim. In 1676 he had agreed to give her a lift on his horse to and from Woburn. On their return when they were still about one and a half miles from Wyman's farms, it grew dark.[40]

The said Wilkinson turned one leg over the horses neck and sate sidewise and said to the said Ruth Shed that his yarde was so stiffe[41] that it Hindred him [so] that he could not ride any longer, & slipt off the horse and pulled her down after him and took her in his arms & would have bin lewd with her & said come let mee &c. Shee replyed no not for all the world: come saith hee I will give you five shillings; No she replyed tho you would give me ten: he replyed why, there is no body seeth us: she replyed god seeth us: Well come saith hee I will give you ten shillings. Then she replyed No for how shall I do this wickedness and sin against god. Then he replyed to her, if you will not consent to it I can force you; she said It is true I know you can: but if you do I will make the woods ring. Then said hee The Indians will hear you. She then replyed I would rather fall into the hands of the Indians[42] than committ this great wickedness with you for that Oke Tree would witness against them & with that slipt out of his armes and ran away before him untill they came within sight of John Wymans house & when he saw the house he said How a divell come I hear, or where am I.

She too told her husband who likewise dared not complain "without more witnesses."[43]

Though Wilkinson was plainly a violent and threatening man, he was sufficiently inhibited by puritan teaching and the threat of eternal damnation to be shamed out of satisfying his "greate neede" by force. In both incidents he treated his victims like whores, offering larger fees when they initially demurred. His sole justification was his wife's unwillingness to sleep with him—"while the grass grow the steed starve" was a common English saying. This may just have been a "my wife doesn't understand me" ploy, but it might well have been a genuine description of sexual sanctions on her part against a violent and faithless mate who failed even to make proper provision for his family. We shall meet him in more complaisant company in the next chapter.

Elizabeth Dane of Concord rebuffed similar insistent solicitations in 1680 from John Law, a former Scottish prisoner of war, with similar responses.[44] "When he tempted his . . . pretty rouge to commit adultery" by proposing "to show all he had" she cried, "I will not! I will not! and turned my face from him . . . I said I had never don so in all my life and would not begin now and bid him hold his hand in the fire for half an hour . . . Nobody sees says he. [She replied] But God sees if nobody [else] sees, for God sees in the dark." As "he lay tempting her more and more . . . he asked her to lay down the child for he could soon do what he had to do . . . She asked him if one wife was not enough,[45] he said if he had any thing to spare what was that to any body."[46] In the end, the threat of summoning authority and the bribery of some cider induced Law to depart.[47]

Law's lawlessness erupted twice more before his trial in October 1681. After the March training day, he became so drunk that he fell off his horse and addressed a pregnant woman as "Pretty Rogue. He must stroke the babys head and running towards her with a stick towards her belly, we feared he would have injured her" if not restrained. In August he inveighed against the catechizing of children and against such worthies as Mr. Bulkeley and Major Estabrook[48] and the county bench. "He paid such greate rates to grease such fatt sowes in the Arse that lye droning upon their beds till noon." He was sentenced to twenty stripes or a twenty pound fine and "to stand committed until the sentence be executed."[49]

The wives' responses suggest a close relationship between popular and elite culture. The vivid metaphor of hellfire was not only a commonplace of sermons from William Ames to Jonathan Edwards, but was likewise used by a Maine goodwife to ward off an attacker. Similarly the God who sees in the dark was used both by the humble Ruth Shed and by Charlestown's minister Thomas Shepard, Jr., in his letter to his son in 1672.[50] Law, though possibly emboldened by drink, was sufficiently abashed to abandon the chase.

A new life in the new world offered married men the temptation of a new wife as well. The New England authorities were ever watchful for potential bigamists, and six men were warned to return from Middlesex to their wives.[51] One such was Marmaduke Johnson, printer of Cambridge. The Society for the Propagation of the Gospel had sent him from an unsavory background in London to help with the printing of John Eliot's Indian Bible in 1660.[52] His stay at Cambridge with Samuel Green, the colony printer, was not a success. He was presented to the December 1661 court "for obtaining the affections of the dafter of Samuel Greene without his knowledge or consent . . . and [even when] forbidden her sosiete being a married man." According to Elizabeth Green, one of nineteen brothers and sisters, he was often "pressing her, alluring & insnaring her to marry him." When her father threw Johnson out, "he calls her to [extended] assignations at William Barretts house. . . . He said he loved her as his own life . . . would make her his wife with all his heart . . . he had kiss[ed] the said Elizabeth sundry times." He had even kissed her in front of her father. After her removal, he tore his hair in the classic manner of the frustrated suitor and threatened violence against potential rivals.

The court predictably ordered him to return to his wife, but two years later he had not complied. He had some excuse. His separated wife was a notorious London whore, infected with venereal disease, who later died en route for Barbados.[53] He did visit London in 1664, a "very much reformed" character.[54] Apart from a brush with the censor in 1665, by which time Elizabeth had died, he settled into provincial life, marrying into a church family, serving Cambridge as constable and the colony as an invaluable craftsman.[55] His skill explains the unusual leniency of the authorities. Though this deserted husband's desire for a fresh start excites our sympathy (and, it seems, Elizabeth Green's), the authority of father and bench frustrated him. Only when he adhered to colony norms was he accepted.

The final case of male infidelity in 1690 involved John Walker and Mary Phipps both of Charlestown. He was a forty-nine-year-old bricklayer and mason fairly recently arrived in the colony. His first wife had been ten years older than he, and his second, Hannah Mirrick, had been convicted of fornication with Thomas Mercer in 1670. They had married in 1675, the same year she became a church member. Walker had a daughter by his first marriage, Mary Larkins.[56] Mary Phipps was nineteen in 1690. Her maternal grandfather was Thomas Danforth, and her father was Solomon, a carpenter and church member. Her uncle Samuel was the Charlestown schoolmaster and the clerk of the county court.[57]

On 30 December 1689, Mary Phipps was delivered of a bastard. She named Walker during her travail—"she was on the brink of eternity"— and explained her failure "to cry out when he came to her to bed because his hand was on her mouth. He took severall opportunities to abuse her body in his wicked lustfull manner," she told the midwife. Six weeks later on 10 February 1690, confronted by Walker, who asserted his innocence, Mary reaffirmed his paternity.

There were witnesses to familiarities between them. Bethya Phipps aged seventeen testified that one summer evening, Walker

> went to the side of the house where Mary was wont to sitt & she heard him whisper to her & she thought that he did kiss her . . . [when] the negro boy came with his candle she saw him drawe and slide his hand from under her sisters coats.

The Negro boy "about his out-business in the bright moonlight saw John Walker had Mary Phips in his arms & was sitting her down in her chair . . . he [Walker] fled."

According to Mary's father, Walker's reputation was hardly reassuring.

John Walker came into this country pretending to be a singleman and proposed marriage to the daughter of Lieutenant Tide.[58] Some few years past with Sarah Pore[59] in the open street he would faine have been naught with her, but she looking upon her self as bound to one man resisted his wicked attempt and made her escape . . . One and a halfe years ago he worked at the house of Nathaniel Frothnegem and the maid Ruth Cutler told her consarts that she never see such a wicked wrich as John Walker in all her life and that she had much ado to restrain him from putting his hands under her coats. Walker said to her Why I know love of [wo]men & [they] love me for this & many other such wicked actions he has done . . . he enslaved my daughter with fear that if she did tell anybody he would kill her.

Another servant maid Hannah Gillson said of him that "his carriage was so nasty & his language so base that she would not have been alone in a house with him for all the world hee was so wicked."

The full enormity of Walker's nastiness is only realized after reading the depositions of Hannah Hurry[60] and Hannah Barber. The former had

Mary Phips a lodger for twelve months to learn reading but found her void of common reason and understanding that is in other children of her age, not capable of discerning between good and evil or any morality . . . but she knows persons and remembers persons. She is next to a mere naturall in her intellectuals. . . . She is incapable of resisting a rape have[ing] one side quite palsied. . . . [we] have to help her as a meer child. Whoever did committ that wickedness did it in a most inhumane way, it seeming to be an impossible thing to be done otherwise.

The last sentence was clarified by Goodwife Barber: it must have been "so wickedly & beastlike committed . . . being seemingly impossible for such a thing to be done but in a beastlike & inhumane manner." This presumably means that she was impregnated from behind rather than in the then conventional and "humane" missionary position.

Though Walker's son-in-law, Edward Larkins, tried to foist father-hood on a black,[61] Walker had incriminated himself. He was judged the reputed father with costs, but escaped further obligations as the baby died.[62] When Danforth died in 1699, he left a special bequest for his severely handicapped granddaughter. Walker's estate amounted to only fifty-six pounds.[63]

Conclusion

Like four of the other promiscuous men we have studied, Walker was evidently a marginal and long-suspected character. He too was an

artisan, like Bucknam, Langhorn, Johnson, and Law, with unusual opportunities for soliciting women.[64] As had Johnson, he had tried to
commit bigamy when he had first arrived in the colony, and his second
wife had a somewhat clouded reputation as had Bucknam's. There is no
more evidence of contrition on his part than of the others. In fact in only
one of the twenty-two cases on file has any evidence of penitence survived. This was the confession of John Woodward of Newton, aged
thirty-five and married for twelve years to Rebecca Robbins, convicted
in 1684 of adultery with Hannah Spring, the twenty-seven-year-old
daughter of John Spring, a leading townsman. It was written in his own
hand, which was unusual for confessions, and after a markedly self-
abasing opening, he listed the many people he had let down by his
behavior. The climax reads: "I have broken covenant with my dear
wiffe, who hath been and still is soe tender of me: I confess I cannot be
sufficiently humbled for this my great sin." Hannah, also a church
member, similarly drew attention to the "relation that that person
stood in with whom I did commit this sin and leaving a dear and loving
yoke fellow."[65]

Others were less self-flagellating. Samuel Sprague, having failed in
1698 to ship away the pregnant widow Elizabeth Mellins (a granddaughter of William and Sarah Bucknam) pestered the court with petitions to reduce his maintenance payments and acted threateningly
toward her family.[66] Michael Bacon smuggled his maid to Rhode
Island, and, when eventually presented, broke out of prison.[67] Joseph
Blanchard jumped bail and failed to support his bastard child for over
a year.[68]

The one mitigating factor which can be recovered in a few cases is
that the men involved were unhappily married: Johnson to a London
whore, Wilkinson to a steed-starver, Bucknam to a depressive, James
Knap, accused in 1658, to Elizabeth, later notorious as the Groton
witch,[69] Francis Flashego, a black slave, to a wife who was barren,[70]
Joseph Carter to a wife suspected of witchcraft,[71] the bawdy innkeeper
John Harris to a highminded church member,[72] William Healey, perhaps still bearing the scars of his violent marriage to Phoebe Green.
Rather than resorting to violence or desertion, they turned to serving
maids or other men's wives for relief.

Their rationales, where reported, centered on physical needs, on the
assumption that a "man was more suddenly taken than a woman."
Some acted as though they were offering favors: "I know love of
woman and they love me for this," or "he had some thing to spare," or,
rubbing his penis in a woman's belly, "thou lovest me." Though a few
like Marmaduke Johnson or John Woodward were obviously smitten,

most were highly promiscuous, attempting the virtue of "divers" or "sundry" women over considerable periods of time, as though the relief were more important than the relationship.

A few acted like proprietors. Nathaniel Partridge told Phoebe Page, "the woman was made for the man,"[73] much like Christopher Grant's "Why should I not make use of my own?" A fancied manservant could "command his dame to kiss him and then he commanded her to lie with him." John Durrant "commanded" and "for bad" his wife, as we shall see. When we add Sarah Bucknam's defense of her adulterous husband, we seem to be brought back to the lordly patriarchs of the last chapter, Thomas Dutton and William Healey, whose patriarchal disdain and violence toward their wives was calculated to make them the better loved.

Does our trawl of errant husbands reinforce the emphasis on authoritarianism rather than amiability? The answer like that of women thus patronized, solicited, or commanded, is a resounding no. It might be framed as a tactful "All in good time" or "In time convenient," but more usually males got tart answers from other men's wives, who used babies, bribes, shaming, and threats in defense. The likes of Elizabeth Dane, Mary Toothaker, or Ruth Shed took their marriage vows seriously. Others were less scrupulous.

9 / Unfaithful Wives

I N 1699 John Cotton's *A Meet Help* was published in Boston. Its central argument is based on the divine judgment that "it is not good that man should be alone." Cotton's summation has since become famous.

> Women are creatures without whom there is no comfortable living for man: it is true of them what is wont to be said of governments, that bad ones are better than none: they are a sort of blasphemers then who despise and decry them, and call them a necessary evil, for they are a necessary good.[1]

Yet while the protestant reformation thus rejected the Pauline and papist preference for celibacy, no puritan dogmatists took the next logical step of advocating female equality. Too much biblical precedent and too much seventeenth-century experience of women like Anne Hutchinson or the Quaker prophetesses argued against such an undermining of order. Just as English Assize sermons inveighed against "naked Bathshebas" and "descendants of Eve,"[2] so William Gouge issued his typically puritan warning that "she who first drew men into sin should now be subject to him [her husband] lest by the like womanish weakness she fell again."[3] Despite daily and cogent evidence to the contrary, like the "three Maries to one John" in church membership[4] or the womanish strength resisting men seeking to draw maids and other men's wives "into sin," this myth of female inferiority maintained much of its potency in seventeenth-century Massachusetts.

Apart from natural weaknesses for religious enthusiasm, and for scolding, gossip, and extravagance, their archetypal sin was their inability to control their lusts.[5] It followed that husbands, with their greater rationality, must exert full control over their wives. If, nonetheless, wives erred, their crime was inevitably more culpable. Thus Gouge discussing adultery: "I denie not but the more inconveniences may follow upon the womans default than the mans: as, greater infamy before men, worse disturbance of the family, more mistaking of legitimate, or illegitimate children."[6] Thomas Langhorn knew this too and passed it on in more earthy terms to his pupil Elizabeth Holmes.[7] The illicit introduction into the nest of a cuckoo which would deprive legitimate fledglings of their rightful inheritance was commonly dwelt on as a peculiarly feminine act of injustice. Indeed, in folklore that perennial figure of derision—and of unease—the cuckold had no female equivalent.[8]

As we have seen the Massachusetts General Court recognized the distinction in opprobrium in its adultery laws. It also sought to prevent opportunities for female temptation like the law of 1674 against any wife entertaining travelers in the absence of her husband without express leave from the selectmen.[9] The courts carefully appraised women licensed to keep taverns and alehouses and approved the putting out of children of women convicted of moral offenses.[10] Neighbors and relatives kept a sharp eye for breaches of the seventh commandment.[11]

As many cuckolding jests make clear, female adultery was one of the most difficult crimes to detect. In theory, at least, a secretive wife could engage in extramarital amours and "hang the bantling's clouts to dry on her husband's horns."[12] All we have to go on are the cases of wifely infidelity which came up before the court. There are seventeen cases in all. They ranged from kissing, other familiarities, and suspicious company-keeping through the bearing of bastards to wifely promiscuity.

Details in many of the cases are vague or nonexistent, but five of the fourteen women involved had been married less than six years. Three male partners were married and four were servants, though not necessarily in the same household. The peak decade, as with adulterers, was the 1680s with seven convictions. Most of the wives involved, with three notable exceptions, came from poor backgrounds and marginal families. This chapter is divided into three sections: single lapses, multiple offenders, and cases centering on Charlestown.

Case Studies: Single Lapses

When William Wheeler of Concord, married four years, spent the night away from his wife Hannah and their maid late in the winter of 1664, her mother Mary Buss, wife of the town miller, sent her maid Elizabeth Cutler,[13] accompanied by the miller's apprentice, Thomas Seabrook, to Wheeler's. A party atmosphere developed. They played "a play called drawing of gloves" and Seabrook demanded a kiss from Hannah as a forfeit. As a second forfeit "he commanded her to lie with him and she answered All in good time. Then Thomas Seabrook commanded Elizabeth Coller to do likewise and she answered it was not to be suffered (to lie together) before God or man." Hannah and Thomas went up to the chamber to investigate a rumbling noise they claimed to have heard, and after an hour Elizabeth Cutler rooted them out of the unlighted room. At length "Thomas said com shal we not all of us go to bed and my dame said I care not if we doe & she would sleep in his lap. Then she sat in his lap and bid [the two maids] to go warm her bed & then we should go to [the maid's] bed and she and Thomas would go to her bed but Elizabeth Coller refused." Two hours later they got to bed—Hannah, her baby, and Thomas in one; the two maids in the truckle bed. Elizabeth Cutler protested, "Thats not to be suffered, and [Hannah] replyed No matter he keeps my back warm . . . and Elizabeth answered Then my dame [Mary Buss] will say O so have I brought my daughter up to this: to lie with another man & have a husband of her own." Hannah and Thomas invented a series of puerile excuses based on the fact that all four were lying together in the same room.

Hannah Wheeler had been seen kissing Seabrook passionately on another occasion. Overall, her behavior suggests that she had a physical infatuation with the miller's apprentice. Amatory millers[14] and dames getting involved with male servants were the stuff of popular literature.[15] Here the censorious maid prevented serious trouble, as Mary Buss had no doubt intended.

Altogether more serious than this puerile and closely supervised pranking was a case heard by the court just before Christmas in 1680. Susannah Durand or Durrant and her neighbor Thomas Wilkinson of Billerica were presented for lascivious carriages toward each other and each to others. Their story reads like a crude prototype of *Anna Karenina*. John Durrant was an ineffectual and meager husband; his wife, raised in the rambunctious Dutton household, was almost suicidally headstrong; Thomas Wilkinson, a married swineherd cast as Vronsky, we have heard of already.[16] Formal presentment—probably at the instance of the town selectmen—opened a floodgate of testimony which Jonathan Danforth had to take down on page after page.

So far as Susannah was concerned, neighbors depicted her as a shameless hussy. John Whittaker described Susannah's audacity when he and a friend were at Durrant's

> sitting in the chimney corner taking a pipe of tobacco. John Durrants wife came and stood by him and stood and leaned over him, and said Ah Whitaker tis a pritty little rogue, I must have a buss of thee; with that he put her away with his hand, then shee came againe, & of a sudden clapt both her hands upon his face and kissed him whether he would or not.

As to her association with Wilkinson, there were plenty of people who had seen them in compromising situations. John Whittaker one day found Durrant's two children outside their house, who

> ran to the door . . . crying here is goodman Whittaker here is goodman Whittaker . . . when he came into the house there was only them two there and they were going from the bedward towards the fire . . . the woman was very nigh the bed.

He had found them several times at home alone in the house; she once told him she had been across the river helping Wilkinson to husk his corn. Others had seen "them ride abroad together to Chelmsford or Concord & set out in the morning only they two together many hours before day & as late home at night: they rid down to the bay and kept severall days together . . . being alone together part of several nights." Her "next neighbour" had seen Wilkinson at Durrant's even when John Durrant was away; once "they were sporting together and she had her hand in his lap."

A man and woman riding home between 10 and 11 P.M. saw the pair on the ground together. When another witness found them in the woods together at dawn, Wilkinson explained that they were retrieving stock, since "Durrant was so idle and lazy that he would not looke after the cowe." Although this sounded like the pot calling the kettle black, the Durrant family had been "in an afflicted condition" four years previously and the Billerica selectmen had asked neighbors for relief contributions.[17]

Durrant was no more successful as a husband than as a husbandman. He seemed totally unable to control the situation. The pastor's slave went to Durrant's on an errand. Wilkinson and Susannah were "playing and sporting. John Durand bid them be quiet but they still continuing he went out and then [I] saw Thomas Wilkinson hugg & imbrace Durand's wife in his armes & kissed her several times." The ubiquitous Whittaker reported how they "made themselves very merry in scoffing at her Husband how hee would act when hee came into the house . . . crying hooh [a Durrant mannerism] in way of derision."

No wonder Durrant "made a very sad complaint, how wilfull & disobedient his wife had bin to him, since Wilkinson kept company with her, & that shee would go with him tho hee for bad; & she took the cannoe & would fetch Wilkinson over the river, altho hee commanded her expressly that shee should not." He could have effortlessly changed places with a dozen cuckolds in contemporary chapbooks or ballads.[18]

This dangerous liaison had been going on for at least a year because one witness reported that the couple's familiarity was already well known the previous spring. Susannah had spurned warnings "that God would discover them; they would not be preserved from wickedness when they kept company so much." She replied that "there was none that had bad thoughts of them but such as were as naught than themselves . . . that where she had bin in Wilkinsons company one hour, shee would bee in his company two houres, & shee would do more for him than ever shee had done . . . and that shee was willing people should know it." When official action was finally taken and testimonies were to be given in, Jonathan Danforth, in keeping with colonial practice, "gave notice of it to goodman Wilkinson, and desired him that hee would come at the same time, that they might speak before his face, and hee should have liberty to object what hee could, but hee refused to attend it." On 21 December 1680 the court imposed forty pound bonds on him and Susannah—half of which her husband had to pledge—for not companying with each other and for good behavior. Susannah was released from her bond in April 1681; of Wilkinson and punishment for either, no more is heard.[19]

Goodwife Durrant is one of the few women in Middlesex who might conform to the feminist interpretation of adultery as "a declarative act . . . in a society which allowed women few opportunities to exercise control over their lives."[20] Even when discovered, she persisted in her rebellion blatantly challenging the mores of the community. On the other hand we could view her cleaving to a macho male as a desperate and pathetic little fling after a violent upbringing and ten years of grinding poverty yoked to a mate she despised.[21] How many more wives less headstrong than she were set back on the rails by informal pressure before the court was called in, it is impossible to say.

Case Studies: Multiple Offenders

There were three women whose promiscuity brought them into court several times or was reported when they were finally caught. Elizabeth Downe Brown was born in 1638. She married William Brown in 1665 and had three children between 1667 and 1673. He developed a drinking problem and on 24 April 1672 the Charlestown selectmen formally warned him about frequenting taverns.[22] Her first brush with the law occurred in 1671, when she and Sylvester Hayes were convicted of "uncivil companying together on Lords Day in time of publick exercises in the absence of her husband in such a way as renders them vehemently suspicious of further wickedness to be committed by them." Witnesses reported that six months previously at Hannah Salter's place, Hayes had asked Brown to wash his shirt. The pair went to a chamber together and remained there some time before she finally emerged with his "foule" shirt. After this had happened a second time, Hayes was seen at her house one sabbath. When the wardens came, she denied that any men were there. Instead of taking recognizances, the court in December 1671 sentenced Hayes to the stiff penalty of twenty stripes or a ten pound fine, and Brown to a three pound fine and to be committed till the sentence was performed.[23] This harshness may have reflected Hayes's record. He had already been convicted in 1668 of taking part in a drunken assembly at the Salters' and of throwing stones at the watch. He would go on over the next twenty-four years to commit petty offenses like assaulting a constable, living from under family government, theft, threatening arson, and in general betraying "a dissolute, idle and unruly carriage."[24]

Five years later she was on trial for her life before the Court of Assistants in Boston. With Thomas Davis late of Boston she was indicted that she "not having the fear of God before her eyes and being instigated by the devil about the beginning of June last did committ Adultery." The jury brought her in "not guilty according to the indictment but doe finde her guilty of prostituting her body to him to committ Adultery." The pair were sentenced to stand on the gallows in Boston with ropes round their necks and then to be whipped thirty-nine strokes each; the following lecture day they were to be whipped thirty stripes each in Charlestown.[25]

After this conviction her three children, aged three to nine, were put out to service by the town. William died in 1678 and the next year his widow was convicted in the Suffolk County Court of "lewd, wanton and uncivill carriages, sentenced to bee forthwith whipped with twenty strokes and then returned to prison, there to remain one month and then to be conveyed to Charlestown and again to be whipped severely twenty stripes."[26] It is not certain who her partner was on this occasion but it seems probable that it was Moses Parker, another Middlesex resident. Although the son of a pillar of the Chelmsford church, Parker had already been convicted of selling liquor to Indians and "obsceen carriages drawing out his yard [penis] in the presence of many persons at Roxbury ordinary [inn]." In October 1682 he was convicted of "deflowring" Mary Barrett.[27]

Bess Brown's finale in the Cambridge courthouse had occurred six months before this. At the April 1682 session, she was first convicted of selling liquor to the Indians and "for her proud contemptuous carriages in open court" spent three days in Bridewell.[28] Then she had to answer "for some carriages between William Everton and her self that give ground to suspect their wicked practices between them." Once again Hannah Salter was a leading witness for the prosecution. On a fast day, when Everton's wife, a recently elected church member, had gone to meeting, Bess Brown arrived at his house.[29] A servant saw her go down into the cellar and fetch drink for herself. After about three hours together they were interrupted by a group of neighbors. First Brown, then Everton slipped outside, according to this version. "I vow there is something working," said one of the visitors, and, sure enough, heavy panting was heard coming from the stable. Brown was heard to whisper, "Where is your wife?" Everton reassured her, "She wont come home for a great while." As the investigators approached, Everton emerged from the stable calling "Bidde, Bidde," ostensibly to feed the chickens. Unfortunately, "he had no meate for the fowles when he called them." His skeptical observer demanded, "What stable do you keep? I am resolved to see." What he saw was Bess Brown standing up in a corner "like a woman surprised somewhat."

Other evidence was presented against Everton. He had outraged Goody Barber[30] by "showing of her his privat members working it in her Belli saying Thou lovest me." He had also shown "his negedness" to Anna Phillips,[31] pinched the lower parts of Edward Johnson's wife, and put his hand under Elizabeth Robinson's apron proposing to kiss her.[32] In fact, the fifty-eight-year-old Everton emerged as a worthy successor to William Bucknam. Because other deponents raised doubts about the credibility and motives of prosecution witnesses, Everton was discharged with an admonition and payment of costs.[33]

Between the ages of thirty-six and forty-seven Elizabeth Brown kept some distinctly insalubrious company on both sides of the Charles River. Her back and her purse suffered for her indiscretions. Her drunken husband seems to have been as inadequate a spouse as John Durrant. She may have been framed in the Everton case, but her acquittal on the adultery indictment represented the jury's refusal to pronounce a capital verdict rather than belief in her innocence. Though the evidence is far from conclusive, she may well have provided sexual solace to three young men during this period. There may have been more. The jury verdict in 1678 hints at the fact that she may have been a prostitute. Draconian punishments do not seem to have deterred her, and her contempt of court in 1682 hardly argues contrition. She seems to have clung to a diametrically opposed set of values, though whether as an advocate or a victim it is hard to say. The defense witnesses in the last case suggest that she may have been the latter.

The colorful career of Mary Atherton, wife of Thomas, was spotlighted in evidence sworn in court in April 1690. The particular incident presented had taken place on 1 November 1689. "About one hour into the night" Mary Atherton had arrived at "Captain Wings garason at Worchester" in company with Richard Deacon.[34]

> Mary Atherton cast Richard Deacon round the neck and kissed him many times . . . and she said she would be true to him or else she wished her hands might drop off from her body. . . . Deacon put his hands under Mary Atherton's apron and pulled up her clothes and knelled between her legs as she sat upon her blok and were in that posture about half an hour. They then went into the chamber.

One or two hours later three men arrived

> and two of us went to the chamber which we found locked and demanded that the door be opened. Deacon swore he would be the death of any one who opened it Robert Wing said he would break it open and said to them Come down you shant play the whore in our house. Mary Atherton said I am no more a whore than your mother and your sister be whores and you a bastard. I am none. To which Robert Wing replied what do you there then locked up? Daniel Peirce fetched an ax and Thomas Bull broke down the door and Richard Deacon made to stab him who first entered the room [Susannah Hall saw Atherton take Robert Wing by the throat] Mary Atherton sat upon the bed with her apron soiled and all unlaced and Decon with shoes and stockings off, both of them just as if they had rose out of the bed & stepped in their clothes. We threw them down the stairs. . . . Some say Richard Deacon and Mary Atherton were in drink, they were well anof.

The court had two character references on Mary Atherton. The first described her as a woman who "set neighbor against neighbour . . . [did] curse and swear, a sabbath breaker, drunkard and opposed to authority. . . . As for her honesty [i.e., moral behavior] I wil not trust her with a negor." The second elaborated on this.

> Some years ago Mary Atherton and her now husband were servants to Major Thomas Savage.[35] She suffered a negro to ly with her by whom she

was with child and thereupon she suffered Thomas Atherton to ly with her
and then told Major Savage who forced him [Atherton] to mary her. She
had a mulatto child now living at Hingham. In 1683 Thomas and Mary
Atherton came to Worcester where she was frequently drunk. . . . She
followed Charles Williams into the woods and was as common with him as
with her husband. She was sick and miscarried a child which she after
admitted was Williams and was privately buryed. She then went to
Weston[36] where after two years she was taken a bed between 2 men her
husband being but at the ? neighbores. Capt. Hinksman[37] was told and
issued a warrant but she ran away deserting her husband for a year. She
went to Mollbery [Marlborough] where she continued to cekall [cuckold]
her husband. Her husband came there and took her again.

For her "hainous wicked accompanying . . . and committing whoredom" and his "most beast like carriage," they were each sentenced to
twenty stripes or a fine of twenty pounds and to stand committed until
performed.[38]

Mary Atherton had spent much of her married life in frontier settlements—Worcester, Weston, Marlborough. In the last quarter of the
century these often new townships were under threat of Indian attack.
The 1673 foundation of Worcester had been destroyed by an Indian raid
on 2 December 1676.[39] Reference to the garrison emphasizes its continued vulnerability. Other cases in the records suggest the undermining effect that war could have on sexual morality. At Woburn during
King Philip's War, a witness reported:

> In the garrison or fortified house of the Widdo Simons was soe much
> disorder and rudeness . . . and uncivill carriages as in particular of
> Benjamin Simons and Mary Tids being laide on a bed together. . . .
> Benjamin Simons and Mary Tids [did] dance together. . . . Mary Tids
> [did] sit in the lap of Benjamin Simons and smoke to baco and these things
> they did freely practise.

Mary Tids was not the only woman to dally with Simons that year.[40]
The bastards born to Elizabeth Coburn and Dorothy Hildreth in garrison houses at frontier Dracut in 1696 had been begotten in similar
circumstances.[41] The threat of attack and the lack of well-established
institutions on the frontier loosened the tightly woven moral control of
more settled times and places.

Case Studies: Charlestown

As well as frontier areas under stress, there was one other part of Middlesex which offered greater temptation to married women because of
its peculiar circumstances. Charlestown, on a peninsula on the north

bank of the Charles River, a brief ferry ride from the Boston peninsula to the south, grew into an important port and shipbuilding center during the seventeenth century. As such it faced problems unique in a predominantly agricultural county.[42] Not only did it have to contend, as we noted, with adolescent apprentices learning crafts associated with the sea, but also with periodic influxes of seamen from England and other colonies. During the often lengthy turn-round of their vessels they would have time on their hands, time for trouble, as they lounged in taverns or walked the wharves "where noys and strutt pass for whitt."[43] In May 1687 there were two riots there involving seamen from England and townsmen. The sailors had set up a maypole, and when this was demolished by the watch it was replaced with a larger one with a garland upon it.[44] Many of the townsmen were sailors or traders forced to leave behind wives or sweethearts during long or frequent voyages. With so many unattached men and women it is hardly surprising to find the court having to deal not only with women left pregnant by transient seamen,[45] but also with the disorderly houses of wives temporarily deserted by seafaring spouses. At least two married women, Susannah Pike[46] and Mary Stanwood,[47] bore bastards fathered by visiting seamen during their husbands' absences. Four other prosecutions of married women—one of which is deferred to a later chapter—cast a revealing light on the temptations of a port town in the last two decades of the century.

Susannah Goose Cross was the daughter of a sea captain. Her mother, a church member, had died when she was six. In 1682, aged twenty-four, she married John Cross, a mariner, and within nine months had her first baby.[48] On 21 July 1684, while her husband was away at sea, she, the Elizabeth Mancers, mother and daughter, and Sarah Candige had been rowed to Boston by seamen from Captain Fowle's ship.[49] Their errand was to inquire after Robert Mancer who was thought to be on a ship recently arrived from Providence. That night the women returned, and four or five seamen went to Cross's house where, fortified by wine, they made a great disturbance. There had been "desorders in her house severall times by company being there by night and by day."

Susannah was on particularly intimate terms with Walkden, the doctor of Fowle's ship. He often stayed at her house, but not always in his own chamber. A maid told how

> the doctor came, put out the light and made a noys with the bed more than usual which did awaken me and I heard Susannah Cross say Doctor get you off & so he lay there and slept to near dawn. Then he went to the door & came & kissed her and bid her farewell pretty soull.

On other occasions when maids were awake in the bedroom, Susannah had made a public show of rebuffing him, but when "He asked her whether he should come down when [the maid] was asleep, she answered yes if he would." When he left one dawn, she was eager to know when he would come again. She confessed to being "sleppy [another morning] because the Doctor lay uppon her Bead."

The court was suitably scandalized by her "keeping of a disorderly house in her husband's absence, and lascivious and wanton practices . . . not without vehement suspicion of uncleanness committed" and sentenced her to be severely whipped or pay a fine of five pounds and costs.[50]

The Mancers had escaped prosecution, probably because the thirteen-year-old Elizabeth had provided key prosecution evidence. They were not so leniently treated five years later. In the meantime, the mother had been widowed and in 1687 had remarried. Her second husband was Thomas Pope, like her first, a seaman. Her daughter, by then eighteen, had followed in the family tradition and married a mariner of the Ives family.[51] At their trial for "lascivious and debauched accompanying together" with James Stanhouse, a sailor, in October 1689, two vivid testimonies were presented.

Hannah Perkins aged 16 or thereabouts testifieth and saieth that on the last night of August last about ten at night she . . . saw through the window a man in bed with Pope's daughter and his arm over her very lovingly & Pope sat on the bed laughing at them. . . . in their naked bed as far as she saw of them out of bed and his arm over her and was kissing of her.

The story was then taken up by John Row who three years previously had been the defendant in a scandalous breach of promise action.

Being called out by . . . [the watch] . . . he saw through the window a man in bed betwixt Elizabeth Pope and Elizabeth Ive. . . . [Once in the house] I saw a man buttoning up his breeches, with no coat or stockings or shoes on in a maze he could not find them in a considerable time the old woman being naked to her shift but before she came out of the bed I saw her draw on her petticoat. Her daughter was in her shift and all of them dressed themselves in my sight railing and scoulding to their neighbours and denying what was visible enough to all present. Elizabeth Pope said to John Tylers wife that nobody would lye with her except it were to cuckold the Devil.

This perhaps extreme self-denigration did not save her from the same fate as her bedfellows—"to be severely whipt on their naked backs at

Charlestown on Lecture Day at the carts tail 30 lashes apiece." This punishment was customarily awarded to whores or bawds.[52]

The constable of Charlestown was awakened about midnight of 18 December 1695 by Edward Carter, a seaman of H.M.S. *Surloin,* with the warning that there would be murder if he did not come to Sarah Smith's house.[53] There he found Sarah, whose husband was in Barbados,[54] Mary Harris, a visiting prostitute,[55] and another sailor, John Chittendon, "in a very unhansom & lascivious manner all imbraced in said Chittendons lap."

At 2 A.M. the quartet were examined by the local magistrate James Russell. Carter testified that Chittendon "had layen with Sarah Smith severall times, last Friday and in the Sallutation [a Boston tavern] and last night a great part of the night naked on the bed together." Chittendon countercharged "that Edward Carter had layen with Mary Harris severall times" and that the clerk of their frigate had forged a marriage certificate for them.

Despite denials in court, Smith was found guilty of "lascivious and wanton carriage . . . entertayning ill-company, drinking and wantonising . . . as also of wicked cursing." After trying to escape she received fifteen stripes. A full year later Mary Harris was convicted of fornication; she named as father of her child William Whiting, seaman, impressed aboard the Newport galley.[56]

These married women of Charlestown, catering to the off-duty needs of sailors as bawds and prostitutes or enthusiastic amateurs are a far cry from the meek, pious, chaste wives of conduct books and sermons. So were the other faithless huzzies described here who repudiated prevailing respectability in words and actions. They were the other side of the biblical coin to the Ruths, Sarahs, Hannahs, or Deborahs—those virtuous wives who kept faith with their husbands even when tempted by adulterous men like Bucknam, Law, or Everton.

Conclusion

When the highly repressive plantation of New Haven was incorporated into the more tolerant Connecticut in 1665, John Clarke was heard to remark that now "he might live merrily and sing and daunce etc."[57] Merriment, which in seventeenth-century usage had strong sexual undertones, was at the heart of English popular culture: "Eat, drink and be merry, for tomorrow we die."[58] This hedonistic enjoyment of the world and the present was in diametrical opposition to the deepest-felt puritan attitudes. Their sights must be set on the hereafter; they must be in the world but not of it. Otherworldly, they were taught to fear and despise the "world's people."[59]

It is tempting to see some of our adulterers and adulteresses, with their frank sensuality, their contemptuous rejection of authority and pooh-poohing of puritan sexual morality, as representatives of this cult of merriment, reinforced by foreign elements in the last two decades of the century as Massachusetts was dragged kicking and screaming into the embrace of empire. Perhaps the subversive youth culture was less transient for some than others—a persistent counterculture gnawing at the vitals of puritanism. Yet the relatively rare number of cases, the untypicality of Charlestown or of wilderness Dracut and Worcester, and the social marginality of most offenders should give us pause. Even more, we should weigh the shocked reactions of ordinary people like Elizabeth Cutler, John Row, Ruth Shed, or Robert Wing. None of these was a church member, yet they were outraged by what they saw and took action to stop it. Often enduring persistent poverty and forced or lonely or loveless marriages, most offenders emerge far more as victims of circumstance than as active advocates of a hedonistic life.

While some sex-starved husbands tried to excite cooperation by describing their great needs, straying wives whose own words have survived expressed genuine love. Mary Atherton told Deacon "she would be true to him or else she wished that her hands would drop off from her body." Hannah Wheeler found the young miller physically attractive. Susannah Cross was eager for Dr. Walkden to return. Of Thomas Wilkinson, Susannah Durrant said "she would do more for him than ever she had done." Neighbors spoke similarly of the relationship of Sarah Bucknam and Robert Burden: "She was ready to do any thing for him as he was for her."[60] Love, devotion, and admiration for the other were an important need for these women, a necessity of life their husbands were not providing.

Should we then conclude that this very absence and inadequacy confirms the argument that most husbands who were present and adequate stood between weak-willed wives and sexual anarchy? Given the outrage of most solicited wives, the number of women who actively prevented, reported, or helped prosecute unfaithful wives, and in most cases the greater culpability of men, that contention is extremely improbable. Contrary to male myth, women were numerically, and probably psychologically, less "beastlike," or promiscuous, than men.

It is surely not sheer coincidence that disordered or distempered minds were so often blamed for marriage breakdowns. Not being able to live comfortably together was a kind of madness. Was disengagement the answer? Not according to the testimony described here. The lubricant of a successful marriage was mutual affection. Provision of necessities by the husband and efficient running of the household by the wife were not enough. He must love her as much as she must love him. In a less compulsively articulate society, tenderness might be shown in actions more than words. It was no less romantic for that. Emotional and sexual needs were recognized as important; sexual consummation was the sine qua non of marriage fellowship. A husband who failed his wife in bed was an object of derision.[61] Marriage was an intimate relationship; even in a world short in privacy, the marriage bed should keep its secrets. Because of this, sadly, we can only glean rather than harvest relevant evidence. From our modest gathering, it does appear that for ordinary people the Winthrop they followed was Winthrop the affectionate romantic rather than Winthrop the chilly patriarch.

PART THREE / FAMILY AND COMMUNITY

Up to now we have analyzed relationships between both the unmarried and the married. We found that in courtship and marriage, love and affection played a far more vital role than some historians allow. From what we have presented it is difficult to imagine that the death of a cow or a horse would cause the typical Middlesex farmer more anguish than the death of his wife or sweetheart. We also posited the existence of an adolescent culture, transient in its impact on most individuals, but subversive of adult values while young people were passing through it. Looked at from an adolescent point of view, the role of parents was envisaged as letting them have their way and only intervening when something went seriously wrong.

The adolescents' point of view was not the only one, however. Though they might like to think of themselves as autonomous individuals, they were also members of families and communities. In this section we examine the outlook on family life from another vantage point—that of parents, masters, dames, and kin, and that of neighbors, elders, and selectmen who made up the communities of Middlesex County.

VERYONE in Middlesex was required to live in a family. In fact, most people during a life span would live in three at least: their family of birth or orientation, the family where they were put out as servants to be trained, and the family of marriage or procreation. Some young people might serve in more than one family.[1] Elderly widows or widowers might move into the families of married sons or daughters.[2] Some families might be highly complex structures. Goodman and Goodwife Healey and their family sound a straightforward enough group. In 1666, however, the household included the offspring of four marriages, the eldest of whom was almost the same age as the wife, the youngest only six months, as well as two live-in servants.[3] "The daughter of Evan Thomas his wife of Boston called Mary" was the court's clumsy designation of Mary Kirtland of another hybrid family.[4]

The family in seventeenth-century Massachusetts was much more than "a haven in a heartless world." It was first and foremost a firm, an enterprise: most often a farm, but occasionally a workshop, a mill, a shipyard, a store, or a tavern. It was also a key social institution. The family regularly fulfilled functions nowadays performed by such diverse agencies as residential children's homes, juvenile detention centers, industrial, domestic, and agricultural training schools, banks, hospitals, mental institutions or old people's homes, social service departments, Sunday and elementary schools.[5]

We know that life in these little firms must have been, by modern standards, unbelievably cramped, primitive, and uncomfortable. With half the population under sixteen it was probably noisier too.[6] Privacy was a luxury. Only bed curtains might separate married couples from servants on a truckle bed or young children in a cradle. In this material sense, at least, "domestic relations were then nearer the cave than now."[7]

What we are looking for in this chapter is whether domestic relations were "nearer the cave" in the psychological sense as well. We focus on two types of relationships: those between parents or masters and their dependents within the household, and those between the nuclear family and the extended family of relations by blood and marriage, the kinfolk. We have already summarized one version of these interactions in which the powerful boss of the firm had his dominion made absolute by the minimalization of the countervailing forces of community and clan. He ruled his little enterprise with a rod of iron, breaking the wills of children and servants as though they were dogs or wild horses. The prevalent custom of putting out young adolescents to other households demonstrated the frigidity and ruthlessness of parent–child relationships.[8] When they most needed parental sympathy and guidance, vulnerable teenagers, confused by the onset of puberty, were shipped off to alien households to be whipped into line by loveless masters or dames.

Case Studies: Domestic Violence

There is some corroboration for this bleak view of the lot of servants in the court records. The vulnerability of servant maids to the sexual advances of their masters or masters' sons has already been described.[9] As well as seduction or rape there were other hazards. On 3 October 1654 Richard French of Billerica was fined three pounds for "shamefull abuse offered to the body of Jane Evans" and ordered to pay her two pounds damages. Jane was the servant of Richard Hildreth who seems to have loaned her to his neighbor French, a recently married man. One incident occurred

> in the woodes as shee was comeing down behind him on horseback & he caried her out of the path to a dessolate place, & . . . he told her that if shee would take up her coates her selfe she should have the lesse [whipping], otherwise he would fetch bloud, & he did turne her upon her backe & discover her secret parts & kneeled on her side to keep her down when she lay on her backe, and shee is affrayd to go out least this ffrench should kill her, & that since that time she hath been troubled with very sad fitts like unto the falling sickness . . . when she is quite senceless in her fits then she cries out of this ffrench and sayeth oh this ffrench will kill me.

Another witness had seen Goody French "strike her three or four strokes on the shoulder with a hoggs yoake and the wench went about to hold the yoake." French admitted that "his wife and he whipt her the day before in the cellar." There was obviously a strong element of sexual sadism in French's attack and he had terrorized the poor girl.[10]

Most other cases of cruelty to servants were the result of unadulterated anger. In 1660 Peter Tufts of Malden tied his servant Henry Swillaway to a tree and set about beating him with the thick end of a goad stick. When a neighbor remonstrated, Tufts told him "he was his servant and therefore he would beat him with what he list." Later both Tufts and his wife had to apologize for outbursts against the deputy governor and witnesses in the case.[11] Another sadist, Isaac Richardson of Woburn, was fined two pounds in 1675 because he burned his servant Joseph Anderson's "breech by fire." The servant was sent to another master and his period of servitude reduced by a year "for recompense of his smart and payne endured."[12]

The violence of Andrew Mitchell of Charlestown toward Consider Sampson in 1690 called forth a complaint from Joseph Pratt, whose maidservant she was. When she made a minor mistake in milking a cow, Mitchell beat her several blows with an unreasonably large stick. Although when weeding in the garden "she could not help standing on things," Mitchell beat her so hard that he broke his stick and fetched another one. "He then licked another maid who called for mercy for Consider Sampson." Various people had seen her crying in the street her back "black and blew" with only her shift and petticoat on. The battered state of her back could only have been the result of "great cruelty." When Consider complained to authority, Mitchell broke another stick in punishing her. Her last resort was to run away and part of Pratt's complaint may have been caused by the loss of his maid's services. The court's decision in this case is not recorded.[13]

Two other cases of apparently wanton cruelty to servants deserve our attention. The first concerns the treatment of a Negro boy in Sudbury by his master Goodman Crane in 1665 and 1666. Witnesses described the boy wearing "a geer of wire," presumably a kind of muzzle, and a chain hobbling his feet. He had been heard screaming, "O Lord! O Lord!" from a distance of a quarter of a mile off, and he had "many stripe wounds, some raw, some healed or partly healed." In other words, he had been severely beaten at least three times.[14]

The richly documented case involving Thomas and Priscilla Crosswell

and their daughter Silence of Charlestown came to the court in 1691.[15]
They had been complained of for the cruel usage of their twelve-year-
old servant Rebecca Lee, deceased. The complainants were Rebecca
Pounding, the girl's mother, and Christopher Goodwin.[16] They con-
tended that because the maid had been "horribly abused . . . [it] had
shortened her days." A decade before, in 1681, Thomas Crosswell had
been accused of cruel treatment and unreasonable whipping of a boy
called Daniel Edmunds;[17] no doubt the memory of this incident was
green in the Charlestown community. Several witnesses testified to the
violence and the paranoia within the Crosswell household. Goodwin,
for instance, had felt "bound in conscience" to investigate "a great
screching or crying" as he passed Crosswell's in 1690.

> Goodwife Crosswell presently said What is there another spie come & I
> told her I came not for a spie and she told me she had been beating the gairl
> for not bakeing a batch of bread well, which was with a stick about as bige
> as a mans finger. I told her she was but a gairle; she said I know not what to
> doe; my husband will be soe angry (showing me the bread on a tray or
> bole) & I went out & she followed me, & having more discourse with her
> concerning the gairles having time to lerne such things, she said she would
> make her know or else she would sell her I replyed that she was not a horse
> nor a negro: then goodman Croswell came & said: We leave my daughter
> to correct her when we are gone abroad; & she will not be corrected by her.
> I said I cannot understand that you leave one gairle to correct another: what
> you and your wife doth in Reason is some thing but this I thought strange,
> I told him; soe I went to my worke at Cambridge.

One of several other witnesses to have heard similar outcries, Mistress Perne Broughton,[18] inquired at a neighbor's. "She said They were
cruell people and had heard terable crying. . . . She would have her
[mother] take her daughter away from Thomas Crosswells." Two girls
reported a conversation with Rebecca Lee shortly before she died.

> She said lately she had gon to Thomas Crosswells barn and had not
> fastened the door and the cattle had gone in and killed a lamb. Thomas
> Crosswell said: The pickbox peek Lee, a town brat . . . and fetched a stick
> from the chamber or staircase and beat her untill she thought she was all
> most dead. On her deathbed we heard Rebecca Lee say Her paines came
> through her hard usage at goodman Crosswells.

Priscilla Crosswell had told another neighbor that "Rebecca Lee was
a nasty slut & she had given her daughter Silence leave to beat her as
long as she would so that she had but breath to breathe or life to sturr."
The dame's short fuse was described by two maids sent by Rebecca's
mother who had "heard she was very sick."[19]

Goode Crosswell looking very angrily asked How came her mother to
hear? We tould her Mary Goodwin and Mary Lee had been at Mrs Backs
and Thomas Crosswell told her so. Goode Crosswell then broke out in
a great rage and said what good in one of them devills; they are the
devilleshest cretors that ere was. My sperit rises against him where ere I see
him: I can never luk comfortably upon him where ere I see him.

Two other girls inquiring "How Beck Lee did" were furiously charged
with spying. She would be placed out of reach of her mother's agents.

In rebuttal, the Crosswells called daughters, sons-in-law, employ-
ees, neighbors, and visitors, who all testified that they had seen "no
cruell yousedge" and that Rebecca had appeared "allwais as cheerley
& as merry as any of their own children." A daughter described a confrontation when Rebecca's mother had used "uncomly and abusive
words. My father said that they [the Crosswells] were liaber to any way
for it and bid said Pounding to bring them out for it."[20] Instead she soon
admitted "the stories . . . to be most parfit lyes spread about by my
mothers malitious neighbours." These stories included Silence's alleged disciplinary powers, which were granted "in Jeast."[21]

Rebecca Lee was shown to be far from faultless. Her father and uncle
had said "if she came home she would do a great deal of mischief." She
had been caught stealing a loaf for her mother "who had not eaten in
five days" and, though she denied it "over and over," had also taken
some spice. Rebecca's pains did not coincide with her alleged ill-treatment, and medical evidence from a doctor[22] and midwives[23] favored
a fall from a horse as the cause of death.[24]

Although the seriousness of the case had been signalized by the enor-
mous £200 bond taken for Crosswell's appearance, the jury reached
a verdict of "not guilty of cruelty by the evidence produced."[25] The
jury may have been swayed by the disreputable or prejudiced backgrounds of several prosecution witnesses, not least Rebecca Pounding
herself, who was much lower down the social scale than the Crosswells. She might have been emboldened to make a formal complaint by
the possibility of a large monetary compensation.

A social worker would recognize in the case of Rebecca Lee many of
the classic features of modern child abuse referrals: the credible alternative explanation for injuries or death, conflicting evidence from neighbors, the accused family producing evidence of marked similarity and
charging neighbors with malice and snooping. In this case evidence was
given by no less than seven relatives claiming daily or frequent familiarity with goings-on at Crosswell's.

The Crosswells, especially Priscilla, appear aptly named. She distrib-

uted her rage liberally, not sparing her husband. Other masters and
dames seem equally violent. Yet, as with Rebecca Lee's petty thieving,
some of them did have sore provocation. Tufts's servant had "a great
stone to throw at his master. . . . I herd him cal his master base
Rouge."[26] Crane's Negro boy had been muzzled because "he did frequently suck the cows, not from want of victuals" but from sheer devilment. He promised a neighbor that "if he would give him 3d he would
suck cows no more." Four neighbors claimed that he ran away (thus the
hobbling), lied, stole, and broke into houses. Their damning opinion
that he was "as full of bad qualities as it is possible for a boy to be" was
corroborated by a nineteen-year-old maidservant: "For knavish tricks
I never see the like of him."[27] Consider Sampson was convicted of
fornication and sentenced to the unusually harsh punishment of twenty
stripes shortly after running away from Andrew Mitchell.[28]

Master-Servant Relations

There were other incorrigible servants in Middlesex. William Eager of
Cambridge was plainly at the end of his tether when he complained
about his servant John Salter's "stubbornes & incorrigiblenes therein
against his master & dame. . . . Idlenes, Night walking, Robbing William Bullards orchard and lying." The punishment reflected the long-
term nature of the problem: twenty stripes, imprisonment in the house
of correction until he humbled and submitted himself to his master and
dame, double recompense of time lost to his master, and no release
without the order of two magistrates. The same sense of enraged frustration comes through the long list of misdeeds and expenses which the
master of John Creete presented to the court in 1660. Creete seems to
have absented himself regularly for whole nights and days, and sometimes disappeared for longer periods.[29] Paul Wilson, James Ross,
Jerathmeel Bowers, Andrew Robinson, Sylvester Hayes, Elizabeth
Dickerman, Sarah Crouch, Susannah Coburn, and Elizabeth Wells
were other violent, refractory, insolent, or persistent offenders we have
already met. As reiterated, clerical complaints about "unmortified
pride" and disobedience in the young demonstrated that "the servant
problem" was not a Victorian invention.[30]

Were these mutual antagonisms, these cold, cruel, suspicious relationships, typical of interactions between the generations? Statements
by witnesses suggest not. People like Christopher Goodwin or Perne
Broughton were plainly appalled by the possibility of cruelty to a
twelve-year-old girl and expected other people to respond similarly.
Goodwin's "she was but a gairle . . . [needing] time to lerne such

things . . . she was not a horse nor a negro" reflect this revulsion and a sense of prevailing leniency, tolerance, and patience toward young apprentices. Other witnesses expected the usual behavior of children to be "cheerley and merry." Neighbors or fellow servants remonstrated with provoked masters. The selectmen of Sudbury were careful to check that Crane's slave was not being underfed. The people of Charlestown "spied" to keep a check on the suspected Crosswells. The court's sentencing—under the 1641 law prohibiting "unnaturall severitie towards the young"—reflected official revulsion, as did the phrasing of presentments.[31] The most persuasive argument for atypicality, however, is the rarity of cases: five in all, or an average of one per decade.

Many scholars, especially those who have worked in personal records such as diaries and letters, have come to the conclusion that sadism among masters was exceptional and that warm and affectionate relationships were common. Thomas Tusser, an East Anglian gentleman, had plenty to say about servants in his *Five Hundred Points of Good Husbandry,* which remained a best-seller well into the seventeenth century. Although masters and dames should beware of their potential for thieving, wandering, and gossiping, and their need for firm discipline, nonetheless, "Good servants hope justly some friendship to feele, / and look to have favour what time they do weele." Dames were advised that "good servants looke dulie for gentle entreating."[32] In Massachusetts in the late seventeenth century, Samuel Willard shed this ambivalence: "Masters must love their servants."[33]

Such demands, with a Creete or a Swillaway, might prove a tall order, but, as Morgan points out, "a master who wished to save his house from fire and his goods from theft had to make some effort to win the goodwill of his servants, for he frequently had to leave them alone in the house, and unless they loved and respected him, no amount of care would secure the cupboard or the cellar against them."[34] What Demos found for Plymouth rings true for Middlesex: "Kindness, loyalty, deep affection: surely such things formed a central part of many master-servant situations . . . there are many instances [in wills] in which a master left to his servant a generous gift of property."[35] When scandal besmirched the Charlestown household of the seafaring Captain Richard Martin, a servant feelingly told a neighbor: "My master does not deserve this."[36] Thomas Danforth left an endowed forty-acre farm in Lexington to a faithful servant in 1699.[37] Mary Ball expected "good councell" from her master.[38]

It was not uncommon for a master to give a testimonial for a servant. Thus, for instance, the Day and Boardman families provided their former servant Mary Waters Davis with glowing references when she was accused of prenuptial fornication in 1656.[39] Richard Hildreth supported Jane Evans's account of her assault by Richard French. Many such examples could be given, as could instances of servants supporting their employers' testimony in court. Goodman Varnum willingly forgave Susannah Coburn for her disrespectful rudeness and incorrigible disobedience, and she seemed genuinely heartbroken to have caused so much anguish in the household.[40]

The putting out of adolescents may have been an economic necessity for poorer families, and it may too have been a way of easing generational conflict within the family, yet it had its positive side as well. It showed parental concern about the training of their children. It could provide a means of social advancement and potential guardians in the event of parental death. The "disposing" of teenagers to other households did not cut them off from their families.[41] The idea that Goody Crosswell should prevent Rebecca Lee from seeing her mother was plainly regarded by witnesses as outrageous. During her illness Beck Lee had plenty of concerned visitors, both family and friends. When Martha Beale got into trouble in the Row household, her father was quickly there to support her.[42] In 1654 the court returned Rebecca Shadow to her mother who had complained of the "great neglect and want of due care" by her master William Toy.[43] A few masters were cruel, a few were lecherous, and a few more were provoked to violence by disgracefully disobedient servants, but the Middlesex evidence, taken as a whole, supports the idea that masters and dames saw themselves much more as guardians and foster parents than Gulag guards and fearsome floggers.

Parent-Child Relations

One family's servant was another family's child. Much has been made by some historians of parental cruelty both mental and physical to their offspring. Two illustrative quotations will suffice: "More children were being beaten in the . . . early seventeenth century over a longer age span than ever before."[44] Puritan "parents were engaged in war with their children, a war which could end only with total victory by parents and unconditional surrender by the children."[45] These are by no means the most sensationalist interpretations of past childhoods.[46] Recent historians, however, have called into question this bleak view of parenting. Analysts of English and New England diaries are generally of the opinion that relations between parents like Ralph Josselin,

Increase Mather, Cotton Mather, or Samuel Sewall and their children were normally warm and affectionate.[47]

The most recent survey of such materials by Linda Pollock comes to the conclusion that "parental care is a variable peculiarly resistant to change." Arguing that proponents of generational warfare have often lifted untypical passages out of context to compose their black picture, she agrees with Keith Wrightson that children "were clearly desired" and that seventeenth-century parents derived "emotional satisfaction and pleasure in pleasing children." They formed strong emotional bonds and lasting attachments which children reciprocated. Punishment for these "comforts and blessings" was much less harsh than previously assumed, and, in seventeenth-century America, protection was far more important than discipline. Parents experienced "searing grief" at the death of infants;[48] as Michael Macdonald has written, "What was familiar was not easily borne."[49]

Support for this thesis can be culled even from prescriptive literature. The main reason why that oft-quoted proponent of infant will-breaking, the Pilgrim pastor John Robinson, advertised his ruthless regime was that parents were naturally "tender-hearted and over-partial."[50] That tireless exhorter to parental discipline, Cotton Mather, was tirelessly patient with his tiresome son Cressy whose death he mourned so pitifully.[51] His contemporary, Samuel Willard, sometime minister of Groton, wrote of "the love of parents to their children . . . so intense and influential."[52] Why, we might well ask, would parents need to be told to "maintain shame" in their offspring if they were already doing so?

It would be incredible if some parents and children did not get on. Michael Wigglesworth, pastor of Malden, confessed to hating his father.[53] Phoebe Page's revulsion was reciprocated by her father, as we shall see.[54] Pregnant Sarah Crouch was worried her father would "knock her on the head." Her lover's father threw him out of the house.[55] One Martin daughter said that her mother and her sister would both go to hell, but not together "because they would fight by the way."

Elizabeth Martin's regrets about child management are instructive: "If I had beaten her bones out when she was young, she would not have that sin to answer for that she now has." But, despite sore provocation, she had not. In fact, the wild behavior of the Martin girls suggests that she had been far too permissive;[56] like Elizabeth Holmes and other young people we have documented, they were past their parents' government.

There is, however, a middle way between the extremes of antago-
nism and permissiveness. Evidence of mutual affection within families
is not hard to come by. Thus a petition of James Cutler's to reduce
his daughter's fine explained how he "in the bowels of compassion
towards his child did engage to pay."[57] When Christopher Grant escaped from prison in June 1669, his parents asked the court to show him
mercy "that we may hope to regain our lost son again and he regain his
lost reputation by his good life and conversation."[58] Jacob Farrer and
his wife, confessing their premarital fornication in 1670, included the
death of his father as one reason for their "great and crying sin." Otherwise, he "might have bene a comfort to us in this houre of our temptation & trouble."[59] Joseph, Caleb, and Christopher Grant, Jr., petitioned the court to allow corporal punishment on Joseph to be commuted, "on behalf of our aged parents that the sorrow of it may not
bring them grey-headed to the grave."[60] In 1676 Robert Pierce went to
great lengths to defend his daughter Elizabeth's reputation from the
imputation that she had willingly submitted to Benjamin Simons's
importunities,[61] as did the Hastings parents when their son Thomas
was named father of Susannah Woodward's bastard in 1671.[62] Other
examples of parents in supportive roles of their children have been
given throughout this study and could be further multiplied.

There is rather less to go on in the records about attitudes to babies.
William Healey was depicted as cruel and unusual in his rage at his
infant daughter's crying in the night, and Sarah Crouch's reputation
was further blackened by evidence that she had neglected the child she
was charged with caring for.[63] Jane Bowen's petition from prison in
1662 asks to be "restored to her child as dear to me as any thing in the
world. [She would] undergoe any thing rather than to have the child
taken from me."[64] Goodwife Dutton not only sent her ten-year-old
daughter to refuge from her father's anger, but was outraged that he
should threaten her while she was holding their baby. Usually women
holding or sleeping with babies automatically escaped attack from lecherous males, however otherwise antisocial.[65] No cases of infanticide or
baby-battering have come to light in Middlesex. Children from war-
ring or neglectful families were ordered to be cared for by other families
as precautionary measures. Several of the confession relations of early
Cambridge settlers applying for admission to the church specify that
a major reason for making the hazardous venture to the new world was
family preservation, giving their children the opportunity for a good
life.[66] These relations also support the view that the death of babies was
seen, not coldly as a predictable fact of life, but as a "sore affliction" to

both parents, just as it had been to their pastor, Thomas Shepard, and his wife.[67]

If, as we have suggested, an adolescent culture developed in Middlesex in the late 1650s and became an accepted part of social life for young people in the county, family dynamics would inevitably have been affected. Parents or foster parents would have to rely less on orders, rigid discipline, and obedience, more on tolerance, mutual understanding, and affection. The 1660s decline in prosecutions and savage punishments for violent attacks on masters and their property—probably for reciprocating violence to servants—would support this change of attitude.

There is plenty of evidence from the sermons of the 1660s onward. Typical was Increase Mather who frequently complained that "parents are so sinfully indulgent"; children were not being "kept in due subjection."[68] Peter Bulkeley of Concord advocated fines for permissive parents and masters in 1655. "It's time to begin with more severity than hath been unless we would see a confusion and ruin coming upon all."[69] Patriarchalism was breaking down in the second generation not just because children were becoming more rebellious; parents were refusing to be authoritarian. Perhaps Michael Wigglesworth, so racked with guilt about his hatred for his authoritarian, first-generation parents, and Cotton Mather, so dependent and affectionate toward his parents, who were Wigglesworth's contemporaries, may stand as symbols of the changing familial relationships of seventeenth-century Massachusetts.[70]

Extended Family Relations

The great majority of families that are known to us through the court records lived in nucleated households: father, mother, children up to about age fourteen and, in one house out of three, servants. Occasionally an aged parent or a lodger lived in; sometimes the servant was a relative.[71] The nuclear family, however, was the norm. Thus Middlesex adhered to the pattern which demographers have plotted for most of Western Europe and North America in the early modern period.[72] The fact of residence under one roof, however, is not particularly revealing about family dynamics, as Lawrence Stone has recently pointed out.[73] The crucial question of family loyalties needs other sources.

What our sources demonstrate time and again is that loyalties across the extended family were extremely strong. Earlier in this chapter, for instance, we saw no less than three sons-in-law and their wives rallying

to the defense of the beleaguered Crosswells. Their testimony demonstrates that though they lived in separate nuclear households of their
own, they had daily contact with the parental household. There is no
need to reiterate the many other examples in previous chapters of this
extended family cohesion at work in defense of "the house" in the sense
of the clan. They reveal frequent meetings between parents and married
children and with more distant kin.[74] When Elizabeth Mellins was
widowed, for instance, her nephew Samuel Bucknam came to live in
with her. It was Samuel Townsend's custom to "visit Elizabeth Mellins
to see how she did do and what she wanted as he used to do once in a little while being related to her" even though distantly and by marriage
only.[75] One of the few personal letters of the Danforth family to have
survived is an affectionate note from Samuel in Roxbury dated 30
March 1670 to Thomas in Cambridge urging him to hold on to a horse
he had borrowed earlier.[76] When a brother-in-law returned to England
to live, Thomas not only acted as his attorney in Massachusetts but also
looked after his nephew when he became a Harvard undergraduate.[77]
Just as Sewall always records the relationship of quite distant kin as
though it were an important consideration to him, so extended family
loyalties were strong and cohesive in Middlesex. "My family right or
wrong" was the motto of these ordinary people; the sense of obligation
to siblings, cousins, aunts, or uncles held even when all the evidence
suggests they were blatantly in the wrong.[78]

This extended family loyalty had its price. The nucleated family had
to have permeable walls. Potential cottage despots had to vie not only
with interfering community "spies," but with countervailing kinship
opinion. Thus William Healey's brutality was challenged by his wife's
kin and Elias Row's arrogance by the clan of his maid. Such checks and
balances obviated patriarchal tyranny; the boss had to be accountable.

Conclusion

The family, then, was a key unit in early modern society. Though it had
more extended loyalties and many more functions than the modern
family, its cement, like today's, was expected to be mutual respect,
understanding, and support among members. Despite repeated calls
for discipline from preachers, synods, and legislators, most people
seem to have thought love the best means of achieving peace, harmony,
and order within their households. As today, that expectation was not
always met. Behind the family stood the community, a federation of
families. When one of its units broke down or stepped out of line, the
community intervened.

ETER LASLETT has defined communities in *The World We Have Lost* as "households in association."[1] In Middlesex that association was formally represented by town covenants, which drew much of their inspiration from Winthrop's "Model of Christian Charity." The basis of communal life was to be "that most perfect rule, the foundation whereof is everlasting love."[2] Thus the founders of Lancaster in 1653 had agreed "to end all difrenc by arbitracon. And for the better preserving of peace and love . . . we covenant not to goe to lawe one with another in actions of debt or damages."[3] Another preserver of peace and love was the practice adopted by many towns of screening candidates for town membership and warning out unwanted newcomers.[4] Thus would purity be maintained. The underlying philosophy of the covenants was, in Winthrop's words, that "the care of the publique must oversway all private respects . . . it is a true rule that perticular estates cannot subsist in the ruine of the publique."[5] The community transcended the individual.

The town as a covenanted community was a New England invention.[6] In old England towns had emerged through the mists of time, received royal charters, grown or contracted according to economic or social conditions. Villages, the English equivalent of most Middlesex towns, were part of the feudal manorial structure and the national parochial system. Yet the newness of the New England town should not be exaggerated. Many migrants to Cambridge or Watertown or Sudbury came from the same region in England.[7] They often brought with them experience of the workings of manorial and ecclesiastical courts, poor law, and parochial administration.[8] The behavior sustaining English village life was not dissimilar to that required in the covenants: "Fair dealing, honest labour, respect for social superiors, mild language and kindliness towards neighbours."[9] Nor did Englishmen in America abandon their deep-seated acceptance of rank and degree; in their associations, some households were more equal than others.[10]

Town covenants represented "policies of perfection," utopian hopes of fellowship, of "all knitt more nearly together in the bond of brotherly affection," a literal obedience to the divine command to love one's neighbor as oneself.[11] How these communities worked out in practice is a matter of considerable contention among historians. Some claim that they were "peaceable kingdoms" or "Christian utopian closed corporate communities."[12] Others argue that once the first flush of idealism waned, they lapsed back into the alleged European pattern, a Hobbesian jungle rife with envy, spite, and malice, wracked by feuds and suits, by bitterness and suspicion of neighbors.[13] The cramping of households, the absence of privacy and of traditional release rituals like the Twelve Days of Christmas, Shrovetide, or the summer festivals, built up explosive charges which the inevitable abrasions of town life could ignite into outbursts of violence, physical or verbal.[14] One version of puritan child-rearing adds the catalyst of resultant aggressiveness in adults to the mixture.[15] Unless intended love nests declined into nests of vipers, how else are we to explain the huge amount of legislation to control personal behavior, the fact that litigation was New Englanders' "second favourite indoor sport,"[16] and "the incredible frequency of slanders"?[17]

Certainly, in coping with some of the characters we have encountered in previous chapters, the towns of Middlesex could hardly rely on ideals of neighborly love and fellowship. There quickly developed, as already recounted, a multilevel system of social control, reaching down from the General Court and Court of Assistants, through magistrates and county courts to town officials like selectmen, grandjurymen, constables, commissioners for small causes, militia officers, later, tythingmen, and a host of petty posts like fence-viewers, highway-surveyors, and pound-keepers. Their functions involved the day-by-day administration of the town; many of these activities like stock-herding, bridge or road repair, defense, maintenance of schools, meetinghouses and their staff, remained communal responsibilities. Often such officials had formal disciplinary and law enforcement functions; they dealt summarily with petty offenses, for instance, or presented law-breakers, contentious or neglectful couples, masterless men or women, or executed the county court's judgments. This was the formal apparatus of social control.

There was furthermore a formal system of conflict resolution: litigation.[18] Massachusetts effectively implemented one of the planks of the English legal reform movement by giving county courts jurisdiction over civil actions, thus decentralizing equity and making it far more accessible to ordinary people. Unlike most criminal hearings, civil suits were tried by elected juries. Peers representing their communities formally arbitrated between plaintiffs and defendants over such questions as debt, trespass, contracts, and ownership.[19]

Survey of Evidence

Before this cumbersome apparatus of formal social control and conflict resolution was lumbered into action, there were informal agencies for crime and conflict prevention. We can demonstrate their activities—foreshadowed in the town covenants—by illustrations from the records. Take, for instance, the indiscretions of Susannah Durrant of Billerica, a married woman with young children, who was seeing far too much of her disreputable neighbor Thomas Wilkinson. Her husband tried prohibitions and commands; these she greeted with derision. But that was not the end of preventive measures. Neighbors warned her that Wilkinson was "a base fellow" and "that the cheife of the towne were much troubled at it." When this advice was rebuffed with "they are a company of babling fooles," Mr. Whiting the pastor tried to use his influence to deter her, but with no more success than the three selectmen who visited her. Only when three lines of informal authority—husband, neighbors, and "chief men"—had been repulsed was official action taken and the county court brought in.[20]

We saw the same process in Reading when Benjamin Knowlton was "vehemently suspected" of fathering a bastard on Mary Pike. First the girl's father tried to get him to admit his responsibilities; then neighbors approached him, and finally the minister, deputy, and deacon confronted him.[21] The Beales provide a third example. When William Beale's agreement with Elias Row was treacherously broken, he used his Bradstreet connections and informal arbitration through Samuel Hunting before the last resort of formal litigation.[22]

One final instance, out of many, comes from the events in Sudbury in 1699. In September the court approved and confirmed an agreement between Captain John Goodenow, on the one hand, and Joseph Noyes, Sr., and William Brown, on the other, arrived at with the "friendly advice" of Thomas Clarke of Chelmsford and Ebenezer Grout of Concord.[23] Noyes and Brown were acting as spokesmen for a body of townsmen in setting forth dissatisfaction with Goodenow's public and private behavior.[24]

Publicly Goodenow had monopolized town offices and corruptly misused his power. Privately, he had cheated at horse trading, been censured for drunkenness by his fellow church members, and attended only half the services. What he did during the other services is implied in the complaint: "When he is absent from meeting the wife of John Brooks is absent also." Mary Clap was more specific:

> Being at John Brooks house during meeting Capt. Goodenow entered. When he thought me asleepe he went to the bedside where Goodwife Brooks lay. I did hear them discorse in such a manner as was not mete for any but a man and his wife. The wife of John Brooks said that the custom of women was uppon her and that her body was much swollen. Capt. Goodenow said he hoped not so. Goody Brooks said it is & if you will not believe me . . . [25] how it is.

Another witness had seen them "in an uncivil maner liing all along [*sic*] in the hovil together, *the womans coats up above her knees. I saw her naked.*"[26]

Three years previously John Brooks, economically vulnerable as a tenant of Goodenow, had complained that his landlord "had as much to do with his wife as himself and he wold beer it no longer . . . he asked some of the company to go with him to demand his house from Capt. Goodenow" but found no volunteers. Another Sudbury housewife deposed that the man who was concurrently militia captain, town clerk, town assessor, first selectman, and moderator of the town meeting had lustfully "tempted me with the command of his estate . . . to committ adultery with him."

Scandalized by this behavior Noyes had started formal accusations in May. In the summer months, however, informal mediation produced a solution. "Being willing to secure my repputation as far as I may which is dear unto me," Captain Goodenow agreed to resign all offices and pay eight pounds court costs in return for the withdrawal of the accusation.[27] Sudbury secured peace after two years of fratricidal wrangling.[28]

Such satisfactory solutions to town antagonisms and to crime prevention were not always forthcoming. Hostilities between neighbors might prove unamenable to compromise or conciliation. The behavior of individuals might be so antisocial that patience was exhausted.[29] This was where defamation might come in. Those people who uttered libels or slanders in Middlesex seem to have had two rather different aims in view. The first was to release pent-up anger against someone. It was a verbal assault. The second was more studied. It was a warning shot to tell the victim that his or her behavior had overstepped acceptable bounds. At times the two divergent aims might coalesce; outrage and premeditation can go hand in hand.

The plaintiffs who brought actions in the county court had one primary end in view. They "waged law" to protect or restore their reputations. Some reputations, of course, were insulated by the raiment of church membership.[30] Nonetheless in face-to-face communities, people tended to individualize their problems and setbacks. Apart from the providences of an inscrutable God, impersonal forces like economic recessions or social change played little part in explanations. If something went wrong it was somebody else's fault.[31] Where gossip was endemic and privacy at a premium, a "good name" was of paramount importance.[32] Iago's maxims on reputation were instinctual to seventeenth-century New Englanders, as Captain Goodenow demonstrated.[33] Not only "the psychological security of villagers depended on communal approval," but also, where so much labor required group assistance, did their material comfort. To be ostracized or even gossiped about by neighbors meant being cast out into an outer darkness of isolation; it also meant no help at harvest time or no bondsmen prepared to give security for a court appearance.[34] If the gossip and innuendo were malicious or groundless, the target had a very understandable sense of grievance.

The towns of New England were by no means free of scandalmongers. Thomas Langhorn described Elizabeth Holmes as "a slanderer of divers persons at several times" who persisted in "her lying and taletelling" despite parental correction.[35] The Carter family of Woburn were accused by their neighbors of exaggerating the matrimonial problems of the Duttons.[36] Thomas Hall described one of the many crimes of Mary Atherton as "setting neighbour against neighbour."[37] The Crosswells believed that they were being spied upon and information was being collected to blacken the family name.[38] Joseph Bent confessed that "he was well pleased" that a false imputation of fornication "was layd unto another, and he somtyme of such a family whose honour and good name I should not have suffered so to have been violated."[39] Defense witnesses suggested that Elizabeth Brown and William Everton had been framed by scandal-sniffing neighbors led by Hannah Salter.[40]

A slander suit could effectively silence false or dangerous accusations, as witchcraft suspects demonstrated.[41] The threat of one might be used for less praiseworthy ends. Thomas Wilkinson, who, unwitnessed, had earlier tried to seduce Mary Toothaker, threatened her husband that "if he spake a word of it it would cost him all his estate" in damages for defamation. Fear of similar repercussions probably deterred some of William Bucknam's and John Law's victims.[42] William Healey's and Thomas Crosswell's daring of critics "to bring them forth" probably had the same ends.[43] It has been suggested that the huge increase of defamation suits in England was the result of similar preemptive strikes, but these are the only examples of such forestalling tactics in the Middlesex Records.[44]

Although less frequent than in seventeenth-century England, defamation suits were not uncommon in Middlesex. On average the court dealt with one action at three out of its four sessions each year.[45] In many cases it is impossible to recover the cause or the nature of the defamation; in others nonsexual imputations were made: "thief," "cheat," "liar," or "drunkard" were words complained of. Because slanders were on the borderline between crimes and torts, one or both parties to a quarrel would occasionally be prosecuted for breach of the peace.[46] Since we are here concerned with community dynamics, I have selected eight cases which help to show how town life worked.

Case Studies: Defamation Suits

The first two cases are typical of those abusive confrontations which arose from outbursts of rage. Both were heard at the court sitting on 16 June 1663. The grounds for the action brought by Sarah Pemberton against James Mellings,[47] both of Malden, were described in the testimony of John Pemberton, aged twenty-one, and Isaac Ong.

> As Sarah Pemberton was driving James Mellings hogs out of Goodwife Barlows garden, he told her He had a good mind to knock her brains out & called her Base liing Jade[48] and furder said He had a good mind to foot her about the place; and sd. Sarah did answer Youre a fine man to stand caling Jade Jade & he answered again Jade! What are you else but a base liing Jade & still kept threatening of her & caled her Bas liin Carion.

The Court awarded Sarah Pemberton twenty shillings damages and costs.[49] She appeared in the record as a twice-injured party, both from hogs and from insults to her honor and honesty. There are some grounds however for believing that Mellings was giving voice to a more widely held opinion of her character. She did not marry until the age of thirty, in 1668, and then not to a fellow townsman, but to the disreputable glover of Cambridge, Samuel Gibson.[50]

The occasion of the second case, heard in June 1663, was the warning given to Thomas Tirrell of Charlestown by Elizabeth, wife of John Mousall,[51] not to make "love to the mayd servant without orderly leave." Tirrell's companion John Fosdick, a thirty-seven-year-old married man, seems to have responded the more volubly to this prohibition.[52] He called Elizabeth "a base jade . . . whore . . . he was in debt to her but he would be even with her." He had also slandered John Mousall, saying:

> All that he had was the devills for he stood by his beds side & caused his members to rise . . . & mead his [cock stand] *flesh to rise*[53] to the maydes & all soe hee bid him goe and show his [cock] *members* to good man Bullyard again & further hee caled him Rog & beastly Rascoll & tould him that he showed his [cock] *members* to good man Bullyard 2 or 3 times the other day when they were a shearing of sheep.

Tirrell and Fosdick were each fined five pounds for "violence and scurrilous and reproachful expressions," and ten pound bonds were taken for good behavior.[54]

Both these contretemps were a culmination of hostile relations as in English examples. Mellings described Pemberton as a liar, referring to some previous grievance, and Fosdick admitted his prior indebtedness to Elizabeth Mousall. Tirrell would hardly seek to court the maid unless he had some familiarity with the household.

The dispute set off by Mellings's errant swine was a commonplace of town records and town memories. The regular appointment of fence-viewers and hog-reeves underlines the potential threat that escaped livestock posed in a mixed-farming community. In a subsistence economy, good fences and properly controlled animals could make the difference between a well-fed and a hungry family. Even the pious and equable Rebecca Nurse had threatened violence when a similar invasion occurred in Salem Village.[55] Thomas Danforth's poor relations with Henry Dunster in the 1650s began with an ox getting loose.[56] A Groton town order of 10 January 1670 emphasized the point later made by Robert Frost: "To the intent that we may preserve love and peace in the town . . . all the out sid fences . . . shalbe a sufficient five raill fence."[57]

The Mousall–Fosdick case is altogether more intriguing. We know that unapproved courting was a sore point between the generations.[58] Yet Fosdick was the same generation as the Mousalls. His outburst at Goody Mousall's prohibition seems both disproportionate and totally irrelevant. His allegations about her husband's exposing himself may have had some factual basis; the couple had only had one child in eight years of marriage. If Mousall were an exhibitionist, however, he would hardly have wanted the fact broadcast in court. The only clues to this colorful but baffling case are that Fosdick's father had been excommunicated from the Charlestown church in 1643 for reading Anabaptist books and fined twenty pounds. He remained an outcast until just before his death in 1664. Both Mousall's father and uncle had been deacons of the church, the uncle in 1643. Second, Mousall's father, Ralph, a carpenter, had died six years earlier. Fosdick's father, Stephen, was still alive with an estate worth £500. Fosdick, a housewright and carpenter, may have had to borrow from the Mousalls, who had already inherited, because he was short of capital. To be a debtor to such a family may have exacerbated ill feelings. This fracas, then, may well have been another round in a simmering family feud, rather than a simple altercation about courtship.[59]

We turn now to cases involving more premeditated insults.

That of Phoebe Page in April 1650 originated from her suing Deacon John Fleming and his wife of Watertown for saying that she was with child. This led to her being medically examined by "skilled women" in March 1650. The Flemings had undoubtedly uttered the statement, but claimed in defense

> that these speeches did not procure the search but other [speeches], and that the deffendant spake these words from the common practise of Phebe Page & the report of her own friends.

To support their contention that if Phoebe was not pregnant she deserved to be, the Flemings produced sixteen witnesses. Ten of these were watchmen or travelers who had caught Phoebe and her father's servant John Poole[60] in various compromising situations the previous summer. She had confessed to one witness that she must "either mary within a month or rune the country or lose her witts." Goodwife Page "wished her daughter had never seen Poole for she was afraid she was with child."

Evidence was produced that she had been involved with other men. Returning "from Boston in the middle of the night . . . Nathaniel Partridge[61] and shee fell once and were downe two other times off the horse and . . . he attempted to lie with her saying the woman was made for the man & she answered: In time convenient . . . Shee had one five shilling piece of old Knap for a kisse & old Knap[62] said that young men would only give a touch but he would give her a cleaving kisse and old Knap did afterward desire to kisse her again uppon that five shillings & she answered no." During her recent sojourn on Long Island she had been whipped for provoking a young man to keep company with her after curfew, and confessed that "shee had carnal copulation" with him.

The Pages were a bitterly divided family. Phoebe told a neighbor, "My mother I can love and respect, but my father I cannot love."[63] Advised to return home, "shee answered Noe, before I will doe soe I will goe into wildernes as far as I can & ly downe and dy." Her father "constantly affirmed [to a sister in the church] that what with his wife and his daughter, he was afraid they would kill him . . . if shee knew as much as he Phebe deserved to be hanged." In the face of this mass of evidence, "the plaintiffe with drew her action." The long-suffering John Page had to pay the Flemings' costs and enter bond for Phoebe's good behavior. She was released six months later in October 1650.[64]

Despite this collection of irrelevant tittle-tattle, hearsay, and innuendo, the fact remains that Phoebe was not pregnant; she was never presented for fornication. Technically, therefore, the Flemings were guilty of slandering her. The seventeenth-century legal mind was not this precise, however. Presentments were often made merely on grounds of rumor or "common fame."[65] The fact that the deacon of Watertown church spread this particular "fame" may signify that there was official disapproval of Phoebe's behavior, which more friendly warnings had failed to correct. He could even have been in collusion with his "brother" Page, who had evidently lost control.

The Bucknam family is already familiar to us through the extramarital exploits of the wanton William, brought to book in 1662. Nine years previously, his wife's association with her sometime lodger, Robert Burden, was in the limelight. Although the records of the case are highly defective, we know that a slander suit precipitated the publicity.[66] The principal surviving evidence to support the innuendo came from Jonathan and Elizabeth Webb, in 1653 aged about thirty-six and thirty respectively, who lodged with Burden for a year, once he had his own establishment. They observed that Sarah came often to Burden's "by day & by night" and Robert often went out of his house with her. He

sent his best victuals to be dressed and his washing to be done at Bucknam's, a quarter of a mile away, when Elizabeth Webb was on the spot
and willing. Jonathan Webb carried a message from Sarah for Robert to
meet her at the South Spring two or three hours before night; he did not
return from this rendezvous until late at night when they were in bed.
Calling unexpectedly one evening at Bucknam's, Jonathan spied his
landlord sitting by the fire and meat upon the table; but Burden did
"presently run into the corner by the chimney and hid himself all the
time this deponent was there."

Elizabeth Webb twice took a message from Sarah "to desire Robt.
Burden to come and lye at her house for her husband was from home at
Charlestown and accordingly [he] went." Goody Webb "observed
much familiaryty betwixt them & spake to Sarah Bucknam about it."
When Sarah's sister stayed at Bucknam's one night, Burden "lodged
(as it seemes) almost all night and [her sister] did wonder at their
familiaryty and late sitting up together." Alice Larkins recounted how
Sarah, her next-door neighbor, "would some tymes take a gerlec herb
& say looke here is a short neckt gerle is she not like Robert Burden."[67]
Their familiarity was commented on by many neighbors; "he was
reddy to doe any thing for her and she was ready to doe any thing for
him and they were observed to oft togeather."

Much testimony originally presented against the pair seems to have
disappeared, but Sarah's point-by-point rebuttal gives some idea of its
contents. Five women had voiced suspicions about the two in a hay-
stack on the marsh; two claimed to have seen familiarities among some
sumac trees; another alleged that they had traveled together in a boat
from Boston; a woman had been asked not to disclose something to her
husband. "A Defence of Sara Bucknam" deals with this assorted cal-
umny with the mastery of a Norman Birkett or a Clarence Darrow.
Some witnesses are proven liars, others could not physically have seen
what they claimed to see. Other witnesses, including Joseph Hills,
assistant and ruling elder of the church, testified to the innocence of suspected encounters and the good character of a much maligned woman.

The reason for Burden's frequent visits, according to a friendly
neighbor, was that William Bucknam, as an artisan, "had much occation of carting and plowing and had neither cattle nor skill of his owne
to doe it and could sheldom gitt others to doe it though often prest
my selfe and others." We are left with the impression that there never
was "any familiaryty more than Christianity and Honestie between
them." Nonetheless the court took bonds from each of them on
5 March 1653 to abstain from all private meetings.[68] In October they

were discharged, just in time for Burden to marry Hannah Winter the next month.

The underlying grounds for suspicion were probably twofold. Sarah, who was thirty-one in 1653, had become Bucknam's second wife around 1640, shortly after arriving in the colony as a servant to Mistress Glover (who brought the first printing press from England). Sarah brought her husband, who was seriously indebted, a considerable dowry.[69] This consideration may have counterbalanced the fact that she was fifteen or twenty years younger than him, but it was the kind of age gap beloved of writers of cuckolding tales and may have led to gossip in the town. Nine years later Elizabeth Payne asked her how she "could have such a ould blackbearded man as he?"[70] Second, we know that Bucknam spent a lot of time away from home and that he had already begun his philandering career among the goodwives of Malden. One of his first victims was Elizabeth Webb. In people's minds, this would provide the still young Sarah with a motive and an opportunity for revenging herself.[71]

There was, however, a much more sinister element in the business. Sarah's best friend in Malden had been Hannah Barrett, her neighbor who was two years older. They had both subscribed to the women's petition of 25 August 1651 in favor of the heretical minister Marmaduke Matthews. Then, when Sarah decided to move, they fell out. Attempts at mediation by William Sargent, the Malden lay-preacher, failed. Though neighbors pressed Hannah "not to defame" Sarah and "to lay aside all these contentions and live in peace and love," the Barretts started "a racking and gathering of witnesses together against Robert Burding and Sarah Bucknam." James Barrett was shown to be a man convicted of lying; he had subscribed to a petition against the Commonwealth and had refused to take the oath of fidelity. This was another family feud.[72]

This case had immediate and long-term repercussions. While it was being decided, Thomas Squire, referring to "the base buisness of Bucknams wife," stated that "Mr. Hills is one day in the Deacones chair & the next day pleading baudy buisness in the court; will you say he is an honest [i.e., moral] man? Is he fitt to sit in the place of a ruling elder that will plead the cause of rogues?" For this Squire in his turn was sued for slander.[73] Nine years later when Bucknam was presented, he spoke darkly of prejudice: "This hath been a thinge searched out . . . not spoken freely nor doeth it appear to be conscience in a religious way moveing them thereunto."[74] Among the women who deposed against him were five who had conspired against Sarah, including Elizabeth

Webb and Hannah Barrett.[75] Two defenders of Sarah spoke in William's favor.[76] Another of his supporters had been in a fight with James Barrett three years before.[77] Several of Bucknam's accusers were connected by marriage;[78] six, unlike Bucknam, were church members, most of whom came from the leading families of the town.[79] So the Bucknams' court appearances were results of more than a neighborly tiff; they were events in a town feud.

Libels were much rarer than slanders, but on 8 March 1664, the commissioners for small causes in Concord summoned John Slater, a young immigrant to the town from England during the 1650s to appear before them as "supposed author of libels writ in papers & set upon a post on the meeting house."[80] The first, containing ninety lines of smutty doggeral and a mock warrant, is addressed "To our dreadfull & most sovereign Lord Haywood high cunstable . . . The cunt searcher." Its opening lines give some impression of its quality.

> Now all you madames in this town that dwell
> Read & marke my story well.
> Looke & observe all your wayes
> Lest the constable brings you to dispraise.
> See unto your primest load
> Lest the constable search you when you come abroad.
> O when he would see your cunts apparent
> Let him not go home without his arrant [errand *sc.* performed]
> For he is the arrant'st rogue
> That ever searched a cunt abroad.

John Heywood told the commissioners that if Slater "did freely confess . . . he'll freely forgive him. . . . John Slater in an humble frame said some others did join with him." The commissioners offered lenience if "he would discover all," but with expressions of sorrow and shame Slater took all the blame on himself. The commissioners wrote "we have passed it by for this time if it will please the honoured court to do the same."

The second libel, in Slater's hand, was directed to "My dear & most loving friend Sir Thomas Pinion"[81] and concerned his relationship with Mary Edwards.

> Her natures fury[82] does so run
> That she thinks it will never be done.
> She standeth up with horrid face
> And thus she argues of the case:
> My knock[83] doth piteously itch

O prethy Penion set to a stich.[84]
His answer being thus to her
I will not prove false to thee my dear
But as thou didst desire me
Thy groaning hole Ill steech and see
And looking on in strange wise
She wet his nose and pist in 's eyes.
So thus served she poor pinion
When he was doing his conjunction.
Oh now quoth she take what is dropt
And let nothing hereof be lost.
From hence issues vertue for your nose,
From hence issues healing for your eyes.
This jut[85] of wonder being burst
Into her hole your head may thrust.
If all this will not serve her turn
Then afterwards put in your tongue . . . [86]
Oh kind sir be not discouraged
But follow on till I am purged
For if you ever mean to be a father
Do your work well before you give over.

At the bottom of this unedifying patter is a response in a different hand.

If natures purll bag[87] does burn
Then quickly send for thy pinion.
If sick thou art and like to die
Get pinion to fuck thee quickly.
If sick thou be and lack a purge
Borrow Pinions gleister pipe and bagg.[88]
If thou art Troubled with the staggers
Borrow Pinions baskett stones[89] and daggers . . .
If ever thou art troubled with Dixens booke[90]
Never spear but let him thee often fuck.

Slater ends with a note about his intention to publish on 14 February 1664, Valentine's Day, but "it did fall out contrary" and had to wait until 1 March.[91]

The accompanying mock warrant provides a clue to the stimulus for this excursus into verse. It concerned a maid with child by a "tailor by occupation[92] or trade." Just as a surgeon might need to follow the tailor in stitching "a cunt that is torn and rent," so "who more expert about this work of searching the privie members of a maid than a tailor. . . . Let Tom wash his tongue in her breech and lick the sore till its well."[93] Heywood as well as being constable was also the Concord tailor. Of

Pinion I can discover little. He was in Sudbury, the neighboring town to Concord, in 1661. He was also presumably a tailor and may have been Heywood's apprentice. In 1661 Mary Edwards had been a maid-servant in Charlestown and had accused another servant Samuel Starr "of haveing the carnall knowledge of her body about the latter end of October last. He confessed he was in her company . . . but denieth he committed such a wicked act with her." Mary reiterated her charge, but seems not to have conceived. Starr was the son of a surgeon.[94] Either Heywood may have had some investigatory function in that case, or he could have been ordered to follow up a "fame" that Mary was pregnant by Pinion, whom she subsequently married, and set about his task in an over-enthusiastic or voyeuristic manner. The idea of repairing vaginas to make them appear virginal was a commonplace of court satire and Restoration bawdy.[95]

Although the author of these limping and lubricious lampoons was devoid of poetic skill and taste, he was reasonably well educated. There is a reference to "Mellpomene, thou famed goddess of poetry," and as well as "conjunction" in the passage cited, he uses such words as "orthographie," "articulate," or "promotion" which hardly sprang to the lips or pens of the average Middlesex deponent. The tone of his two pieces suggests some familiarity with the type of scurrilous lampoons that Grub Street hacks and court satirists were producing in late Protec-torate and Restoration London. There are some precedents for libels of this type in the English records. The best known are probably "The Chelmsford Ballads" for which two men were prosecuted in Essex in 1602.[96] "A foolish and reproachful Rime casting reproch upon the Towne & the maids" of Springfield was prosecuted in 1671,[97] and a defamation case shortly to be discussed involved a verse lampoon. There was plainly a strong element of youthful devilment in this par-ticular episode, and the prurience of the libels may well owe something to Slater's English upbringing. However, it seems likely that other young people of Concord joined with enthusiasm in the ridiculing of authority and the shocking of respectability.

If ever a defamation suit was ill judged, it was that brought by Elizabeth Martin[98] against Hannah Long,[99] both of Charlestown, on 20 Decem-ber 1681 for "taking away Margaret Martin's good name and reputa-tion by reporting her with child which is very much to the plaintiffs damage." Long had further alleged that Margaret, who was only four-teen, was to have her pregnancy terminated; "they were going to make her miscary . . . gave her Phisick three days together . . . gave her boyld Saffin . . . that the child might not be laid to her charge." It was, of course, a vile slur on the family of a wealthy sea-captain. Yet it blew open a can of worms which the Martins would have much preferred to keep sealed.

As to the slander itself, various women came forward with a mass of circumstantial evidence. A maidservant thought Margaret had looked first pregnant and then like a woman after delivery. Margaret had borrowed a skillet from a neighbor to boil up penny royal, horehound, nip, and marigolds—all abortifacient plants. She did "look as bad as a woman that had a naty conscience." There had been two extra washes at a house in Charlestown in the week in question—in early November 1681—and "the washing was as bad as a woman that did lie in . . . abondance of stained clothes more than ordinary." Two men described "a great noyse and crying from women and Elizabeth Martin cryed Elizabeth Drinker [a neighbor] come away or my daughter Margot will die."[100]

Some of Margaret's loose talk came back to haunt her. Michael Long deposed that he had heard her say to Lobdall "she did believe that he did catch her by the cunt twenty times." Rebecca Lee reported her to have "told me that a man might lye with a maid a dozen times and not gett her with child and my answer was let not you and I trust to that but if you've had experience you may lawfully speak it." Two former maids testified to their "seeing Margaret Martin and her fathers boy ly together on the floor upon a Matt, attempting etc. & . . . Margaret said [to the] boy a little higher and then a little lower at last there etc in their wicked actions." She had told one of the maids that "she would cut little when she did it." When Hannah Long had sore eyes, Margaret had opined that "he that knoked her laste knoked her eyes oute." She called Long and her sister "that impudent hore" and "bould hore and impudent hore and damde hore severale times." One day Margaret had put her cold feet on her mother's lap and refused to move them. "Her mother hit her on the mouth and said of Margaret that if she had beaten her bones out when she was young then she would not have that sin to answer for that she now has. Elizabeth Martin Johnson said that both her mother and sister would go to hell, but not together because they would fight by the way. Margaret said the path is wide enough."

To add to the unwelcome publicity, the sins of Margaret's sister and mother also got a thorough airing. Goody Martin was alleged to have entertained visiting seamen from New York one Sunday when her husband was away. She had given an elaborate and thoroughly implausible explanation for missing sabbath services, and there was strong evidence that her guests had stayed the night.[101] Elizabeth Johnson had been married off when only sixteen to a mere seaman, grounds for suspicion. In her case memories proved long.

Hannah Salter recollected how "many years ago" Betty Martin had told the manservant to move his bed so that she could entertain a neighbor's lodger. "He heard [Betty] say it is enough and thrust him from her. The next morning [he] came to my house for fire and said The devils in our children my master does not deserve this." Betty, looking "sad and frightfull" posed a hypothetical question to her grandmother[102] about a "man in Boston . . . who strived with a woman and had so much to do with her as to spill his seed upon her whether the woman sinne. To which it was answered if a woman could not be heard when she cried out it was no sin." The older women were not fooled; the question was "Base all over" and the alleged woman of Boston would "prove to be a woman of Charlestown."

Another frequent visitor was Mr. Holman, a privateer. Goody Martin, who had herself "played the whore with him upon the staircase," often altered sleeping arrangements because "the pore man pined for [Betty] and was desirous he should ly with her . . . and when he had been with her Goody Martin would say Oh how fresh and red she looks what a colour she hath gott and would be peering in her purblind manner upon the sheets they had been lying upon and laughing at what they had been doing."

A cousin, William Whiting,[103] had been seen several times lying on Betty's bed, as had John Long.[104] "Last Thanksgiving," after heavy drinking, according to a maid, he "kept pleading with me to come to him for he said he had had a boute with the other three and I must have a boute with him too." Another girl was likewise being harassed: "That base rogue John Long he wants to play the rogue with me." Drinking, "uncivil songs," and "chambering and wantonising" created "rout and disturbance and much disorder in the house. . . . I never did see the like in any house that ever I lived in in my life."

What had precipitated the slander action was Betty Johnson's news

that her mother and Margaret were published to the privateers at Rhode Island by a paper set up at Mr Longs porch.[105] . . . Her mother was a little abashed for a while then said This may thank you, you young whores, to which Betty replied You are as much talked of as we. Margaret Martin said Why mother you were talked of as bad before we were born and wil be when you are dead. Goody Martin said These [Longs] are the people of God . . . the [church] members a crew of Devills of them . . . sister Foster, sister Taylor and your sister Smith[106] that gather together under pretence to pray, but it is to kill and slay and doe all the mischief they can.

The Martin women may have won modest one pound damages for Hannah Long's slander, but, thanks to the revelations, they were in turn prosecuted "for their many lascivious and wanton practices unto a high degree of prophanes and of neglecting to attend Gods public worship but instead thereof scorning and reproaching the people of God." Elizabeth Martin and Elizabeth Johnson were each sentenced to pay fines of twenty pounds, Margaret, ten pounds; they had to enter sureties of £100 and stand committed until the fines were paid in cash. It had not proved a good bargain.

There are several familiar elements here. There was obviously considerable ill feeling between the Long and Martin households. Five members of the Long family, also wealthy and influential in town affairs for two generations, testified for the defense. The libel about Margaret and her mother and the privateers was put up on the porch of "The Two Cranes," the Longs' inn. Hannah Long and her sister had been called whore by Margaret more than once, and Martin evidence further blackened the already sullied reputation of John Long.

Once again, however, this was more than a family feud. Elizabeth Martin spoke of a conspiracy of church members against her family. Several Martin servants testified against their employers,[107] but at the same court two of them were convicted of stealing gold and linens from their dame.[108] Finally a key defense witness was Sister Hannah Salter, who had already testified against Elizabeth Brown, and would again the following year, when the accuracy of her evidence would be impugned.[109] Since no one had actually seen Margaret miscarry, the jury found for the plaintiffs. Yet the Martin ménage was plainly seen by both bench and respectable opinion in Charlestown to be a disorderly house similar to those of Cross, Mancer, and Smith.[110] Their profane and amoral enjoyment of sexuality, their uninhibited domestic quarreling and late night parties all point to a dangerously subversive set of values. They would no doubt have applauded the erection of the Charlestown maypole in 1687. As a threat to the good name of the town, they must be suppressed.

Details of the last libel are sparse. The Malden grandjuryman reported in April 1685 that Elizabeth, the wife of Stephen Payne, had recently published "a kind of rythme" containing "reproachfull speeches against the Reverend Mr. Wigglesworth of Maldon." Nevertheless, at her trial the jury found her not guilty. No record of either the libel or the defense has survived.[111]

Elizabeth Payne born in 1639, married to Stephen Payne in 1657 or 1658, and now forty-six, has already been encountered in previous cases.[112] According to Sarah Bucknam she was the prime mover in the welter of accusations against William Bucknam in 1662, to whom she had acted in an "unseemlie" manner.[113] In 1669 she had twice cross-questioned Elizabeth Wells about who was the father of her bastard, how many times she had slept with him, when and where, and whether any inducements had been offered.[114] She therein betrayed all the characteristics of the town scandalmonger: nosiness, sharp sarcastic tongue, malicious delight in spreading gossip, and hypocritical self-righteousness.[115]

What her "kind of rythme" was about can only be conjectured. The Rev. Michael Wigglesworth, celebrated author of *The Day of Doom*, had been the minister of Malden since 1656. Racked by psychosomatic invalidism, he had not proved an effectual leader of the township. In 1679, at the age of forty-six, this grandfather who had been a widower for almost twenty years, announced his intention to marry Mary Mudge, his servant maid "of obscure parentage, & not 20 years old, & of no church, nor so much as Baptised." Despite scandalized opposition from his fellow clergymen and from "the good people of Malden,"[116] the marriage to a girl six years younger than his own daughter went ahead. Although Mary, who bore Wigglesworth six children in nine years, appeared to have a therapeutic effect on his health, she was never accepted by the town. In the mid-1680s, when he was contemplating resignation, the minister wrote:

> I discern such an envious and spiteful disposition in some towards my wife (& those not of the meanest either) as argueth little love or respect for me. The old proverb is, love me & love my Dogg; which if it be true, certainly they do not love me that hate my wife; & are glad when any dirt is cast upon her or affront offered to her.[117]

It seems probable that Wigglesworth's marriage, of which "the like never was in New England . . . [nor] in the Christian world,"[118] and his reactivated sex life were the subject matter of the libel Elizabeth Payne published—a grudge against Mudge.

Conclusion

The picture of community life glimpsed in these cases was hardly one of loving neighborliness. In both Charlestown and Malden, there were vendettas between groups of households, with servants acting as informers, spiteful individuals stirring up scandal, and lots of dirty washing (both figuratively and literally) hanging out in public. Yet before jumping to the conclusion that Middlesex replicated one view of old world communities as so many hornets' nests, we should ask how typical they were.

We have already suggested that Charlestown was quite different demographically, socially, and economically from the rest of the towns in the county.[119] Malden, its neighbor and offshoot across the Mystic, was, however, much more typical as a farming community. Yet in other ways it did diverge from the norm. Its popular first pastor, Marmaduke Matthews, had been accused of heretical leanings, which the wealthy resident magistrate and ruling elder, Joseph Hills, shared. The prosecution and departure of Matthews produced fratricidal strife feelingly described in a letter of 19 June 1658 by Wigglesworth:

> Consider whither there be no havock made of Brotherly love amongst you. For Brethren to be like two flints that they can never meet but they must strike fire together, becaus neither part wil yield a little or condescend that they might gain upon each others infirmity by a spirit of meeknes! for Brethren to be so estranged that they know not how to fast and pray together for common mercies; for Brethren to interprete every word & action of one another to the worst sence, to make mountains of mole hils & think evry smal greevance intollerable! for Brethren to intermeddle with strife that belongs not to them, as if there were not jarrs enough already! For Brethren to censure one another for their private communications & actings which they that censure cannot be privy too, & out of a spirit of jelousy to conclude that such was their carriage in such a private or secret proceeding, because it use to be such at other times! for Brethren to give one another the ly & provoke one another in their speeches as becometh not men, much less christians! For Brethren to be so incensed against each other that they cannot lie together in a Town! For Brethren whilest the Lord hath some under the rod and all under his frown! to be quarrelling at such a time . . . Brethren you add affliction to the afflicted by such things; you need not ask then what keeps me weak so long.[120]

Thanks to Hills's subsequent prosecution and departure, Wigglesworth's illness and tactlessness, and a series of unfortunate assistants, the town was virtually leaderless. As the town historian, Deloraine P. Corey, writes "A spirit of ill will and strife seemed to pervade the whole community; slanders, assaults, domestic broils and other evils kept the people in a state of unrest."[121] Several of those who defended Sarah Bucknam were Matthews supporters, including Elizabeth Payne's father. The traumatic breach of the 1650s seems to have lasted for a generation.[122]

The abnormality of Malden's anarchic feuding becomes obvious when it is contrasted with Cambridge, just upriver. It too had its bad apples and its differences, but it also had two strong-willed and efficient resident magistrates and a series of outstanding ministers. Troubles in the town were not allowed to slip out of control.[123] Something like the pacification of Sudbury was theoretically perfectly possible in Malden, but the will and the authority were missing. Outsiders' comments on Malden's broils demonstrate that it was untypical of the county and the colony as a whole.[124]

What then were the motivations of defamers? For some there was an element of spite, for others it was a joke. For those involved in sudden outbursts of rage against neighbors it was probably cathartic. The bench recognized this by offering defendants in such cases the option of a public apology before church, town meeting, or militia muster as a means of reestablishing harmony within the community.[125] But in many cases in the records there remains a deeper purpose.

The premeditated types of malicious words could be described as the verbal equivalent of more physical forms of folk ridicule—the charivari, rough music, riding the stang or rail, or the cuckold's horns.[126] In these cases the main object of the exercise seems to have been to shame those who deviated from the accepted conventional behavior of the community. A sexually deviant "child of the church," an over-familiar constable, a girl convicted of fornication, a suspected bigamist, an erring wife, a disorderly family, or an elderly man marrying his young maid were fair game.[127] They required a shot across their bows to make them alter course and rejoin the convoy. In the language of cultural anthropologists, gossip and, by extension, slander performed the function of "normative restriction."[128]

There was, moreover, a strong religious element in the maintenance of conformity. From childhood, New Englanders were constantly reminded by catechists, preachers, and exemplars that they were their brothers' keepers. The saints were taught to keep a "Holy Watchfulness" over each other.[129] If they neglected this duty, they too sinned and the whole community would suffer for it. "God has . . . committed to us the care of our neighbours . . . shall we run upon God's displeasure to avoid men's?"[130] "If the neighbour of an elected saint sins, then the saint sins also," wrote Cotton Mather, enjoining "watchfulness to admonish one another."[131]

Communal vulnerability was taken seriously by ordinary people. Trial Pore confessed in 1656: "By this my sinn I have not only donn what I can to Poull doune Jugmente from the lord on my selve but allso apon the place where I live."[132] Similarly important was the obligation to be watchful. Edward Carrington deposed that he, "hearing of sum claimes about Robb Burding and Sarah Bucknam did the more narrowly take notice of theire carragis than before." Will Brackenbury affirmed that "having more than ordinarie occation to inquire concerning the life and carriage of Robb Burding" he could find no fault.[133] These were not private detectives; they were townsmen concerned about the reputation of their town. An English countryman told a visiting nobleman in 1602 that "every citizen is bound by oath to keep a sharp eye at his neighbour's house."[134] In Middlesex every church member had formally contracted to keep "holy watchfulness" on their brethren. This helps to explain why church families in Watertown, Malden, and Charlestown were prepared to invite defamation suits. There is a mass of evidence that the common folk too kept a sharp eye open for suspicious behavior. The community memory bank stretched back for years, as was the case in witchcraft accusations, of which defamations were a less lethal relation. John Demos has recently argued that the former were a desperate means of preserving group life.[135] In their way, a lampoon or a slander often had the same end in view. Gossip has been called "the politics of the officially powerless."[136] If the powers-that-be failed to take formal or informal action against antisocial behavior, then the scandal and the odium mushroomed into a communal challenge. Thus could the allegedly "inarticulate" assert community control.

Conclusion

E have been treated in the foregoing pages to a feast of talk. We have eavesdropped (as did they) on the men and women in the country lanes of three centuries ago. Even bearing in mind all the caveats about the evidence culled from court records, this has proved a highly informative listening post on the world we have lost. What does their speech tell us about them?

In everyday conversation, their mode of discourse is usually blunt and direct, but the range of tones is wide and varied. Young girls accosted by unwelcome suitors are derisively dismissive: "What is that to you?" or "Get you gon!" or "It was nothing to me what he had drunk." Young men in trouble with the law could talk touchingly about vain vows they had made in times of stress or danger; or apologize plaintively for lies they had told, passions they had indulged, or innocents they had implicated. Married women respond with astonishment or asperity—"She would see him hanged first"—which unmans would-be seducers, as do inconvenient reminders of matrimonial vows. Older men brag of their sexual prowess and transparently rationalize their indecent advances. There is plenty of pathos and tragedy: young girls betrayed or crossed in love or repenting false accusations, wives deserted by despicable husbands, widows left alone with young children, men brought face to face with the outcome of their folly. Given the nature of the better-documented cases, much of the reported speech is adversarial in tone. This may give a misleading impression of normal discourse, yet enough accounts survive of unstressed conversations to cast doubt on the alleged aggressiveness of puritanism.

No one familiar with the depositions could deny that the ordinary men and women of Middlesex had a sense of humor. The older women of Charlestown quickly see through a hypothetical question about a petting session which got out of control. Their menfolk show a similar sense of irony in questioning a man about carrying a peahook in November, or what stabling—a two-legged mare—another has. Testimony is regularly flavored with salty wit. An older woman claims "that nobody would lie with her except to cuckold the Devil." A young wench diagnoses eye trouble as "he that knoked her last knoked her eyes out," and drolly opines that the path to hell is wide enough even to accommodate her and her antagonistic mother. An elderly seducer attempts to flatter women with "I made his hart leap in his briches" or "I come to see how rich [your husband] is." A frustrated wife ridicules her husband's inkless pen and a frustrated husband quotes the adage "While the grass grow the steed starve." The women who blush at Cotton's double entendre are less literal-minded than their preacher and far from sexually innocent.

In retrospect, some incidents take on the qualities of farce: the assaulted milkmaid hanging on for dear life to the cow's udder; the salacious, short-sighted matron busily inspecting the sheets; the trio caught in the act vehemently but vainly denying the obvious; the horseplay of the young wench teasing an old lecher; the children posted as lookouts by their dallying mother; the maid urgently summoned only to be confronted with a penis. Sometimes the humor—as in much popular literature—is painfully puerile: the tedious jokes between wife and servants about who was lying with whom, the "hoohs" of the cuckolders imitating the approaching husband, the stale puns on hole and commodity, or the limping libels at Concord. Yet overall these people come through as canny and worldly-wise, skeptical of self-serving arguments and explanations, and accomplished readers of character. Middlesex people were nobody's fools.

The Middlesex County Court Records confirm the judgment of Edmund S. Morgan that it is anachronistic and misleading to think of the puritans of seventeenth-century Massachusetts as squeamish about sexuality.[1] Although there are half a dozen cases where testimony appears to have been bowdlerized, there are as many cases where crude Anglo-Saxonisms are faithfully recorded.[2] Nevertheless, there is pervasive evidence of a strong sense of modesty. For instance the act of sexual intercourse is usually described by such circumlocutions as "had to do with her" or "used her as if she was his wife" or "had fellowship with her" or "unfitted her for another man." Exposure of a penis becomes "laid out his negedness." A woman who told a man about her period was felt to have indulged in an intimacy which should have been restricted to the conversation of a wife with her husband. Even partial nakedness was considered deeply embarrassing. Young people appear to have been kept in ignorance of sexuality and several girls who had been molested had no clear idea of what had been done to them. The sexual curiosity of several groups of young people had to be satisfied by recourse to books rather than to parents or elders.

Two other impressions emerge from the record. However much a Danforth or a Gookin might have been confused by the differences of business, procedures, and priorities of an English Quarter Sessions or Ecclesiastical Court, they would have immediately recognized similar types in the dock and witness box. For anyone familiar with the court records of the old country, the behavior of Middlesex seducers, ex-posers, cuckolds, wanton wenches, wayward wives, defamers, dirty-talkers, gossips, and scandalized onlookers gives an overpowering sense of déjà vu.[3] The accused in New England use the same kinds of pungent language, of sexual stratagems and inducements, of ration-alizations and justifications, of enraged outbursts and satirical derision as their English cousins. Accusers display the same kinds of moral self-righteousness and communal self-interest. In this sense, Perry Miller's famous judgment that "if we . . . take puritan culture as a whole we shall find, let us say, that about ninety per cent of intellectual life, scientific knowledge, morality, manners and customs, notions and prejudices was that of all Englishmen" is certainly borne out by the Middlesex records.[4]

Second, footnotes scattered throughout the preceding pages have drawn attention to real-life behavior which reflects the antics of the heroes and heroines of ballads and street literature so popular in the sev-enteenth century, be it the man whose testicles were exposed through a tear in his breeches, or the surprised lecher escaping with the wrong clothes, or the cavalier's daughter excusing her amours,[5] or the inter-loping suitor who finds his prized bride is already pregnant. Similarly, the verbal responses of unsatisfied wives, cuckolded husbands, or part-ners of either sex rationalizing their infidelities could be taken almost word for word from the literary sources. The same could be said of several cases in the Somerset, Essex, or Wiltshire court records. It has often been assumed that the escapades of picaresque characters were fantasies invented by hacks to lighten the boring grind of everyday lives, an early modern equivalent to the soap opera or domestic situa-tion comedy. However, all of this evidence raises the distinct possibility that literature imitated life rather than compensating for it.

Do these impressions mean that as time passed Massachusetts was becoming more like England? Were the people of Middlesex reverting from that purifying zeal of the pioneers to moral and materialistic pollution? Certainly, many contemporaries there thought so, and not just the oft-quoted Jeremiahs. Peter Bulkeley of Concord called for tougher action against backsliding in 1656. A decade later, William Healey twitted his young wife at the poor quality and superficial commitment of new church members. Meanwhile, Charles Chauncey in Cambridge bewailed the pollution of the sanctity of the pure church of saints by the adoption of the Half-Way Covenant. Thomas Danforth complained in 1665 of "a new generation risen up who know not their fathers primitive interest nor the God of their fathers . . . New England is grown too too wanton against all order in Church and Commonwealth and stands in need of a whip to reduce them to the old primitive resolution and affection."[6] Three years later he publicized to all towns the General Court's order about the neglect of wholesome laws for education and training in families which "doth occasion much Sin and prophanes to encrease among us."

We have seen certain signs of moral decline in the records. We noted, for instance, the striking increase of dishonesty and moral irresponsibility in fornication cases, starting in the 1660s. By the 1690s young people who frankly admitted their crimes were exceptional, and flight was not uncommon. Moral discipline broke down in some frontier settlements under the strain of warfare and wilderness conditions in the last quarter of the century. Adolescents, as groups, became increasingly uppity after the late 1650s, and, as family discipline slackened, tythingmen had to be institutionalized. Newly-arrived English immigrants, a Marmaduke Johnson or an Elizabeth Wells, a John Slater or a John Walker, introduced corrupting influences into their communities. As the colony was drawn inexorably into the ambit of the English empire,[7] certain households in Charlestown came to resemble the seedier outports back home.

From the 1660s the ratios of bastardy and prenuptial fornication were on the rise. In the 1680s marital infidelity reached a peak unimagined a generation before. Similarly, litigiousness grew after the Restoration, a sign, perhaps, that pioneer ideals of brotherly love were on the wane.[8] Wholesome laws against fornication and adultery had to be diluted in the face of noncooperation, and as court business became increasingly routinized, the careful fitting of punishment to criminal suffered. The population of the county spread out in search of land or furs. Mobility militated against moral control. After King Philip's War poverty became a disturbing social problem.[9] The court began having to arbitrate in settlement disputes, those hoary perennials of English quarter sessions business. In the last decade of the century young men began trying to exclude the authorities from interfering in sexual peccadilloes by entering into private financial arrangements, for all the world like English gallants "putting away" their mistresses.

Although all this points to declension being a reality rather than the myth recent scholars have depicted, we need to see the other side of the coin and to put change into perspective.[10] The younger generation never comes up to the expectations of its elders; they always seem to have it easier, even if they are in fact pioneering new settlements, or fighting Indians, or resisting Stuart tyranny. Certain crimes actually declined over time, notably domestic violence, and, after the 1680s, marital infidelity. The rise in fornication ratios was relatively slight. Admissions to full church membership, particularly of men, revived between 1675 and 1690, in Charlestown of all places, and probably elsewhere.[11] The division of court business in the 1690s gave the general sessions more time to consider criminal cases. Dispersion took place in new group settlements, not in isolation.[12] The social "odiom," the "scandal and reproach," and "the laish of the law" were feared and felt in these new communities as much as the old and in the 1690s just as strongly as in the 1650s. Attempts at private settlements on behalf of bastards were normally rejected. Recent arrivals from the old world stuck out like sore thumbs initially, but they were eventually integrated into the different ways of the new. Civil litigation and settlement disputes were to some extent the results of increasing complexity and population. Poverty was still rare by European standards, and mobility took place over short distances.[13] Middlesex largely escaped the horrific witch craze of 1692, a sign of continuing social cohesion and consensus.[14] Declension, or adaptation, was inevitable over three generations, but its proportions were modest.

Placed in a broader perspective, the statistics of criminality assembled here and elsewhere point to a crucial difference with the old country. New Englanders in general, and Middlesex people in particular, were markedly more law-abiding, both in the 1650s and in the 1690s.[15] The great majority of men, women, and children were never presented or complained of. We examined the possibility that this silent majority simply did not get caught. With the possible exception of company-keeping or masturbating adolescents and thwarted attempts at seduction, we came to the conclusion that for most crimes and misdemeanors formal and informal law enforcement and conflict resolution worked efficiently. The silent majority behaved themselves and sustained the New England Way.

The major question we have posed in this study is why this was so. We have been particularly concerned to test the hypothesis advanced with such panache and widespread learning by Lawrence Stone. Did most people in Middlesex conform to high standards of personal conduct because of the discipline imposed by the physical and psychological force of the family patriarchs, "the priest-rulers of microcosmic empires"? Were dependents so suppressed and repressed in the little prisons in which they lived that any sense of personal autonomy was crushed out of them? Did they conform because they could no longer conceive of any other line of conduct?

We cannot give a conclusive answer to questions such as these. Why most young women did not bear bastards, most brides were not pregnant, most husbands and wives were not unfaithful, most marriages not violent, most children not incorrigible, most masters not batterers, we do not finally know. All we can do is to adduce tentative answers from the small sample of deviants available and, especially, from the reactions they provoked. To a considerable degree Middlesex criminals and witnesses are representative of society at large; in the main they were emphatically not an atypical subculture. They came from all backgrounds and all walks of life.

What these hints and clues suggest is that Stone's depiction of plebeian life in his era of the restricted patriarchal nucleated family bears little resemblance to plebeian life in Middlesex County. In the teeth of lay and clerical injunction, ordinary people appear to have followed the devices and desires of their own hearts. Though the laws of Massachusetts invested patriarchs with power to control courtship, the courters chose their own partners, circumventing parental supervision by guile or by gall. Their choices were dictated not by economic factors but by physical attraction and love. Patriarchs might be called in if the girl became pregnant, but not in a dominating role, rather as persuaders and facilitators. The unmarried, far from being erotically repressed, were fascinated by sexuality. They read and talked about it; they seem to have relieved sexual tensions by various means short of, or including, intercourse. Through group activities, cemented in the militia, abetted or at least tolerated by adults, they developed an alternative youth culture often at odds with puritan mores and expectations, wholly at odds with the model of brutalized, will-shattered, neurotic adolescence. It was marriage and parenthood which returned them, of their own volition, to the New England Way.

What of their conception of marriage and parenthood? Tenderness, love, care, helpfulness were their watchwords, not just wives and mothers, but husbands and fathers equally. Wife- and child-battering were as exceptional and exceptionable then as now. Women were not the subordinated and powerless gender. They had important official functions as midwives. They do not speak in their testimony in the tone of an oppressed group. They could see off the most unsavory men. They chose their mates and expected them to satisfy their emotional and sexual needs; they knew the power of sexual sanctions. As witnesses, they were often the community's conscience. Normal parents expected their and other people's children to be cheerful and merry, not flogged into subservience.

Since the family had far more functions, the home was relieved of the traumas of the modern emotional hothouse. The household had to be a team if the firm was to prosper. It was not an insulated unit ensuring unchecked patriarchal despotism. The extended family retained great psychological cohesion. It could be relied on for support; it could counterbalance the potential despotism of a patriarch. So could and did the community. Individuals saw themselves as their brothers' keepers. Communal functions of charity, counsel, conformity, crime prevention, and conflict resolution had not been taken over by institutions; neighbors still felt them as obligations. Many townspeople fell short of the ideal of loving their neighbors as themselves, but the ideal retained its potency. None of this is to deny that the attitudes and environment of people in the early modern world were very different from our own. Individualism was still a luxury. Equality of opportunity was inconceivable. Standards of living were meager and discomfort endemic. Superstition was rife and death was ever-present. Their world was a capricious and less apparently controllable place. The past *was* a foreign country, but it was not the lost planet some historians would have us believe.

If not patriarchal despotism, what then produced such comparatively high moral standards? A major factor, encountered time and again in this study, was popular piety. The great majority of men and women encountered in the court records were, quite literally, god-fearing. Their threatening and unpredictable world was theocentric: God controlled their uncertain destinies. A young man faced with death at sea makes a vow to God to mend his ways if He will save him. Another, meeting resistance to his advances, desists because "God smote him with a trembling." A threatened woman tells her abuser that "God sees, if nobody [else] sees, for God sees in the dark." Confessors describe how "God withdrew his protection" or "God permitted me to fall into temptation" or "Our great and crying sin cries aloud in the ears of God for vengeance." A woman who successfully resisted attack explained that "it pleased God to keep in me a resolution not to yeeld" and another who did succumb described herself as "justly left of God." "As God is my witness" or "As in the presence of God" or "Before God and man" reinforced solemn assertions or denials; they were not empty phrases. A suspected liar is told "God and his conscience did know how far he was guilty."

The devil and hellfire were just as real. Indictments in the superior court conventionally spoke of the accused as "not having the fear of God before his eyes and being instigated by the Devil." Individuals referred to "this beast he tare [God's commands] in pieces" or to "Sathans temptations in persuading me to deny it." Those who swore by the devil were liable to prosecution. A married man threatened a pregnant Negro that "if she layd it [the bastard] to him he wold sett the divel to work upon her . . . she should never have a quiet life again." The Martin women are alone in their apparent nonchalance about going to hell. The woman who told her tempter to hold his hand in the fire for half an hour was describing more graphically what a midwife implied when she reminded a woman in childbirth that "this might be her last breath." The woman who rebuffed a harasser with the words "that Oke tree would witness against him" was reminding him of the day of judgment. The invisible world was real enough to such people.

That spiritual world was real too to those apparent subversives, the seducers and harassers, a Bucknam or an Everton, who claimed "it was no evill" or "it was a small sin and might be repented of." If they met resistance, as they usually did, their internalized shame inhibited them. If, like John Row, they went ahead regardless, their subsequent sense of guilt was patently genuine. There is little evidence in Middlesex of a thriving counterculture to puritan values.

Recent studies of popular piety in New England stress the extent to which the ordinary men and women in the pews of the meetinghouse understood post-Calvinist theology. They were not mere passive listeners to a "speaking aristocracy." Far from there being a "chasm" between ministers and congregations, "the rhetoric of clerics was 'intrinsic to a collective mentality they shared with ordinary people.'" Religiosity pervaded everyday life in fact as well as prescription. "The servants, farmers and housewives . . . were in part the makers of their own faith." Yet if the evidence of Cambridge is typical—and there is material in the court records to suggest that it is—these people looked to their ministers as spiritual mentors rather than to the patriarch. He was spokesman rather than priest.[16] Malden's minister might be less influential in the everyday life of the town than his brethren, but the phenomenal popular success of *The Day of Doom* compensated. The plebeians of Middlesex likewise saw themselves as conscience-armed against the wiles of the devil; their consciousness of their own unpredictable but unavoidable days of doom had a profound impact on their everyday behavior.

Other forces outside the family played their part in making sexual misdemeanors such a rarity. The most obvious is the high standard of law enforcement. We have already paid tribute to the unremitting public service of magistrates like Danforth, Gookin, and Russell. They were the watch spring of the whole formal mechanism of ensuring good behavior. Their leadership in the county was tested by vote, and they were reelected year after year. Perhaps because of this, there was remarkably little evidence of sedition.[17] What there was came from marginal individuals already deeply suspected by their communities. The only riot in Middlesex was in favor of the status quo, against a hated symbol of English folk culture, the maypole. Without this social cohesion, the magistrates' task would have been impossible. As it was, their burden was lightened by the pervasiveness of informal community control. Middlesex was well stocked with moral monitors who did not miss much in the goldfish-bowl existence of daily life. The very use of the word "uncivil" to describe immoral behavior suggests that it was regarded as an offense not only against God but also against civic standards. A court appearance, then, was often a last resort for the intractable.

Even a court conviction was not the end of the line. Given the absence of long-term prisons, these people had to go on living and working together. Practical considerations thus reinforced the puritan emphasis on contrition, reclamation, and reintegration. Except for heinous or persistent sinners, punishments were relatively light: the short sharp shock of a public whipping or a modest fine. Commutations were fairly easily obtained by the contrite. Much of the punishment consisted in the shame of presentment, examination, court appearance, and sentence. In certain adversarial cases, defamation, for instance, public apology was offered as an alternative to damages. In criminal cases, notably premarital fornication, confession was encouraged. Thus was reclamation and reintegration begun. In many cases it seems to have worked. Examples of recidivism were rare. Many convicted young women went on to marry; many convicted youths later served their communities in elected or appointed offices. Even such an unspeakable young rogue as Jerathmeel Bowers eventually became a representative in the General Court.[18] Where the object of justice was not simply punishment or protecting society from criminal behavior, but also the reform of the criminal in which society had a vested interest, breaches of the moral law would be reduced, and the growth of a criminal class deterred.

Many scholars have drawn attention to the comparatively benign economic conditions in Massachusetts as a further crime deterrent.[19] A chronic labor shortage obviated vagabondage or an underemployed urban proletariat. After the 1650s there was a relatively even balance between the sexes and thus unmarriageable young males were rare.[20] There was no great gulf between rich and poor; everyone had food, clothing, shelter, and a recognized place in the social hierarchy. We only encountered one questionable case of petty theft due to hunger.[21] In Middlesex, only marital stress seems to have been the prerogative of the poor; sexual misdemeanors were spread across the social classes. The deacon's son was just as likely to go off the rails as the day laborer's. The presence of economic opportunity and the absence of endemic pauperism must have helped to reduce criminality.

Finally, and in starkest contrast to Stone's paradigm, tolerance, mutual regard, affection, and prudent common sense all played their part in reducing tensions and nipping criminality in the bud. Where relationships between husbands and wives, parents and children, masters and servants, neighbor and neighbor were based on interdependence and trust, criminality was unlikely to flourish. Despite the protests of clergy and legislators, most parents seem to have decided to let youth have its fling. Having flung, youth returned voluntarily to the fold. Jurors, more humane than legislators, refused to send adulterers to the gallows. When neighbors fell out, other neighbors interceded. When a constable was obscenely libeled by rambunctious youths, he asked only for apology. The case was discreetly dropped. If a widow with a jaded reputation was being victimized, fellow townsmen stepped in to defend her from prejudiced allegations. They likewise intervened to prevent a busybody turning a domestic tiff into a major crisis. A girl beaten black and blue or a Negro boy wearing a muzzle excited pity and concern. These are but a few examples culled at random to make the point that, far from being a brutal, suspicious, intolerant, and bigoted crew, most of the people of Middlesex were concerned, considerate, and cooperative. Consensus and common sense helped to make it a law-abiding place.

The remarkably high standards of popular mores in this Massachusetts county in the second half of the seventeenth century owed far less to oppressive patriarchalism than we have been led to believe. This conclusion coincides with the findings of other recent studies on both sides of the Atlantic.[22] Modern relationships and group dynamics would be far less alien to our early modern ancestors than has been suggested. The provocative and challenging theses of the 1970s simply do not stand up under detailed testing and examination.

Notes

Preface

1 / *The Wonder-working Providence of Sion's Saviour*, ed., J. Franklin Jameson (New York, 1910), 24.

2 / *The World We Have Lost*, 3d ed. (London, 1983).

3 / Notably Roger Schofield, E. Anthony Wrigley, John Harrison, David Cressy, Karla Oosterveen, and others affiliated with the Cambridge Group for the History of Population and Social Structure.

4 / On this phenomenon in America, see Lawrence Stone, "Family History," in *The New History* ed. Theodore K. Rabb and Robert I. Rotberg (Princeton, 1982), 52; for England, see Linda Colley, *Times Literary Supplement*, 16 Dec. 1983.

5 / Stone, "Family History," 60–72; Miranda Chaytor, "Household and Kinship: Ryton in the Sixteenth and Seventeenth Centuries," *History Workshop Journal* 10 (1980): 27–34; Daniel Blake Smith, "The Study of the Family in Early America," *William and Mary Quarterly* 39 (1982): 1–7; E. Anthony Wrigley, "Reflections on the History of the Family," *Daedalus* 106 (1977): 71–75; Moses I. Finley, "Progress in Historiography," ibid., 139; Laslett, *World We Have Lost*, 115, 121.

6 / *Times Literary Supplement*, 7 Dec. 1983.

7 / On interpretations based on prescriptive literature, see introduction to part 2; on the problems of using popular literature, Roger Thompson, "Popular Reading and Humour in Restoration England," *Journal of Popular Culture* 11 (1976): 653–71; Margaret Spufford, *Small Books and Pleasant Histories* (London, 1981), 42–84.

8 / R. B. Outhwaite, ed., *Marriage and Society* (London, 1981), 7, 10.

9 / Lawrence Stone, *Family, Sex and Marriage in England 1500–1800* (New York, 1977), 123–218.

10 / Ibid., 151–59; cf. Christopher Hill, *Society and Puritanism* (London, 1964), chap. 13.

11 / E.g., John Demos, *New York Times Book Review*, 16 Dec. 1977; Keith Thomas, *Times Literary Supplement*, 13 Dec. 1977.

12 / E.g., Lyle Koehler, *A Search for Power* (Urbana, 1980); Peter C. Hoffer and N.E.H. Hull, *Murdering Mothers* (New York, 1981).

13 / Alan Macfarlane, "Review Essay," *History and Theory* 18 (1979): 103–26; Outhwaite, *Marriage and Society,* 7–11; G. R. Quaife, *Wanton Wenches and Wayward Wives* (London, 1979), 243–49.

14 / "Family History," 76

15 / *New York Review of Books,* 14 June 1984.

16 / "Family History," 72.

17 / Ibid., 72, 83; Stephen Innes, *Labor in a New Land* (Princeton, 1983), 128; Chaytor, "Household," 27; Wrigley, "Reflections," 75–76.

18 / John M. Murrin, "Review Article," *History and Theory* 11 (1972): 226–75; James A. Henretta, "The Morphology of New England Society," *Journal of Interdisciplinary History* 2 (1971–72): 379–98.

Introduction

1 / Quarterly courts had been created by the General Court in 1636. They were to meet in Boston, Cambridge, Salem, and Ipswich. Until 1648 the seat of the Middlesex County Court was Boston. On these early developments, see D. T. Konig, *Law and Society in Puritan Massachusetts* (Chapel Hill, 1979), 26–27, 32–36; N. B. Shurtleff, ed., *Records of the Governor and Company of Massachusetts Bay* (Boston, 1853–54), 2:38.

2 / Cambridge, Charlestown, and Watertown were the original foundations of the great migration of 1630–32. Subsequent towns were either founded as offshoots, like Sudbury of Watertown in 1637, Woburn or Malden of Charlestown in 1642 and 1650, or Billerica and Newton of Cambridge in 1655 and 1688, or by fresh grants of land by the General Court, like Concord in 1635 or Lancaster in 1653. W. Haller, Jr., *The Puritan Frontier* (New York, 1968), 36, 43, 44, 66–69. The Hookerian migration to the Connecticut Valley recruited a large proportion of its following from Cambridge and Watertown.

3 / See Sumner Chilton Powell, *Puritan Village* (New York, 1965), chaps. 5, 9; Bernard Bailyn, *The New England Merchants in the Seventeenth Century* (New York, 1964), 28, 55–56; Johnson, *Wonder-working Providence* (see pref., n. 1), 68, 110–15, 212–18, 225, 227, 250 has contemporary descriptions of Charlestown, Concord, Woburn, Reading, Chelmsford, Malden, Cambridge, and Watertown.

4 / Samuel Eliot Morison and Zechariah Chafee, eds., "Records of the Suffolk County Court 1671–1680," *Publications of the Colonial Society of Massachusetts* 29 (1933): xix–xx (hereafter cited as "Suffolk Records").

5 / Supplementary justices, created in 1642. T. H. Breen, *The Character of a Good Ruler* (New York, 1974), 85.

6 / Danforth sat on the bench from 1659–1699; Gookin, 1652–1686; Willard, 1654–1676; Richard Russell, 1659–1676; James Russell, 1680–1699.

7 / The most detailed description of the colony's judicial system and criminal jurisdiction is in J. H. Smith, ed., *Colonial Justice in Western Massachusetts* (Cambridge, Mass., 1961), chaps. 5, 7.

8 / Breen, *Good Ruler,* 16, 46.

9 / Bradley Chapin, *Criminal Justice in Colonial America* (Athens, 1983), 3–4, 10.

10 / Smith, *Colonial Justice,* 80. In the period between the fall of Andros in April 1689 and the arrival of the second charter in May 1692, the judicial system reverted to the practice of the first charter period.

11 / The division was ordained in the second charter and enacted by the General Court in Nov. 1692. Konig, *Law and Society,* 194.

12 / G. B. Warden, "Law Reform in England and New England," *William and Mary Quarterly* 35 (1978): 668–90; Robert Ashton, *Reformation and Revolution* (London, 1984), 390–91, 403; Chapin, *Criminal Justice*, 18.

13 / Chapin, *Criminal Justice*, 19; John M. Murrin, "Trial by Jury in Seventeenth-Century New England," in *Saints and Revolutionaries*, ed. David D. Hall, John M. Murrin, and Thad Tate (New York, 1984), 153–67.

14 / Testimony of Hannah Coburn, Middlesex Court File 201; Murrin, "Trial by Jury," 164; Page Smith, *As a City upon a Hill* (Cambridge, Mass., 1973), 59; Konig, *Law and Society*, 88; Jules Zanger, "Crime and Punishment in Early Massachusetts," *William and Mary Quarterly* 22 (1965): 471–77.

15 / Adultery committed by a woman was a capital offense, and as such was tried before the Court of Assistants in Boston. The death penalty was only rarely pronounced, however; a common sentence was for the guilty "to go to the place of execution next fifth day after lecture and there to stand on the gallows [for one hour] with a rope about your necke and tied to the gallows and thence at the cartes tajle to be severely whipt not exceeding 39 stripes." J. Noble and J. F. Cronin, eds., *Records of the Court of Assistants of the Colony of Massachusetts Bay* (Boston, 1901–28), 1:70 (hereafter cited as *Court of Assistants*).

16 / Chapin, *Criminal Justice*, 50.

17 / George Lee Haskins, *Law and Authority in Colonial Massachusetts* (New York, 1960), 188; Edwin Powers, *Crime and Punishment in Early Massachusetts* (Boston, 1966), 188; David Grayson Allen, "In English Ways" (Ph.D. diss., University of Wisconsin, 1974), 388, 393–94, 401. The greater severity of punishment for moral offenses in the 1670s may have resulted from the clerical campaign which culminated in the Reform Synod of 1679.

18 / "Suffolk Records," xlviii–xlix.

19 / The four original order books were transcribed in the nineteenth century by David Pulsifer, an extremely accurate copyist. His last volume has been lost, but I have used his transcriptions for 1649–1663, hereafter cited as Pulsifer 1, 1671–1680 as Pulsifer 3, and 1681–1686 as Pulsifer 4. The original records for 1686–1689 will be cited as Sessions Records A, for 1689–1692 as County Court Records 5, and for 1692–1699 as Sessions Records 1.

20 / Files 201, 203, and 205 also have documents relating to cases in the late 1690s. Otherwise the files are in rough chronological sequence. The Works Project Administration of the 1930s sponsored the compilation of a card catalogue of cases in the files, cover notes to individual documents, and lists of matters covered in each file on its envelope. The New England Historic Genealogical Society has a two-volume manuscript calendar by T. B. Wyman of the documents in the files between 1649 and 1671. I am most grateful to David Dearborn of the Society for bringing this to my attention and for his help in general.

21 / Presentments by the grand jury for fornication or premarital fornication which never came to court (usually because the accused escaped) are not listed.

22 / Under the Andros regime from 1686 to 1689, the newly created superior court went on circuit quarterly to the county towns and heard criminal cases which would previously have been tried by the county courts. Konig, *Law and Society*, 160–61.

23 / "The Massachusetts Franchise in 1647," *William and Mary Quarterly* 27 (1970): 136–44; "The Decline in the Massachusetts Franchise," *Journal of American History* 59 (1972): 303–10. Rather than simply quadrupling Wall's totals of male population over the age of twenty-one, as suggested by E. B. Greene and V. Harrington (*American Population before the Federal Census of 1790* [Gloucester, Mass., 1966], xxiii), I have first doubled his

figures to produce complete adult population, then added 25 percent to include the sixteen to twenty-one age group, and finally doubled that total to arrive at the complete population. This method produces a larger but, in my view, more accurate total. The doubt raised about Wall's totals by B. K. Brown in "The Massachusetts Franchise," *William and Mary Quarterly* 33 (1976): 212–41, seems to me convincingly laid to rest in Wall's reply in *William and Mary Quarterly* 34 (1977): 453–58. Figures for towns founded after 1647 are taken from individual town histories cited below. Most of Medford's population in 1647 was probably included in Charlestown's total.

24 / The average birthrate of forty per thousand is based on the calculations in R. Higgs and H. L. Stettler III, "Colonial New England Demography: A Sampling Approach," *William and Mary Quarterly* 27 (1970): 282–94, esp. 288.

25 / Greene and Harrington, *American Population,* 19–20; militia totals have been quintupled.

26 / D. S. Smith, "The Demographic History of Colonial New England," *Journal of Economic History* 32 (1972): 165–83, esp. 175. The 29 percent increase calculated by W. S. Rossiter in *A Century of Population Growth* (Washington, D.C., 1909) is far higher than the 6.7 percent in S. Sutherland, *Population Distribution in Colonial America* (New York, 1936) which would produce a 1699 population of 9,972, a bastardy ratio of 1.04 percent and premarital conception ratio of 0.63 percent. This would represent a greater increase on the figures for 1649–63, but would still be less than the English figures. As we shall see, fornication may well have been under-recorded in the 1690s.

27 / Bridal pregnancies are traditionally measured as a percentage of marriages. A rough calculation based on a marriage rate of 12 per 1000 would produce a rate for the early period of 1.1 percent and 1.7 percent for the 1690s, compared with an average 20 percent for contemporary England.

28 / Peter Laslett and Karla Oosterveen ("Long-term trends in Bastardy in England," *Population Studies* 27 [1973]: 255–84) arrive at the following decadal ratios for bastardy: 1651–60—0.5%; 1661–70—1.6%; 1671–80—1.6%; 1681–90—1.8%; 1691–1700—1.9%. The low in the Commonwealth and Protectorate period of puritan dominance in the 1650s coincides with serious blemishes in the parish records. P.E.H. Hair ("Bridal Pregnancy in Earlier Rural England," *Population Studies* 20 [1966]: 233–43 and "Bridal Pregnancy Further Examined," *Population Studies* 24 [1970]: 59–70) found that on average in seventeenth-century Britain one out of every five brides was pregnant. Daniel Scott Smith and Michael S. Hindus ("Premarital Pregnancy in America 1640–1971," *Journal of Interdisciplinary History* 5 [1975]: 537–70) compute the American rate for the same period at less than 10 percent. Cf. Chapin, *Criminal Justice,* 139.

29 / Some of these cases, in the form of defamation suits, may have been heard in the inferior court of common pleas after 1692. The relevant records were not available.

30 / Pulsifer 1 has 44 female witnesses to 42 male; Files 33–57 have 50 women to 54 men; Pulsifer 3 has 38 women to 33 men; Pulsifer 4 has 45 to 29; Sessions Records A has none; County Court Records 5 has 35 women to 30 men; Sessions Records 1 has 42 to 38.

1. Fornication: Detection and Evasion

1 / Stone, *Family* (see pref., n. 9), 608.

2 / Pulsifer 1:39; File 7. Cf. Pulsifer 4:51, 59, 63; File 102.

3 / Pulsifer 1:229; File 28, 2 April 1661.

4 / Testimony of Cooper and Towne, 29 Jan. 1667, File 44.

5 / Pulsifer 3:217; Sarah Fiske's confession, 22 Oct. 1677, File 80.

6 / File 52, June 1669.

7 / E.g., MacDonnell and Dawes, File 15; Clarke and Greene, File 38; Smith and Grant, File 44; testimony of Martha Faulkner, File 52; Crouch and Grant, File 52; Hastings and Woodward, File 59. Cf. David Flaherty, *Privacy in Colonial New England* (Charlottesville, 1972), 62.

8 / Pulsifer 1:53; File 1, 4 Oct. 1653. Cf. Lathrop and Beresford who "did the act" in Hannah Lathrop's brother-in-law John Goodwin's house "in the daytime," File 77; Jones and Crouch, File 56; Hastings and Woodward, File 59; Tufts and Wells, File 52.

9 / E.g., Brown and Everton, testimony of Hannah Salter, File 99.

10 / Hastings and Woodward, testimony of John Chadwick, File 59.

11 / Pulsifer 3:120; File 70. Cf. Pulsifer 1:218; Grant and Crouch, File 52; Shepard and Smith, File 44; Johanna Negro's confession, File 123.

12 / "Manner & Frame of Words and Actions between James Tufts and Elizabeth Wells, servant of Peter Tufts," File 52. We may doubt whether Wells, with her English reputation, was quite the innocent party of her account. Cf. Pulsifer 1:64; Flashego and Smith, File 9. Several attempts at intimacy, to be mentioned later, were made when maids were milking.

13 / E.g., Sarah Blake's confession, 9 July 1689: "Joseph Winn jr. got her with child in the leanto of her fathers barn. Having persuaded her to the act she came into the house by one way the other [Winn] another." File 134.

14 / Pulsifer 4:45; testimony of Hannah Salter, letter of John Betts, File 99.

15 / File 38. Hannah denied any sexual relations with Clarke; Sherman was not sure the object he had seen was a petticoat. There is no clue in the documents on file as to Clarke's motives; perhaps he desperately sought marriage with the unwilling Hannah. Cf. Roger Thompson, *Unfit for Modest Ears* (London, 1979), 78, 79, 113.

16 / Testimony of Goodwife Grant, File 44.

17 / Tufts and Wells, testimony of Samuel Blunt, File 52.

18 / Examination of Elizabeth Frost, File 167; examination of Sarah Crouch, File 52.

19 / Testimony of Isaac and Joanna Johnson, File 57.

20 / Testimony of Mary Davis, File 40.

21 / Testimony of Thomas and Daniel Barney, File 162.

22 / "Law and Morals in Early America," *Perspectives in American History* 5 (1971): 225.

23 / Lilly and Sawyer case, File 203. Settlement disputes were less common than in England, but they did increase during this period. A typical example occurred in 1672 when Elizabeth Parker returned to her father's home in Lancaster after bearing the bastard of Silvanus Negro, late servant of Deacon William Parks, in Roxbury. Although Edmund Parker had "land & catle sum what considerable & him selfe & his son able bodied for labor," he lived in "a mean habitation with no dry place when it rains . . . before she went from him to live in service it was said they all lay together which occasioned her to ly at neighbors houses." Nor could the selectmen "cause Parker to get his son Abraham, 20 to get a little learning nor attend public ordinances on the Lords Day for a whole year & when delt with he was full of froward and peevish and provoking language." What proved far more provoking, however, was that Edmund Parker "violently took in his daughter against the order of the town" and that Silvanus "violently & forcibly if not fraudulently forced [the bastard] upon us." On 1 Oct. 1672 the court ordered Parker to enter bond for £100 to exempt Lancaster from charges or to return the child to Suffolk County. Pulsifer 3:32; H. S. Nourse, *Early Records of Lancaster* (Lancaster, 1884), 92–93.

A similar case occurred over Robert Webber's daughter in Cambridge in Aug. 1699. *Cambridge Town Records 1630–1702* (Cambridge, Mass., 1901), 324.

24 / Pulsifer 1:53; File 1. Injunction to marry, enacted in 1648, was a dead letter before the new fornication law of 1668.

25 / I.e., named.

26 / File 39. Cf. Sessions Records 1:79, 90; testimony of W. Symmes and J. Poole, File 66.

27 / On English usage, see M. J. Ingram, "Ecclesiastical Justice in Wiltshire 1600–1640" (D.Phil. diss., Oxford University, 1976), 241; Quaife, *Wanton Wenches* (see pref., n. 13), 105; M. J. Gretton, "Oxfordshire Justices of the Peace in the Seventeenth Century," *Oxford Record Society* 16 (1934): 72; R. Gough, *The History of Myddle* (Fontwell, 1968), 72. By the new law, the reputed father was liable for maintenance, but if he denied paternity he escaped other punishment. E. S. Morgan, "The Puritans and Sex," *New England Quarterly* 15 (1942): 699.

28 / Testimony of Elizabeth Jefts and Mary Tufts, File 52.

29 / Midwives in England took an oath "that they would endeavour to extract the name of the father from any unmarried girl they assisted." Quaife, *Wanton Wenches*, 105. On the similar role of the midwife in Plymouth, see John Demos, *A Little Commonwealth* (New York, 1970), 152–53.

30 / Pulsifer 1:230; File 26.

31 / File 43. See chap. 3 below.

32 / E.g., Sessions Records 1:59, 67, 74; Hastings case, File 89; Johnson case, File 102; Johanna Negro case, File 117; Barnard case, File 156.

33 / County Court Records 5:8; File 134.

34 / Sessions Records 1:74; File 169.

35 / Sessions Records 1:79, 86; File 170.

36 / Sessions Records 1:44; File 163.

37 / Sessions Records 1:53; File 201. Hannah Coburn alleged, however, that her mother told Susannah "she would have her send for Mistress Wolder the other midwife and for her grandmother once and againe. Susannah prayed her earnestly to do the office of midwife for her and then she did." Cf. the cases of Johanna Negro, File 123, discussed below, and of Hannah Brackett in 1685; her stepmother Ruth was her midwife and her aunt Elizabeth an assistant when she accused John Eliot, Jr. of seducing her. Pulsifer 4:225.

38 / Sessions Records 1:20; File 156; WPA card catalogue (see intro., n. 20), s.v. John Dunster.

39 / File 30.

40 / Testimony of Mary Tufts, Sr. and Jr.; Elizabeth Jefts and Mary Tufts, Jr., File 52.

41 / County Court Records 5:78; Files 140, 141, 143.

42 / County Court Records 5:80; Fay's will exhibited, File 141.

43 / Sessions Records 1:46; File 162. On the Bloods' background, see E. Faber, "Puritan Criminals," *Perspectives in American History* 11 (1977–78): 133; V. A. May, *The Plantation Called Petapawag* (Groton, 1976), 1–4.

44 / Pulsifer 3:231; File 79. The outcome of the case is not recorded. Henry Willard was the younger brother of Rev. Samuel, sometime minister of Groton.

45 / William Snelling was a leading Boston obstetrician, consulted in the celebrated *Lane v. Lane* divorce case in March 1659. E. S. Morgan, "A Boston Heiress," *Colonial Society of Massachusetts Transactions* 34 (1942): 500–12.

46 / Testimony of Mary Tufts, Jr., age about 14, File 52.

47 / *Martin v. Long*, File 105; Blood, File 79; Carter, File 123. Cf. Ingram, "Ecclesiastical Justice," 238.

48 / Testimony of Mary Davis, File 40.

49 / Grant and Drabston, *Court of Assistants* (see intro., n. 15), 1:125–26, 3 Sept. 1678.

50 / Pulsifer 1:230; Wright, File 36; Barnard, File 156. Cf. Winthrop, *Journal,* ed. J. K. Hosmer (New York, 1908), 2:318 and Hoffer and Hull, *Murdering Mothers* (see pref., n. 12).

51 / County Court Records 5:77. Testimony of Hannah Roper, File 143.

52 / The frequency of this solution in Essex, a major recruitment area for emigration to Massachusetts, is discussed in F. G. Emmison, *Elizabethan Life: Morals and the Church Courts* (Chelmsford, 1973), 24.

53 / File 55; Bacon later gave bond to appear in court, but the outcome of the case is unknown. Bacon was tythingman of Billerica in 1677. Mary may have been daughter to the contentious John and Elizabeth, see chap. 7.

54 / Pulsifer 1:230; File 26, 1659. Rose later returned as a passenger in another ship and married Abigail.

55 / Pulsifer 3:120; Paul Wilson, File 70.

56 / County Court Records 5:52, 62; File 135.

57 / File 143.

58 / Sessions Records 1:74; Joseph Lynde's examination, File 169.

59 / Sessions Records 1:80; File 169.

60 / Warrant for Priscilla Ball alias Miller, File 203. Cf. warrant for Susannah Pike, dated 16 Jan. 1693, File 153; warrants for Eunice Shed, Thomas Squire, Deborah Robins, Hannah Bartlett, dated 22 Nov. 1695, File 162; warrant for George Howard and Hannah Chadwick, dated 3 Dec. 1696, File 201; warrants for Mary Cowdry, Hannah Ridgeway, and Hannah Hill, dated 13 Oct. 1689, File 167. In 1695 Sarah Ward's petition took credit that "I have Not fled from the justis of the Law which I might have Done."

61 / Examples of similar evasions and concealments in England at this time are given by Quaife, *Wanton Wenches,* 109–23; Ingram, "Ecclesiastical Justice," 189, 238–40, 324.

62 / John Baker, her father, had been convicted of fornication in 1653, Pulsifer 1:53; for Sarah, see County Court Records 5:76, 85. It is conceivable she mistook the name of Archibald Forrest, who had been convicted in Boston in 1679 of "being in bed with Julian wife of Richard Knight [and] sentenced to bee severely whipt with thirty stripes." Powers, *Crime and Punishment* (see intro., n. 17), 175.

63 / Pulsifer 4:177, 179, 192. Her lover was Stephen Geary, the Cambridge bellman. Similar treatment was meted out by English justices, see Quaife, *Wanton Wenches,* 209. Sarah died in Cambridge prison on 9 Feb. 1687. T. B. Wyman, *Charlestown Genealogies* (Boston, 1879).

64 / Sessions Records 1:69; Files 203, 205. When the midwife, Widow Parker, told Edes that no one would believe her if she said it was her husband's, she answered, "Who can tell?" The examining magistrate had no better luck.
Q. Who is the father of the child? A. My husband . . .
Q. What is the childs fathers name? A. . . . .
Q. What is the childs name? A. Joseph.
Q. Joseph what? A. Silent to that peremptorily demanding proof of her husbands death. (File 203)

65 / Sessions Records 1:67; File 203. The baby died a few hours later; Thomas

Varnum was later ordered to pay half of the costs of the lying-in and the child's burial—£1 19s. 6d. The largest item in the bill of costs, after the hiring of a nurse, was "drink at the childs burial."

66 / Sessions Records 1:74, 78, 79, 80; File 167.

67 / County Court Records 5:40; File 131.

68 / Sessions Records 1:46; testimony of Barney, File 162. Cf. Coburn case, File 201; Mary Harris confession, Files 162, 201.

69 / There are several bills of charges incurred by unmarried mothers on file. Typical was Abigail Foster's, dated 10 Oct. 1695, in File 157:

	£	s	d
Midwife		5	00
Womens entertaynment that were			
at her labor		6	00
Nurse & diet 5 weeks	1	10	00
Wood & candle 5 weeks	1	00	00
Keeping the woman 5 weeks	1	00	00
4 Women sworn at Major Bradstreets			
& his swearing of them		8	00
	£4	9	00

70 / Sessions Records 1:1, 5; File 144. Coller's reference to Canada was probably the disastrous expedition of 40 vessels and 2000 men organized by Sir William Phipps in 1690. Born in 1661, Coller had had a poverty-stricken upbringing in Cambridge, where his father, another John, was on poor relief in 1673. *Cambridge Town Records,* 210. It appears he did eventually marry Elizabeth, who bore him nine children.

71 / She was daughter of a church member and granddaughter of Rev. John Miller of Roxbury, Rowley, and Yarmouth.

72 / Sessions Records 1:79, 86; Files 167, 170. Needham married Mary Jefts in 1703.

73 / She was niece of the notorious Phoebe Page Cutler, whom we shall encounter in chap. 11. He may have been the nephew of William Cheney, executed for rape in Boston on 22 Sept. 1681. Benjamin married Mary Harbet in 1706. Wyman, *Charlestown Genealogies.*

74 / Sessions Records 1:90; File 171.

75 / Cf. Ingram, "Ecclesiastical Justice," 237; half his sample admitted to frequent coitus, half to three times or less.

76 / Pulsifer 1:191; File 15.

77 / Pulsifer 1:15; File 1.

78 / Pulsifer 1:39.

79 / File 43.

80 / File 52, both.

81 / Pulsifer 3:120, 105; File 44.

82 / Pulsifer 3:3.

83 / County Court Records 5:53; File 141.

84 / Pulsifer 4:51; File 102.

85 / File 94; Stone, *Family,* 608.

86 / On law enforcers in colonial New England, see Flaherty, *Privacy,* 189–218.

87 / *Cambridge Town Records,* 52.

88 / Pulsifer 4:13; Sessions Records 1:75, 78. Cf. Winthrop, *Journal* 2:191–92.

89 / Only six were not accounted for. Flaherty argues that law enforcement was lax in New England, but much of his evidence is adduced from English or eighteenth-century New England sources.

90 / Chapin, *Criminal Justice* (see intro., n. 9), 94.

91 / See chap. 11 below.

92 / Cf. a Wiltshire petition of 1606 against a girl's "filthy act of whoredom, by the which licentious life of hers not only Gods wrath may be powred down upon us inhabitants of the town but also her evill example may so greatly corrupt others that greate and extraordinary charge for the maintenance of baseborn children may be imposed uppon us." Ingram, "Ecclesiastical Justice," 239.

93 / Nevers, Pulsifer 3:163; Row, Pulsifer 4:225; Needham, Sessions Records 1:86.

2. Courtship and Patriarchal Authority

1 / Laslett, *World We Have Lost* (see pref., n. 2), 178.

2 / Daniel Scott Smith, "Parental Power and Marriage Patterns," *Journal of Marriage and the Family* 35 (1973).

3 / Pulsifer 1:156; File 17, my italics.

4 / Pulsifer 1:249; File 29. Cf. Pulsifer 1:286; 3:311.

5 / Testimony of Dexter, File 42.

6 / Pinson letter, ibid.

7 / Pulsifer 3:309, my italics.

8 / File 39.

9 / Testimony of Marshall, File 49.

10 / Cf. Faber, "Puritan Criminals" (see chap. 1, n. 43), 100–102.

11 / "The Planter's Wife," *William and Mary Quarterly* 34 (1977): 560.

12 / Pulsifer 3:105, 120; 4:49.

13 / Pulsifer 3:120.

14 / Petition of Mary Parmenter, File 39.

15 / Testimony of Dexter, File 42.

16 / Testimony of Ball, File 55.

17 / Roger Thompson, *Women in Stuart England and America* (London, 1974), 29–30.

18 / William H. Whitmore, ed., *Colonial Laws of Massachusetts 1672–1686* (Boston, 1887), 28.

19 / Gail S. Marcus, "Criminal Procedure in New Haven," in *Saints and Revolutionaries* (see intro., n. 13), 132.

20 / Flaherty, "Law and Morals" (see chap. 1, n. 22), 229.

21 / File 44.

22 / Sessions Records A, 22; File 128.

23 / Fleming et al., File 25; "Harvard College Records," *Publications of the Colonial Society of Massachusetts* 15 (1925): 115–31; Salter et al., File 45.

24 / E.g., Hastings, Pulsifer 3:3; testimony of Woodward, File 59.

25 / File 44; cf. Pulsifer 4:49.

26 / File 163.

27 / Robinson and Wells case, June 1669, File 52. The promise to marry was also a common inducement in England. See Keith Wrightson, "The Puritan Reformation of Manners" (Ph.D. diss., Cambridge University, 1973), 57, 63; Ingram, "Ecclesiastical Justice" (see chap. 1, n. 27), 230; Quaife, *Wanton Wenches* (see pref., n. 13), 59ff.; Michael Macdonald, "Casebooks of Richard Napier" (Ph.D. diss., Princeton University, 1979), 29–30.

28 / Testimony of Richard Temple, File 201.

29 / Testimony of Elizabeth Jefts, File 52.

30 / Pulsifer 1:226; examination, 2 April 1661, File 28. The giving of gifts had sym-

bolic importance, "making clear to the neighbours a contracted couples' new status." Ingram, "Ecclesiastical Justice," 118.

31 / Pulsifer 3:105; testimony of Nathaniel Cutler and wife, 6 Oct. 1674, File 66.

32 / Pulsifer 4:224–25; testimony of Hannah Kelling and William Beale, 6 April 1685, File 125.

33 / File 52; File 55; testimony of Nathaniel Cutler and wife, File 66.

34 / Testimony of Martin, File 17.

35 / Testimony of E. Whitney, File 144; testimony of Moore, File 29.

36 / Daniel Pattison, File 33; File 30.

37 / File 42.

38 / Letter of Increase Mather, cited in Richard Crowder, *No Featherbed to Heaven* (East Lansing, 1968), 212.

39 / File 42.

40 / File 52.

41 / Frank Shuffelton, *Thomas Hooker* (Princeton, 1977), 9, 69.

42 / File 167; File 7.

43 / "Illegitimacy, Sexual Revolution and Social Change," *Journal of Interdisciplinary History* 2 (1971–72): 242–43.

44 / Cf. Cotton Mather's complaint about youth filling the "joy of harvest" with "folly and lewdness." *Humiliations followed by Deliverance* (Boston, 1697), 10.

45 / Quaife, *Wanton Wenches*, 77–88, summarizes English data; see also Richard T. Vann, review of *The Making of the Modern Family*, by Edward Shorter, *Journal of Family History* 1 (1976): 110–11.

46 / Faber, "Puritan Criminals," 142–43; File 56; Wyman, *Charlestown Genealogies* (see chap. 1, n. 63), s.v. Wells.

47 / The sentiment concerning wife and whore may have been conventionally used. Daniel Defoe uses similar words in *Conjugal Lewdness* (London, 1727), 58.

48 / A condition in adolescent girls, much discussed by bawdy writers. It was, according to them, most easily cured by loss of maidenhead. See Thompson, *Unfit* (see chap. 1, n. 15), 74, 76, 97, 108, 160, 166.

49 / Sarah Largin was later imprisoned for fornication and petitioned for release from gaol because of her child's health there in the winter. She was daughter of Edward and Joan Largin, both Charlestown church members; she was adopted by Edward Chalkley when her father died and her mother remarried. Sarah eventually married Henry Streeter. Wyman, *Charlestown Genealogies.*

50 / Goodman Crouch, a Charlestown church member since 1658, was admonished for drunkenness in May 1669 and excommunicated for persistent inebriation in 1674. *Charlestown Church Records,* ed. J. F. Hunnewell (Boston, 1880), vii, viii.

51 / The grand jury presentment of Sarah Crouch is dated 5 April 1670. Danforth wrote a memorandum dated 24 June 1670 of names to be summoned to the September adjournment or to the October sessions which included the names of Sarah Crouch and Thomas Jones accused of fornication before marriage.

52 / Words italicized are interlined in the petition. Files 52, 56.

53 / *Charlestown Church Records,* vii–viii. The three principals in these two cases were all children of church members. On Sarah Jones Smith, see chap. 9.

54 / Pulsifer 1:201.

55 / File 52. Andrew Robinson was convicted in December 1672 of "lascivious cariadges in words and behaviour towards the wife of Joseph Wilson," the Malden blacksmith. We learn from this case that Robinson would have been sixteen or seventeen in

1669. He married Elizabeth Whafe in 1674 and his wife was molested by William Everton nine years later, see chap. 7. James Tufts was killed by Indians at Bloody Brook on 18 Sept. 1675, Deloraine P. Corey, *History of Malden* (Malden, 1899), 327. In April 1673 Elizabeth Wells married Thomas Bathrick. She died ten months later. Wyman, *Charlestown Genealogies,* s.v. Tufts and Wells.

56 / William Symmes was forty-seven in 1674; he was the eldest son of Rev. Zechariah, minister of Charlestown, and brother-in-law of Reading's minister, Rev. John Brock. Jonathan Poole, forty, was the Reading representative at the General Court; he distinguished himself as captain and president of the Council of War in King Philip's War in 1676. Nathaniel Cowdrey was a member of a leading founding family of Reading. His daughter or granddaughter Mary was presented for fornication in 1698 but escaped arrest by flight. File 167; James Savage, *Genealogical Dictionary* (Boston, 1860–62).

57 / Pulsifer 3:105, 120, 125; Files 66, 70. Knowlton appears to have moved away soon after this affair because he married an unmarried mother, Hannah Mirick, in Springfield in western Massachusetts in 1676. File 55. Innes, *Labor* (see pref., n. 17), 135–36, 222.

58 / Sessions Records 1:53; File 201. Richard Graves, "husbandman late of Sudbury now at Chelmsford," had been convicted of fornication with Johanna Perry in Sept. 1695. He was the son of a blacksmith and was apprehended by the constable while working for the Sudbury blacksmith Jonathan Wilson. The constable "being set to victuals, Richard Graves standing and we sitting, he made his escape and sought sanctuary with Zechary Maynard, where he was detained from me despite my requiring him to deliver my prisoner. Goodwife Maynard assisted them." Maynard, the twenty-three-year-old son of a Sudbury selectman, had been convicted of fornication at the same court, but he too had run away! Sessions Records 1:41, 44, 45, 49; Files 163, 201. S. R. Coburn, *History of Dracut* (Lowell, 1922), 3, 67, 371. The religious devotion of Varnum may have been renewed after his presentment with Ezra Coburn in Dec. 1692 for absence from meeting. Wilson Waters, *Chelmsford* (Lowell, 1917), 410.

59 / Peter Burke, "The Imposter," review of *The Return of Martin Guerre* by Natalie Zemon Davis, *London Review of Books,* 19 April 1984.

3. Pregnant Brides and Broken Promises

1 / Quaife, *Wanton Wenches* (see pref., n. 13), 15.

2 / Ibid., 57–58; Smith and Hindus, "Premarital Pregnancy" (see intro., n. 28), 537–70.

3 / Peter Laslett, *Family Life and Illicit Love* (Cambridge, 1977), 130; P.E.H. Hair, "Bridal Pregnancy" (see intro., n. 28), 240–43; "Bridal Pregnancy Further Examined" (see intro., n. 28), 59–70.

4 / Carr and Walsh, "Planter's Wife" (see chap. 2, n. 11), 545, 569.

5 / Hair, "Bridal Pregnancy," 240.

6 / James A. Henretta, "Families and Farms: Mentalité in Pre-Industrial America," *William and Mary Quarterly* 35 (1978): 25, 31; Lutz K. Berkner, "The Stem Family and the Developmental Family," *American Historical Review* 77 (1972): 403.

7 / Vann, review of *Modern Family* (see chap. 2, n. 45), 111.

8 / Laslett, *World We Have Lost* (see pref., n. 2), 173–77; Keith Wrightson and David Levine, *Poverty and Piety in an English Village: Terling 1525–1700* (London, 1979), 132.

9 / The seven-month interval was delineated by Cotton Mather, *Ratio Disciplinae Fratrum Nov-Anglicorum* (Boston, 1726), 143. Although considerably shorter than the

period commonly used by demographers, it was the usual measure throughout the seventeenth century. A prosecution over a child born five weeks early in Plymouth in 1652 is reported in Demos, *Little Commonwealth* (see chap. 1, n. 29), 159, but this was very rare.

10 / Testimony of Matthew Johnson, File 52.

11 / Thompson, *Women* (see chap. 2, n. 71), 134; see chap. 8 below. They could not perform their own marriages, however, as Joseph Hills discovered when the court admonished him in 1656. Pulsifer 1:95; cf. Winthrop, *Journal* (see chap. 1, n. 50), 2, 43–44.

12 / Emil Oberholzer, *Delinquent Saints* (New York, 1956), 13.

13 / File 56.

14 / Pulsifer 3:276; File 84. Her fine was reduced to three pounds.

15 / Pulsifer 4:214; File 123. Thankfull Austin, his wife, died of smallpox on 4 March 1691.

16 / County Court Records 5:97; File 143. They may have been refugees from Dunstable, on the frontier.

17 / Sessions Records 1:59, 62; File 203, dated 23 July 1697.

18 / Sessions Records 1:71; File 167, dated 13 Sept. 1698.

19 / Sessions Records 1:74; File 166, dated 28 June 1698.

20 / File 39, dated 28 Feb. 1665.

21 / File 44, dated 7 April 1668.

22 / File 49, dated 15 Dec. 1668.

23 / File 55, 1671.

24 / File 36, 1664.

25 / Elizabeth Wells, File 52; Susannah Coburn, File 201; also see Sarah Largin, File 56.

26 / The laws and liberties of the colony stipulated that unreasonable denial of a timely marriage gave children the right to seek redress in court. Haskins, *Law and Authority* (see intro., n. 17), 81.

27 / Pulsifer 3:299.

28 / File 56. Cf. the Roys, Pulsifer 1:285, 16 June 1663. In Oct. 1690 Phillip and Mary Goss excused their sin because of delay in granting him a divorce from his first deserting and bigamous wife. File 143; *Court of Assistants* (see intro., n. 15), 3:326.

29 / File 89. Cf. Demos, *Little Commonwealth,* 159.

30 / Testimony of Elizabeth Moore and Mary Noyes, 22 Sept. 1664, File 36. Cf. testimony of Stride, File 102.

31 / Sessions Records 1:13; Files 144, 156. Cf. the Dunster case, chap. 1 above.

32 / File 49, 6 March 1669.

33 / The Wiggins's petition mentions that "they are married together" which may refer to a fresh ceremony. William Marble had been sued for defaming Sarah Bucknam in 1653, see chap. 11 below. Susannah's brother was sued for defiling Elizabeth Procter of Chelmsford in 1680. Pulsifer 3:309.

34 / The midwife's report is quoted in chap. 1 above.

35 / Between these two statements Goody Rutter told Bent that the child, which soon died, was not in her view premature.

36 / Words italicized are cancelled.

37 / A James Taylor is noticed by Savage as marrying in Connecticut in 1641. The James Taylor referred to in Elizabeth's examination would probably have been his son. *Genealogical Dictionary* (see chap. 2, n. 56).

38 / File 43. Joseph was the seventh son of John Bent and was born on 16 May 1641. The Bents had been leading townsmen of Weyhill, Hampshire, and friends of the Noyes

family, but their prestige had declined somewhat in Sudbury. Peter Bent, Joseph's brother, was one of the founders of Marlborough in 1657, whither Joseph seems to have followed him. Those who searched out the providences of God would have had a field day with events on 29 July 1677. Joseph Bent was then killed by "chance medley or casualty" by his nephew Peter, Jr., who was ordered by the Court of Assistants to pay Elizabeth Bent twenty pounds compensation. Joseph's real estate was valued at £431. Powell, *Puritan Village* (see intro., n. 3), 3, 8, 17, 23, 107, 115, 123, 126, 129–30, 157, 206; *Court of Assistants*, 1:86. Savage, *Genealogical Dictionary* (see chap. 2, n. 56); C. Hudson, *History of Marlborough* (Boston, 1862), 45–50, 324.

39 / "They were agreed" or "they were made sure" was how ordinary people expressed it. This status of betrothal was taken from Anglican canon law: after espousals "they were accounted for lawful man and wife before God." Emmison, *Church Courts* (see chap. 1, n. 52), 150. In New England, betrothal was formally defined thus: "By a lawfull contract the court understands the mutuall consent of two parties with the consent of parents or guardians if there be any to be had and a solemne promise of marriage in due time to each other before two competent witnesses." Demos, *Little Commonwealth*, 157. See chap. 7 below.

40 / Whittaker, who moved to Dracut, was later convicted of slander, assault, and fraud. He appears in chap. 9 as a snooper.

41 / This might be an early reference to bundling. Cf. Dexter and Pinson case below.

42 / Pulsifer 1:226; Savage, *Genealogical Dictionary*. Cf. Grant–Crouch case, chap. 2 above.

43 / A man of this name is recorded as living in Lynn, five miles northeast of Malden in 1672. Konig, *Law and Society* (see intro., n. 1), 86. Between 1666 and 1672 he was charged with night-walking, absence from church, uncivil carriages, threatening behavior, assault, and drunkenness. G. F. Dow, ed., *Essex Records* (Salem, 1911–1936), 3:321, 353, 398, 448; 4:292; 5:33–34. Whether this lawlessness was cause or effect of the break-up with Sarah is unknown.

44 / Cf. the fabliau plot adapted in *The Practical Part of Love* (London, 1660) discussed in Thompson, *Unfit* (see chap. 1, n. 15), 76.

45 / File 42. Pinson's first marriage on 2 Aug. 1664 had been to Ann, daughter of Deacon John Cooper of Cambridge. She died on 8 May 1666. Pinson is entered in *Cambridge Vital Records* (Boston, 1914–15), 1:697, as newly arrived in the town in 1666; Lucius R. Paige, *History of Cambridge* (Boston, 1877), 84.

46 / This is the only reference to using an almanac for accurate dating. The common practice was to use events like training or election days as reference points, or else to date things by agricultural seasons like Indian harvest or planting time.

47 / Italicized word cancelled.

48 / Row's violent response to Martha and later to her father might have reinforced suspicions about the death of his wife in 1681. A quarrelsome, drunken woman, estranged from her husband, she was found in bed with "much blood about her so some think she was choak'd with it." No evidence of violence was found, however. Koehler, *Search for Power* (see pref., n. 11), 139.

49 / Joseph, flying the embraces of his mistress, Gen. 39:7–12, seems to have been a commonly used model; cf. *The Mery History of Tom Stitch the Taylor* (London, 1685), 5, reprinted in Roger Thompson, ed., *Samuel Pepys' Penny Merriments* (London, 1976), 282; Francis Osborn, *Advice to a Son* (London, 1656), 57; Anne Yarbrough, "Apprentices as Adolescents in Sixteenth-Century Bristol," *Journal of Social History* 13 (1979): 70, quoting Roger Edgeworth's sermons.

50 / Simon Bradstreet. William Beale, sometime miller, was born in 1630 and had married Martha, daughter of Humphrey and Bridget Bradstreet in 1655. She appears to have been married or betrothed to Thomas Rowlandson, but had obtained an "annulitie of marriage." This led to a court action in 1657 and to two slander suits in 1669 and 1673. The Beales were also involved in a case of battery in 1667. They seem to have come close to separating in 1662 because of violent quarrels over a male servant. From 1676 Beale was elected a selectman of Marblehead and often served as a marshall's deputy. Savage, *Genealogical Dictionary;* Dow, *Essex Records,* 1:332, 348; 2:59; 3:419; 4:161, 269, 280; 5:245; 6:171; 7:130, 297.

51 / This is the only evidence in the case that Martha Beale was pregnant. Had this become evident in the months between the September crisis and the April court case? In September the Rows seemed sure that she was not with child and the Beales had not contradicted them. Had Martha allowed herself to become pregnant since September in order to put pressure on John to marry her? If so, this would be the only example in our records of a girl's using this tactic in order to gain a husband, which has been conjectured as a stratagem employed in England. Stone, *Family* (see pref., n. 9), 607.

52 / Pulsifer 4:224–25; File 125. Wyman, *Charlestown Genealogies* (see chap. 1, n. 63). For two similar cases, see Koehler, *Search for Power,* 97, 99.

53 / Wyman, *Charlestown Genealogies;* Superior Court Records 1686–1700, 2:228; Mass. Hist. Soc. Photostats, 9 Feb. 1697.

54 / E.g., Phoebe Page, chap. 11 below; Hannah Mirick, chap. 2 above; Elizabeth Johnson, chap. 11 below; Elizabeth Holmes, chap. 5 below; Sarah Crouch, chap. 2 above.

55 / Table A represents fornication and bridal pregnancy cases involving church members from 1649 to 1699.

Table A

				Order Book Date			
	1649–63	1663–71	1671–80	1680–86	1868–89	1689–92	1692–99
FORNICATION							
Church Members	4	5	16	6	2	3	9
Others	8	4	6	5	2	10	16
BRIDAL PREGNANCY							
Church Members	5	7	2	10	3	3	11
Others	2	3	7	3	1	2	6

56 / Details are given in chap. 6 below.

57 / *Anatomie of Abuses* (London, 1683), 27.

58 / Quoted in Laslett, *World We Have Lost,* 172.

59 / *Of Christian Oeconomie,* in *The Workes . . . of William Perkins* (London, 1626), 65.

60 / Wrightson and Levine, *Terling,* 132; Carr and Walsh, "Planter's Wife," 544.

61 / Koehler, *Search for Power,* 354.

62 / *Colonial Laws of Mass.* (see chap. 2, n. 18), 28.

63 / Smith and Hindus, "Premarital Pregnancy," 561; an eight-and-one-half-month interval was used here.

64 / Pulsifer 3:75; File 62.

65 / Henretta, "Families and Farms," 25, 31.

66 / Sessions Records 1:40.

67 / Pulsifer 1:53, 125.

68 / Austins, File 123; Cumminses, File 143.

69 / Coller, Sessions Records 1:1; Whiting, ibid., 57; Smith, County Court Records 5:86. On the bitter winters of 1686 and 1690 and the food shortages of 1696–98, see Karen Ordahl Kupperman, "Climate and Mastery of the Wilderness," in David D. Hall and David Grayson Allen, eds., *Seventeenth-Century New England* (Boston, 1984), 30–31, 35–40.

70 / Edward Eggleston, *The Transit of Civilisation* (New York, 1900), 7.

71 / Flaherty, "Law and Morals" (see chap. 2, n. 20), 244.

72 / E.g., Jones and Coller, chap. 2 above.

73 / *Oxford English Dictionary* (hereafter cited as *OED*).

74 / Pulsifer 1:125.

75 / "Suffolk Records" (see intro., n. 4), 959. Testimony of Wing, File 131. In England, Richard Napier did the same thing, see Macdonald, "Napier Casebooks" (see chap. 2, no. 27), 23.

76 / Fifty-three percent; see chap. 6 below.

4. Sexual Deviance and Abuse

1 / J. Hajnal, "European Marriage Patterns in Perspective," in *Population and History*, ed. D. V. Glass and D.E.C. Eversley (London, 1965).

2 / Edward Shorter, *The Making of Modern Family* (London, 1976), 104, 112; Stone, *Family* (see pref., n. 9), 52.

3 / I have found no evidence for coitus interruptus in the Middlesex Records. For one possible reference to anal sex, see the exceptional Walker–Phipps case, chap. 8 below. References to orality in Slater's libel, discussed in chap. 11 below, seem to be scatological.

4 / Jean-Louis Flandrin, "Mariage tardif et Vie Sexuelle," *Annales E.S.C.* 27 (1972); Ingram, "Ecclesiastical Justice" (see chap. 1, n. 27), chap. 6; Quaife, *Wanton Wenches* (see pref., n. 13), 246.

5 / John Demos, *Entertaining Satan* (New York, 1982), 236, 471; Flaherty, *Privacy* (see chap. 1, n. 7), 219; P.E.H. Hair, *Before the Bawdy Court* (London, 1972), 186; Smith, *Colonial Justice* (see intro., n. 7), 103; Thompson, *Women* (see chap. 2, n. 17), 46; Winthrop, *Journal* (see chap. 3, n. 11), 2:84; Robert F. Oaks, "Things Fearful to Name," *Journal of Social History* 12 (1978): 273, 278; Murrin, "Trial by Jury" (see intro., n. 13), 167, 176, 178, 193.

6 / Thomas Cobbett, *A Fruitfull and Usefull Discourse* (London, 1656), 173–83; Samuel Danforth, *Cry of Sodom* (Cambridge, Mass., 1674); Increase Mather, *Solemn Advice to Young Men* (Boston, 1695), 24, 36; Cotton Mather, *Manductio ad Ministerium* (Boston, 1726), 20; idem, *Pure Nazarite* (Boston, 1723); Michael Wigglesworth, *Day of Doom*, ed. K. B. Murdock (New York, 1929), 23; David J. Hibler, "Sexual Rhetoric in Seventeenth-Century American Literature" (Ph.D. diss., Notre Dame University, 1970), 29–36.

7 / Cited in Chapin, *Criminal Justice* (see intro., n. 9), 10.

8 / Samuel Eliot Morison, ed., "Charles Morton's *Compendium Physicae*," *Pubs. Col. Soc. Mass.* 33 (1940): 143; cf. Richard Burton, *Anatomy of Melancholy* (London, 1961 ed.), 2:33; William Prynne, *Histriomastix* (London, 1633), 378; Stone, *Family*, 46, 484, 495.

9 / Edmund S. Morgan, "The Diary of Michael Wigglesworth," *Pubs. Col. Soc. Mass.* 35 (1942–46): 311–40. Cf. Wesley Frank Craven and W. B. Hayward, eds., *The*

Journal of Richard Norwood (New York, 1945), 14, 17, 24, 26, 27, 51, 71, 78, 81; Stone, *Family* (see pref., n. 9), 512.

10 / Worthington C. Ford, ed., *The Diary of Cotton Mather* (New York, 1957), 1:78–79.

11 / Quoted in John Demos, ed., *Remarkable Providences* (New York, 1972), 134.

12 / *Addresses to Old Men, Young Men and Children* (Boston, 1690), 73; *Pure Nazarite*, 1.

13 / Pulsifer 1:169.

14 / Ch E. 10. 36; *Court of Assistants* (see intro., n. 15), 1:87; Pulsifer 3:108.

15 / Murrin, "Trial by Jury," 179–80.

16 / Haskins, *Law and Authority* (see intro., n. 17), 150; *Court of Assistants*, 3:199.

17 / Pulsifer 1:218; File 23.

18 / I have an article forthcoming on this topic.

19 / Thompson, "Popular Reading" (see pref., n. 7), 660–67.

20 / Pulsifer 1:113; Smith, *Colonial Justice*, 389–91.

21 / Pulsifer 4:153; File 112. She was the daughter of James Ross the Scottish ex-prisoner of war.

22 / Pulsifer 1:267; File 30.

23 / Illegible.

24 / Pulsifer 3:46; File 60. See chap. 2 above.

25 / Pulsifer 4:230; File 124.

26 / John Fownell, the Charlestown miller since 1645, had died on 19 March 1673. Montgomery was only eighteen. Savage, *Genealogical Dictionary* (see chap. 2, n. 56); Wyman, *Charlestown Genealogies* (see chap. 1, n. 63).

27 / Used with a sexual connotation?

28 / Pulsifer 3:144; File 72.

29 / *Watertown Records* (Watertown, 1894), 49, 52. Pulsifer 1:124, 126. Phillips, who did not marry until 1681 when he was forty-eight, later became a magistrate. Henry Bond, *Watertown Genealogies* (Boston, 1855). Another brother, Samuel, was involved in the slander suit of *Hall v. Whaley* in 1651. He started the rumor that Elizabeth Hall, whose husband was in England, had claimed that "all things are common as in the apostles tyme, mens wives allsoe." The case never came to judgment. Nourse, *Lancaster* (see chap. 1, n. 23), 17–19.

30 / Chadwick had led a group of apprentices who stole on the sabbath. Pulsifer 1:254, Dec. 1661. On 4 Oct. 1671 John Chadwick was acquitted of fornication with Susannah Woodward, but convicted of unseasonable company-keeping and lying about his prenuptial fornication with his wife Hannah. His evidence incriminating Thomas Hastings, Jr., however, looks distinctly suspect and self-serving. On 5 Sept. 1671 he was formally warned out of Watertown. It appears that the Chadwicks may have moved at that time to Plymouth Plantation. Pulsifer 3:2. *Watertown Records*, 107.

31 / Phillips seems to have been acquitted. Files 40, 42; S. A. Green, "A Local Scandal," *New England Historic Genealogical Society Register* 51 (1897): 68–69. Mary Davis's mother had died in Watertown, aged thirty-three, before she was able to answer charges of adultery with James Knap on 9 April 1656. Mary, then fourteen, had already lost her father. It may have been at this time that she went to live with the Springs. Her grandfather, John Spring of Watertown, had been separated from his second wife for several years during the 1650s.

32 / My italics.

33 / Pulsifer 3:120, 126, 160, 163; Files 72, 75, 76. *Court of Assistants*, 1:100. Savage, *Genealogical Dictionary*.

34 / Bethya was nineteen; she was the granddaughter of Captain Edward Johnson.

35 / *Court of Assistants*, 1:158; Pulsifer 3:311; File 89.

36 / Pulsifer 3:158; File 82.

37 / Cases here do not include alleged force used by Tufts, Knowlton, Row, and Jones already discussed. If included, the average would still be only one case every four years!

38 / "Suffolk Records" (see intro., n. 4), 182–83.

39 / Ibid., 1062; Superior Court Records 1686–1700, 18.

40 / *Watertown Records*, 1:49, 52; Bond, *Watertown Genealogies*.

41 / File 72; "Suffolk Records," 485.

42 / See chap. 2 above.

43 / Pulsifer 3:144.

44 / Nourse, *Lancaster*, 129; County Court Records 5:73, 76, 78, 88.

45 / Testimony of Pierce, File 82.

46 / Morgan, "Puritans and Sex" (see chap. 1, n. 27), also discusses the cases involving Peter Grant and Thomas Hawes, the files of which are missing.

5. *Adolescent Culture*

1 / See Roger Thompson, "Adolescent Culture in Colonial Massachusetts," *Journal of Family History* 9 (1984): 130–31 for a review of recent research.

2 / Flaherty, *Privacy* (see chap. 1, n. 7), 177; E. S. Morgan, *Puritan Family* (New York, 1966), 27.

3 / Morgan, *Puritan Family*, 120–21.

4 / File 49.

5 / Linda A. Bissell, "Fathers, Sons and Wealth in Colonial Windsor, Connecticut," *Journal of Family History* 3 (1978): 141, 148.

6 / Koehler, *Search for Power* (see pref., n. 12), 12.

7 / See chap. 10 below.

8 / Pulsifer 3:290; S. E. Morison, *Harvard College in the Seventeenth Century* (Cambridge, Mass., 1936), 460; Corey, *Malden* (see chap. 2, n. 55), 329.

9 / File 45; cf. chap. 11 below.

10 / Pulsifer 1:156, 193; File 6; Christina Hole, *English Folklore* (London, 1945), 23; Corey, *Malden*, 124.

11 / Pulsifer 1:217–18; File 25.

12 / Pulsifer 1:295; File 24; Thompson, *Unfit* (see chap. 1, n. 15), 166–68; Otho T. Beale, "*Aristotle's Master-Piece* in America: A Landmark in the Folklore of Medicine," *William and Mary Quarterly* 20 (1963): 207–22.

13 / File 36; see chap. 11 below.

14 / File 45; on Salter, see chap. 7 below.

15 / File 52.

16 / Files 47, 49; Robert G. Pope, ed., "The Notebook of Rev. John Fiske," *Pubs. Col. Soc. Mass.* 47 (1974): 209–12. Richard Hildreth challenged the prosecution and called for Fiske's dismissal; for this, Hildreth was presented in the county court in April 1670.

17 / Pulsifer 3:120; File 72. Cf. Thomas Johnson, "Jonathan Edwards and the 'Young Folks' Bible'," *New England Quarterly* 5 (1932): 37–54.

18 / "Suffolk Records" (see intro., n. 4), 485.

19 / These are the only records of a magistrate's acting in a petty sessional capacity that have survived for seventeenth-century Middlesex. "Harvard College Records" (see chap. 2, n. 23), 115–31.

20 / Pulsifer 4:22; File 97; see chap. 11 below.

21 / File 201.

22 / Pulsifer 1:274; File 39.

23 / Pulsifer 4:196; File 113; Morison, *Harvard College,* 460–62.

24 / File 141; Nourse, *Lancaster* (see chap. 1, n. 23), 129; Pulsifer 1:124, 127–28, 187, 197, 254; File 45; Pulsifer 3:244, 291; Files 40, 49, 141.

25 / File 49.

26 / *Watertown Records,* 2:12; S. Sewall, *History of Woburn* (Boston, 1868), 64; *Cambridge Town Records* (see chap. 1, n. 23), 164, 178, 231.

27 / Morison, *Harvard College,* 461.

28 / R. R. Wheeler, *Concord: Climate for Freedom* (Concord, 1967), 19.

29 / Perry Miller, *The New England Mind: From Colony to Province* (Boston, 1961), part 1; Thompson, *Women* (see chap. 2, n. 17), 69–72; Emory Elliott, *Power and the Pulpit* (Princeton, 1975), 50, 116–18, 125, 127; Thomas Shepard, *Eye Salve, or a Watch-Word from our Lord* (Cambridge, Mass., 1673), 44; Increase Mather, *Discourse concerning the Danger of Apostacy* (Boston, 1679); idem, *A Call from Heaven* (Boston, 1679), 69–72; idem, *The Necessity of Reformation* (Boston, 1679).

30 / *The Family Well-Ordered* (Boston, 1712), 117–18. On this theme, see Lawrence R. Towner, " 'A Fondness for Freedom': Servant Protest in Puritan Society," *William and Mary Quarterly* 19 (1962): 279–97.

31 / George Selement, "Elite and Popular Minds," *William and Mary Quarterly* 41 (1984): 38.

32 / File 49; Flaherty, *Privacy,* 177, 196; Mass. Hist. Soc. Photostats, 31 Oct. 1679; R. Frothingham, *History of Charlestown* (Boston, 1845), 199; Paige, *Cambridge* (see chap. 3, n. 45), 97.

33 / Testimony of Hobart et al., File 162.

34 / Ingram, "Ecclesiastical Justice" (see chap. 1, n. 27), 347, 372; Keith Wrightson, *English Society 1580–1680* (London, 1982), 41–43, 75–79.

35 / Cf. Sewall's anger at the celebration of April Fool's Day, David D. Hall, "The Mental World of Samuel Sewall," in *Saints and Revolutionaries* (see intro., n. 13), 84.

36 / Cotton Mather, *Diary,* ed. Worthington C. Ford (Boston, 1912), 67–68; David Levin, *Cotton Mather* (Cambridge, Mass., 1978), 74.

37 / Pulsifer 1:6.

38 / See chap. 7 below.

39 / *Puritan Village* (see intro., n. 3), chaps. 8, 9.

40 / *Four Generations* (Ithaca, 1970), chap. 4.

41 / T. H. Breen, "English Origins and New World Developments: The Case of the Covenanted Militia," *Past and Present* 57 (1972): 74–96; Natalie Zemon Davis, *Society and Culture in Early Modern France* (London, 1975), 111.

42 / Frothingham, *Charlestown,* 204.

43 / Koehler, *Search for Power,* 59.

44 / Mass. Hist. Soc. Photostats, 28 May 1679.

45 / Paige, *Cambridge,* 76.

46 / Winthrop, *Journal* (see chap. 1, n. 50), 2:319; Lilley Eaton, *Genealogical History of Reading* (Boston, 1874), 24; Robert E. Wall, *Massachusetts Bay: The Crucial Decade* (New Haven, 1972), 96–97.

47 / E.g., Pulsifer 3:3, 244; 4:4, 13, 22; Sessions Records 1:87; File 49.

48 / Prynne, *Histriomastix* (see chap. 4, n. 8), 540.

6. Typical Adolescents

1 / Quoted in Breen, *Good Ruler* (see intro., n. 5), 15–16.

2 / Quoted in Stephen Foster, "English Puritanism and North American Institutions," in *Saints and Revolutionaries* (see intro., n. 13), 6, 10.

3 / David M. Scobey, "Revising the Errand," *William and Mary Quarterly* 41 (1984): 12.

4 / Quoted in Chapin, *Criminal Justice* (see intro., n. 9), 81.

5 / *Puritan Family* (see chap. 4, n. 2), chap. 7.

6 / Scobey, "Revising the Errand," 27.

7 / Smith, *As a City* (see intro., n. 14), 61.

8 / Koehler, *Search for Power* (see pref., n. 12), 59.

9 / Selement, "Elite and Popular Minds" (see chap. 5, n. 31), 38.

10 / T. H. Breen and Stephen Foster, "Social Cohesion in Seventeenth-Century New England," *Journal of American History* 60 (1973–74): 5–22.

11 / Smith, *As a City*, 59–60.

12 / Robert G. Pope, *The Half-Way Covenant* (Princeton, 1969), 13–27; idem, "New England and *The New England Mind*," *Journal of Social History* 3 (1969–70): 95–108.

13 / Selement, "Elite and Popular Minds," 32–48. Patricia Caldwell, *The Puritan Conversion Narrative* (Cambridge, 1983), chap. 4.

14 / Chapin, *Criminal Justice*, 139–42; Flaherty, "Law and Morals" (see chap. 1, n. 22), 245.

15 / Bailyn, *New England Merchants* (see intro., n. 3); Paul R. Lucas, "Colony or Commonwealth," *William and Mary Quarterly* 24 (1967): 89–90.

16 / Paul Boyer and Stephen Nissenbaum, *Salem Possessed* (Cambridge, Mass., 1974); Innes, *Labor in a New Land* (see pref., n. 12).

17 / Laslett and Oosterveen, "Bastardy" (see intro., n. 28), 282–84.

18 / Pulsifer 1:125; 3:281; Sessions Records 1:187; on Parmenters, Pulsifer 3:299; Files 39, 50. See chap. 11 below.

19 / George Lawrence, the father of Grace and Martha, had been admonished by the Watertown selectmen for neglecting his children's education in 1670. *Watertown Records* (see chap. 4, n. 29), 102, 128. Sessions Records 1:69, 81. Mary Edes claimed that her husband, a seaman, was the father of her child. Unfortunately a sailor had witnessed his death in the West Indies five years previously. Files 203, 205; Sessions Records 1:75; File 52. She had been a church member since 1680, but was admonished by the church in December 1698 for her obstinacy and impenitence for her sin. *Charlestown Church Records* (see chap. 2, n. 50), xii, 18. Pulsifer 3:276.

20 / Pulsifer 1:7, 127, 230, 255; Files 38, 44, 51, 52; Pulsifer 3:217; 4:138; Sessions Records A, 35; Sessions Records 1:8. *Court of Assistants* (see intro., n. 15), 1:125–26. Christopher Grant's estate was valued at £296 in 1685.

21 / Pulsifer 1:6–8, 23, 100, 124, 127; 3:107; County Court Records 5:5. "Old Knap" had been fined five pounds in 1642 for selling beer for two years without a license. Bond, *Watertown* (see chap. 4, n. 29), 1075. Cf. *Watertown Records*, 1:17, 24, 25, 28, 41, 46, 48, 55, 104, 107. James, also a carpenter, moved to Groton where he made good, often serving as selectman and becoming sergeant of the militia. May, *Plantation* (see chap. 1, n. 43), 1–6.

22 / According to Faber's investigations of *all* criminal cases in Middlesex, "no fewer than 133 offenders or 42.2% of the cohort of 315 came from families with more than one transgressor." "Puritan Criminals" (see chap. 1, n. 43), 133.

23 / Pulsifer 1:113, 191, 302; 3:32, 99; 4:44, 173, 196; County Court Records 5:59; Pulsifer 1:260; File 52; Sessions Records 1:95; File 171. In 1702, the selectmen of Reading exchanged Abigail Lilly for another woman on the poor rate in Reading. Corey, *Malden* (see chap. 2, n. 55), 396. John Cromwell had died in 1661. He had owned an Indian trucking house in Tyngsborough. Seaborne was the daughter of William Batchelor of Charlestown. H. A. Hazen, *History of Billerica* (Boston, 1883), 45. Cromwell was a church member. His wife had been found to be pregnant on 12 March 1657 by a jury of four midwives. Wyman, *Charlestown Genealogies* (see chap. 1, n. 63). Bethia Hyde, aged nineteen, was the orphan daughter of Job and Elizabeth Fuller Hyde. Her paternal grandfather was deacon of Newton; in 1708 she married her cousin Jacob Hyde. Mary Bartlett came from a pauperized Newton family. Her father was convicted of misbehaving in the meeting house in 1691, her brother Joseph for premarital fornication in 1695, and her sister Martha for fornication four times in the early eighteenth century. File 143, Sessions Records 1:46. Sawtle, Lilly, and Wells all eventually found husbands.

24 / Laslett and Oosterveen, "Bastardy," 284.

25 / Dickerman, Ball, Polly, Salter, Row, Fiske, Lawrence, Parker, Coller, Beale, Bowers, Dutton, and Blanchard families. See chap. 7 below.

26 / Dunster, Phillips, Eliot, Hyde, Weld, Graves, Coburn, Holmes, and Cross families.

27 / Dunster, Grant, Knap, Parmenter, Fiske, Marble, Edes, Lawrence, Woodward, Bartlett, Sprague, Mirrick, Harris, Ross, Jones, Wallis, Maynard, Baker, and Page families.

28 / See chap. 11 below. Savage, *Genealogical Dictionary* (see chap. 2, n. 56); Powell, *Puritan Village* (see intro., n. 3).

29 / Bond, *Watertown Genealogies* (see chap. 4, n. 29); Corey, *Malden* (see chap. 2, n. 55), 113, 120–21, 327; Wyman, *Charlestown Genealogies* (see chap. 1, n. 63).

30 / *Women* (see chap. 2, n. 17), 148–53.

31 / Pulsifer 1:10; 3:311.

32 / Pulsifer 1:260; Sessions Records 1:21.

33 / Pulsifer 3:44, 196; 4:153; File 112. Gookin's daughter Elizabeth had married Rev. John Eliot, Jr., of Newton as his second wife in 1666. Eliot died in 1668 at the age of thirty-two, leaving this John, aged one. The latter graduated in the Harvard class of 1685. Hannah was the granddaughter of Richard Brackett, who had been captain of the Billerica militia and deacon of the church. Her father John, however, was in the lowest quarter of the Billerica tax lists in 1663 and 1679. Faber, "Puritan Criminals" (see chap. 1, n. 43), 115; Savage, *Genealogical Dictionary*.

34 / Pulsifer 1:288; Bethia Mitchelson's partner was Daniel Weld, nephew of Rev. Thomas, minister of Roxbury.

35 / Pulsifer 1:288; File 40; Pulsifer 3:75, 190; Sessions Records 1:79.

36 / Goodenow, Parmenter, Johnson, Upham, Shepard, Fletcher, Hills, Norton, Dunster, Wade, Hastings, Gookin, Eliot, Sherman, Bemis, Weld, Mitchelson, Graves, Fleming, Cawdrey, Wainwright, Phillips, Carter, Phipps, Baldwin, Warren, Spring, Grout, Stone, Frost, Sprague, Mason, Barnard, Allen, and Stearns.

37 / *Benefit of a Well-Ordered Conversation* (Boston, 1684), 13.

38 / *Help for Distressed Parents* (Boston, 1695), 7.

39 / Cotton Mather, *Magnalia Christi Americana* (1702; reprint, Hartford, 1820), bk. 3, 103.

40 / See chap. 3 above.

41 / See chap. 5 above.

42 / Pulsifer 4:196; File 113; Morison, *Harvard College* (see chap. 5, n. 8), 460–62; "Harvard Col. Rec." (see chap. 2, n. 23), 115–20. Cf. Sarah L. Bailey, *Historical Sketches of Old Andover* (Boston, 1880), 33–34.

43 / Silvanus Negro was the father to the child born to Elizabeth Parker of Lancaster in 1672. Nourse, *Lancaster* (see chap. 1, n. 23), 92–93.

44 / *The Protestant Temperament* (New York, 1977), 55.

45 / Ross W. Beales, "In Search of the Historical Child," *American Quarterly* 27 (1975): 379–98; Pope, *Half-Way Covenant,* 70, 247, 280–86; Owen C. Watkins, *The Puritan Experience* (London, 1972), 47, 56, 64, 76, 113, 176, 231; Daniel B. Shea, *Spiritual Autobiography in Early America* (Princeton, 1968), 91, 106, 127; Michael McGiffert, ed., *God's Plot* (Amherst, 1972), 42–45; Craven and Hayward, *Norwood Journal* (see chap. 4, n. 9), 12; Michael Walzer, *The Revolution of the Saints* (New York, 1973), 140–41.

46 / Pope, *Half-Way Covenant,* 70; R. C. Richardson, *Puritanism in North-West England* (Manchester, 1972), 112

47 / This phrase was grounds for a slander suit in 1651. Nourse, *Lancaster* (see chap. 1, n. 23), 17–19. Cf. Christine Leigh Heyrman, "Specters of Subversion, the Society of Friends," in *Saints and Revolutionaries* (see intro., n. 13), 68.

48 / Pulsifer 3:4.

49 / Pulsifer 1:296; 3:120.

50 / Quoted in Morgan, *Puritan Family,* 75. Bowers was fostered in the Bowtell family. See chap. 7 below.

51 / In 1667 Nevers had been convicted of turning his back on the ordinance of baptism.

52 / Christopher Hill, *The World Turned Upside Down* (London, 1975), chap. 15.

53 / Ashton, *Reformation and Revolution* (see intro., n. 12), 326.

54 / Savage, *Genealogical Dictionary,* 3:79, 293; cf. P. Ross, *The Scot in America* (New York, 1896), 48–49.

55 / Pulsifer 1:48, 68, 84, 125; 4:153; File 112; Sessions Records 1:1.

56 / Pulsifer 1:83, 240; File 29; Pulsifer 1:272; File 32.

57 / Nicholas Wallis was forced by the court to marry Jane Lindes, Pulsifer 1:83.

58 / Pulsifer 1:280; File 33.

59 / Pulsifer 1:113, 191; Files 15, 20. One of her paramours was a married man, Daniel McDonnell.

60 / Pulsifer 1:158. John Crownwell and Elizabeth, the wife of George Polly, convicted of dalliance in June 1658. She was born Elizabeth Winn and had married Polly in May 1649 and already had four children. In December 1674 he was hauled before the Woburn selectmen for harboring visitors. He riposted: "He wold entertaine them for all the townsmen [selectmen]; and that the woman shold not goe out of towne for any of them." He was fined and subsequently humbled himself. Sewall, *Woburn* (see chap. 5, n. 26), 47. It seems probable that the Edward Polly convicted of fornication with Abigail Lilly in 1691 was their son. County Court Records 5:96.

61 / Pulsifer 1:281.

62 / Pulsifer 3:144, 237; Sessions Records 1:1, 32. In Oct. 1678 James Scott was sentenced for fornication with Mal Negro, twenty stripes. In June 1682 John Levistone and his wife, of Billerica, were convicted of premarital fornication. Pulsifer 4:41. John Law's misdemeanors are described in chap. 8; those of John Roy in chap. 5.

63 / Innes, *Labor in a New Land,* 130, 131, 143.

64 / Edward Randolph reported "not above two hundred slaves" in Massachusetts in 1676. By 1705 Governor Dudley estimated that the black population had increased to 550. L. J. Greene, *The Negro in Colonial New England* (New York, 1966), 79–80.

65 / Pulsifer 1:64, 189; 3:44, 176, 211, 217, 219, 237, 262, 275; 4:139, 209; County Court Records 5:78, 85; Sessions Records 1:95; Files 9, 38, 42, 51. A more serious case of a Negro who in 1676 had privately conveyed away her bastard was tried by the Court of Assistants. *Court of Assistants*, 1:29–30, 33.

66 / In two of these cases the sentences, a forty shilling fine or ten stripes, were the same as for white couples. In the third case, Dorcas Stone, who accused Primus, Mr. Angier's Negro in 1699, was fined three pounds or ten stripes without any explanation. She was the thirty-seven-year-old granddaughter of Deacon Gregory Stone, sometime representative of Cambridge at the General Court. Rebecca Hamlett, the fifteen-year-old daughter of Jacob of Woburn and granddaughter of Thomas Dutton to be met with in chap. 7, was convicted of fornication with William Wyman's Negro Jack "many times" in 1691. She was a baptized "child of the church." The Malden records include the additional allegation of Sarah Howard's "misdeeds" with Samuel Bucknam's Negro Peter. Corey, *Malden*, 395.

67 / Greene, *Negro*, 157. The arrival of a vessel in Boston in 1678 carrying some fifty slaves, mainly women and children, may have had contributory significance. Frothingham, *Charlestown* (see chap. 5, n. 32), 212. Robert C. Trombley and Robert H. Moore, "Black Puritan: The Negro in Seventeenth-Century Massachusetts," *William and Mary Quarterly* 24 (1967): 224–42, allude to an embryonic abolitionist movement in neighboring Essex county in 1690, n. 26.

68 / File 123. Carter, aged about forty, had been married some fifteen years and had six children, one of whom, John, was admonished by the Woburn selectmen in 1699 for misspending his time. Sewall, *Woburn* (see chap. 5, n. 26), 57. See chap. 7 for his father, Capt. John.

69 / Pulsifer 4:209, 227; Files 117, 123.

70 / Examination was conducted by Robert Bridges, the magistrate at Lynn in Essex County, the next town to Reading.

71 / I.e., Indian corn harvest.

72 / Pulsifer 1:64; File 9. This view is endorsed by Trombley and Moore, "Black Puritan."

73 / Pulsifer 1:73. Greene, *Negro*, 19–20, refers to Pequot women and children being enslaved in 1636.

74 / Pulsifer 3:219. Keeny appeared late at the superior court in Sept. 1678 and his case was remanded to the next session. There is no further record of his ever being tried. *Court of Assistants*, 3:126.

75 / Pulsifer 1:71, 218; Files 13, 23. The obvious ignorance of both girls about what was being done to them sexually belies the assumption that in such an earthy, agrarian society children would learn about sexuality from observation in field and farmyard. One of these Indian harassers, Thomas Dublet, later played an important role as a go-between in ransoming Mrs. Rowlandson after King Philip's War and witnessed a deed conveying Indian land to Marlborough in 1684. Hudson, *Marlborough* (see chap. 3, n. 38), 91.

76 / Kai Erikson, *Wayward Puritans* (New York, 1966), part 1.

Part 2. Married Mores

1 / Quoted in Koehler, *Search for Power* (see pref., n. 12), 37.

2 / "Model of Christian Charity," in *Winthrop Papers,* ed. Allan Forbes (Boston, 1929), 1:290–91.

3 / *Journal* (see chap. 1, n. 50), 1:299.

4 / Demos, *Remarkable Providences* (see chap. 4, n. 11), 134.

5 / *Journal* 2:239.

6 / William and Malleville Haller, "The Puritan Art of Love," *Huntington Library Quarterly* 5 (1942): 235–72; James T. Johnson, *A Society Ordained by God* (Nashville, 1970); Edmund Leites, "The Duty of Desire," *Comparative Civilisations Quarterly* 3 (1979): 40–82.

7 / Thompson, *Unfit* (see chap. 1, n. 15); idem, "Popular Reading" (see pref., n. 7); idem, *Penny Merriments* (see chap. 3, n. 49).

8 / Thompson, *Women* (see chap. 2, n. 17). Cf. C. Dallett Hemphill, "Women in Court . . . Salem 1636–1783," *William and Mary Quarterly* 39 (1982): 164–75; she detects a declining status for women after 1670.

9 / Kathleen M. Davis, "The Sacred Condition of Equality," *Social History* 5 (1977): 563–79.

10 / John Halkett, *Milton and the Idea of Matrimony* (New Haven, 1970), chap. 1.

11 / Stone, *Family* (see pref., n. 9), 198.

12 / Ibid., 202; Koehler, *Search for Power,* 15–23, 31, 136, 160, 441; Mary M. Dunn, "Saints and Sisters," *American Quarterly* 30 (1978): 582–601.

7. Marital Problems

1 / See my "The Transit of Civilisation: The Case of Thomas Danforth," to be published in a festschrift for Hans Galinsky by Naar of Tubingen under the editorship of Winfried Herget in 1986.

2 / John Benjamin of Watertown.

3 / Words of Martha are cancelled to illegibility.

4 / Testimony of Richard Wall.

5 / The right-hand side of the document is damaged.

6 / Testimony of wife of John Fuller.

7 / Savage, *Genealogical Dictionary* (see chap. 2, n. 56). A William Clements, Jr., of Cambridge died on 16 July 1669, and may have been either this man or a child of the second marriage. In 1672 William Clements gave Daniel Hudson all his estate "on condition of support for himself and wife Ann for the residue of their lives." This may have been the parents of this William. The family lived on the south side of the Charles River. *Cambridge Town Records* (see chap. 1, n. 23), 128, 161.

8 / Pulsifer 1:71, 85, 101; File 20. Cf. Uffit case in New Haven, Koehler, *Search for Power* (see pref., n. 12), 144, and Miller case in Springfield, Innes, *Labor in a New Land* (see pref., n. 17), 142.

9 / This metaphor for impotence was a cliché of street literature. See Thompson, "Popular Reading" (see pref., n. 7), 653–71, and idem, *Penny Merriments* (see chap. 3, n. 49), 247–76.

10 / Both were inhabitants of Salem, the latter the twenty-three-year-old son of a wealthy and esteemed merchant and town deputy, Walter Price.

11 / A leading witness was Lydia, the wife of Josiah Dustin, an original settler in Reading, and a church member since 1650. Her husband died in 1671. In 1692 she and her daughters Sarah and Mary (Colson) were all accused of witchcraft. She was acquitted at the age of eighty in Jan. 1693, even though, in Calef's words, "if there were a witch in the

world she was one, as having been so accounted of, for 20 or 30 Years." Eaton, *Reading* (see chap. 5, n. 46), 3, 7; Corey, *Malden* (see chap. 2, n. 55), 332; Roger Thompson, *The Witches of Salem* (London, 1982), 153–54.

12 / On the requirements of a husband to provide, see Morgan, *Puritan Family* (see chap. 5, n. 2), 65–66.

13 / File 52.

14 / This was neither the first nor the last time they appeared in Massachusetts courts. In 1649 Samuel had been convicted of provoking a fight in Lynn in neighboring Essex County, where he had lived since 1637. In November 1664 a complaint was heard in the Essex County Court about the couple's disorderly living. Hannah was charged with "oft leaving her husband" and Samuel with "not providing necessities for her." The following year Hannah's father, John Johnson of Andover, brought her according to his bond into court which sentenced her to be severely whipped for lying, cursing, and stealing. In 1670, after their brief stay in Reading, they moved to Andover, where "their uncomfortable living" caused the selectmen endless problems. In 1674 Hannah was convicted of housebreaking in Andover on the Lord's Day and stealing rum, sugar, linen, and money. After a court appearance in 1675, the Essex Court gave the selectmen permission in 1678 "to dispose the children to deliver them from much suffering." Dow, *Essex Records* (see chap. 3, n. 43), 1:95, 174; 3:219, 274; 5:155, 350–51; 6:26, 425.

15 / Pulsifer 1:83, 89, 118, 196. Mansfield, a goldsmith by training, was the son of Sir John, a London goldsmith. According to his brother-in-law, Robert Keayne, he had been shipped out to Massachusetts in the hope that the bracing atmosphere and the ministrations of another brother-in-law, Rev. John Wilson, would work reformation. Yet he frittered away the money the censorious Keayne lent him on "drink and company-keeping" and provoked quarrels and disturbances "in his distempered fits." Disinherited by Keayne in 1653, he tried unsuccessfully to gain a share of the colony minting from John Hull and Robert Saunderson the following year. In 1666 Ezekiel Cheever complained that Mansfield "is suffered to teach and take away his scholars." In 1668 Mansfield was in "extremity of poverty" and left only eight pounds when he died in 1674, aged seventy-four. His wife was Mary, daughter of John Gove, who died in 1648. Frothingham, *Charlestown* (see chap. 5, n. 32), 148; Wyman, *Charlestown Genealogies* (see chap. 1, n. 63); Bernard Bailyn, ed., *The Apologia of Robert Keayne* (New York, 1965), 43–45.

16 / He was a Wiltshireman by birth who had married the daughter of John Peirce of Watertown in the early 1640s. Elizabeth died in the early 1660s having declined into insanity. Savage, *Genealogical Dictionary*.

17 / Pulsifer 1:137, 166; File 16. Their daughter Mary was convicted of fornication in 1671. File 55, and chap. 1 above. The *Watertown Records* indicate that the selectmen had already been involved with the Balls in the winter of 1656–57, when three children were put out. They ordered that "Sister Baall" should card two skeins of wool which her daughter was to spin "with other Business of the family and this to be her dayly taske, the wch if she refuse she must expect to be sent to the House of Correction." Both parents were church members. *Watertown Records* (see chap. 4, n. 29), 48, 49, 50, 57, 67, 85. John Ball and his second wife were killed at Lancaster in 1676.

18 / See chap. 6 above.

19 / Pulsifer 1:300; Savage, *Genealogical Dictionary;* his wife Olive was probably the daughter of James Thompson, one of the first selectmen of Woburn. She died about 1663 and Cutler was briefly remarried to Mary Brown Lewis who died in 1666. By then he was completely deranged. Cutler died of smallpox in 1679 having been for thirteen years in the care of the Woburn selectmen.

20 / Pulsifer 3:80; Files 45, 49, 51, 62. In Oct. 1674 John Salter, one of this neglected family, was sentenced to twenty stripes and imprisonment until he humbled himself. His crime was "high handed stubbornness and incorrigiblenes therein against his master [William Eager of Cambridge], Idlenes, Night Walking, robbing William Bullerds orchard and lying." Pulsifer 3:106. Another son, Henry, moved to Andover as a servant, For running away twice, he was sentenced to be whipped and put in a leg-lock; for stealing, he was fined triple damages, and for breaking out of Ipswich prison, he and his accomplice were whipped. Dow, *Essex Records,* 5:230, 249; dated Sept. and Nov. 1673.

21 / File 156; *Watertown Records,* 83. In 1664, the year of Metup's marriage in Watertown, the selectmen, learning that he and another townsman were "intending to goe to Cape Fear and the town fearing their wives or children may be in want in their absence," insisted that he leave sufficient money and supplies before his departure. The Metups had for some years been residents of Groton.

22 / Macdonald, "Napier Casebooks" (see chap. 2, n. 27), 43.

23 / One other case of domestic violence came before the Court of Assistants, when Eleazur Parker of Cambridge went to stab his wife who was saved by "a book in her bosom." He was the son of James Parker of Woburn and had been born in 1660. He seems to have been drunk at the time of the crime. Koehler, *Search for Power,* 139.

24 / Five of the cases are merely recorded in the order books and they concerned: John Mirriack of Charlestown, 5 Oct. 1652, Pulsifer 1:29; Thomas Boylston, 5 Oct. 1652, ibid., 31; Roger Draper of Concord, 16 June 1657, ibid., 135; Henry Bowtell of Cambridge, 2 April 1663, ibid., 262; John Pemberton of Malden, 19 Dec. 1671, Pulsifer 3:12. Pemberton's offense occurred after he had been found drunk in the streets of Boston and sentenced to the stocks. Corey, *Malden* (see chap. 2, n. 55), 122. Bowtell was warned out of Cambridge on 29 May 1671. *Cambridge Town Records,* 193. His stepson was Jerathmeel Bowers. See Morgan, *Puritan Family,* 126–27 and chap. 6 above.

25 / An early settler of Woburn, he arrived from Charlestown in the early 1640s. He was about forty. It is unclear whether he was related to Rev. Thomas Carter, first minister of Woburn, who preached there from 1642 to 1684. Mary was nearly ten years old.

26 / Dutton, about forty, and his wife Susan, thirty-five, had lived in Reading since at least 1648, but had moved to Woburn about 1658. Savage, *Genealogical Dictionary.* They seem to have moved on again to Billerica. Hazen, *Billerica* (see chap. 6, n. 23), 122.

27 / Pulsifer 1:239; File 27.

28 / He was again a defendant in a slander action in 1668. His other daughter Susannah, wife of John Durrant of Billerica, was convicted of being overfamiliar with Thomas Wilkinson in 1680. Her contempt for her husband and disobedience to his wishes were remarked upon by several witnesses, as was her flouting of popular conventions. Pulsifer 3:332; 4:1; File 91. The case is discussed in chap. 9 below.

29 / Healey's age in 1666 was fifty-three, at most twenty-three years older than his wife. Previously he had been married to (1) Grace Ives, whose first child by him had been baptized in 1644; she had died in childbirth in 1649; (2) Mary, daughter of Rev. Nathaniel Rogers of Ipswich, married in 1650, died in 1653; (3) Grace Buttress, married 1653, who was dead by 1660.

30 / Samuel Green, aged about forty-one, was the colony printer. Langhorn, to be encountered later, had married Sarah Green, Samuel's younger sister. He was forty-nine.

31 / The Healeys had had three children since their marriage in 1661: Samuel born in Sept. 1662, Paul in April 1664, and Mary in Oct. 1665. Mary would have been just over six months old in May 1666.

32 / In Langhorn's case, however, not without good reason. The case involving him and Elizabeth Holmes in 1663 is described in the next chapter.

33 / She had been admitted to membership of the Cambridge church by 1658. Healey had been granted freemanship in 1645 when resident in Roxbury, and church membership was a prerequisite for this. He and his first wife Grace gained dismission when they moved to Cambridge in 1650. S. B. Sharples, ed., *Records of the Church of Christ at Cambridge* (Boston, 1906), 12; Savage, *Genealogical Dictionary*.

34 / Possibly in the sense of a woman's head dress. *OED*.

35 / Make formal complaint against.

36 / She was in fact Phoebe, daughter of Bartholomew Green who had died in 1635 two years after his arrival in Cambridge. She must have been at least twenty-five when she married Healey on 15 June 1661. Savage, *Genealogical Dictionary*, esp. "Genealogical Notes and Errata," comp. Caroline Dall, unpaginated, appended to vol. 4.

37 / The wife of Miles Ives of Roxbury; see n. 29 above.

38 / Born in 1589, and therefore seventy-seven.

39 / Healey's eldest daughter Hannah would have been twenty-two in 1666.

40 / File 42.

41 / No more children were baptized to them after 1665. On 8 April 1672 Thomas Langhorn was keeping Hannah Healey, born in 1671, and receiving five pounds from the town rate. *Cambridge Town Records*, 202. Healey's fifth marriage, in 1677, was to widow and school-dame, Sarah Brown.

42 / Pulsifer 4:59, 63; File 102.

43 / Morison, *Harvard College* (see chap. 5, n. 8), 405; Savage, *Genealogical Dictionary*; Faber, "Puritan Criminals" (see chap. 1, n. 43), 109.

44 / E.g., Susannah Pike, Sessions Records 1:9; Mary Atherton, County Court Records 5:40. In the Plymouth Records, Goodwife Spring, widowed by the death of her first husband Thomas Hatch of Scituate about 1646, was presented in 1659 for leaving her second husband John Spring of Watertown and having returned three or four years earlier to Scituate. The Plymouth court ordered her "to repaire to her husband with all convenient speed . . . or . . . give a reason why she doth not." Quoted in Demos, *Little Commonwealth* (see chap. 1, n. 29), 93.

45 / Cf. Rev. John Wilson's wife. He had to return twice before she would emigrate from England.

46 / Files 37, 41.

47 / She was the daughter of Richard Holden of Watertown. In 1685 she was thirty-nine years old. It comes as some surprise that her husband was with *her* relatives.

48 / Pulsifer 4:177; File 113.

49 / Savage, *Genealogical Dictionary*.

50 / On 1 Nov. 1677 William Pope, described as "Mr.," was convicted by the Court of Assistants for "cursing of the authority here making an order to prevent the spreading of the smale pox; as also defameing all the weomen of Boston" and sentenced to twenty stripes or a fine of twenty marks or £13 6s. 8d. *Court of Assistants* (see intro., n. 15), 1:104.

51 / Sessions Records 1:10; File 154.

52 / My italics.

53 / G. B. Nash, *The Urban Crucible* (Cambridge, Mass., 1979); Stephen Foster, *Their Solitary Way* (New Haven, 1971), 137. After King Philip's War every eleventh family was homeless. Indians wreaked comparable devastation on the frontier in the 1690s.

54 / Mansfield, Clements, Ball, Boyden, Pope, Hutchinson, Cutler, Salter, and Metup.

55 / Salter, Ball, Mansfield, both Hutchinsons, Pope, Dutton, and Boylston.

56 / Pemberton, Parker, Salter, and Mansfield; see also chap. 9 for William Brown.

57 / Clements, Hutchinson, Metup, Boyden, Pope, Dutton, and Ball.

58 / Salter, Bowtell, Ball, and Mirriack.

59 / *A Care-Cloth* (London, 1624), sig. A²v.

60 / Testimony of Pinson, File 42.

61 / Cf. similar expectations in Springfield. Innes, *Labor in a New Land*, 138, 144.

62 / Flaherty quoting John Barrett of Maine, 1666, in *Privacy* (see chap. 1, n. 7), 59; the statement of Beatrice Berry, Dow, *Essex Records*, 5:297–98. Cf. the Ela case (March 1682) in ibid., 8:272–73 discussed in Morgan, *Puritan Family*, 45, and the petition of Sarah Reynolds of Salem for reducing her husband's punishment for beating her in Hemphill, "Women in Court" (see part 2, n. 8), 170.

8. Unfaithful Husbands

1 / Keith Thomas, "Puritans and Adultery," in idem and Donald Pennington, eds., *Puritans and Revolutionaries* (Oxford, 1979), 272–82; Warden, "Law Reform" (see intro., n. 12), 680.

2 / *Histriomastix* (see chap. 4, n. 8), 376–83.

3 / Winthrop, *Journal* (see chap. 1, n. 50), 1:262–63; 2:12–13, 161–63.

4 / Thomas, "Puritans and Adultery," 261–62; Haskins, *Law and Authority* (see intro., n. 17), 80.

5 / Murrin, "Trial by Jury" (see intro., n. 13), 191–92.

6 / Mass. Hist. Soc. Photostats, 1685.

7 / One other adultery case involving Peter Cole of Charlestown was tried by the Court of Assistants. *Court of Assistants* (see intro., n. 15), 1:73. It is discussed in notes on the Sarah Bucknam case in chap. 11.

8 / John Goodenow, discussed in chap. 11 below; cf. Thomas Wilkinson, see chap. 11.

9 / Confession of Mary Ball, April 1671; File 55.

10 / See Healey case, chap. 7 above.

11 / Pulsifer 4:13, 14; testimony of Elizabeth Dickerman, File 94; cf. William Everton in chap. 9.

12 / Totals for other decades are: 1650s—2; 1660s—5; 1670s—3; 1690s—5.

13 / Mass. Hist. Soc. Photostats, 1685.

14 / We have already encountered him in the previous chapter in the Healey case, File 42, complaint dated 30 July 1666. He was subsequently holder of various town offices, surveyor of fences or highways, and in the year 1666–67, constable. *Cambridge Town Records*, 111, 137. C. H. Pope, *The Pioneers of Massachusetts* (Baltimore, 1977), describes him as a butcher.

15 / Holmes, a church member since 1641, died in May 1663, leaving estate of £324, which places him in the status of a prosperous yeoman, similar to Langhorn. Holmes served as Cambridge constable in 1649, 1657, and 1662. Elizabeth's mother Jane had died in 1653 when the girl was eight. Jane Holmes's relation of her conversion experience before admission to the church in Cambridge in 1638 (when her first child was born) is a story curiously similar to her daughter's. Jane's own mother had died early and her stepmother proved "an affliction to me." On the ship coming to Massachusetts she renewed acquaintance with a minister. He sought to persuade her that he could lie with a woman

without committing sin, and, paradoxically, that no one could come to God without having committed some gross act. Jane tried to argue against this self-serving antinomianism (a forerunner of such ranters as Clarkson and Coppe) by rehearsing the evils of "bad women lewd with lusts," but without success. "He by insinuation got within me and I would not leave him which I speake to the horror of that which it left me." Arrived in Roxbury, she was returned to the orthodox puritan way by the teaching of Thomas Weld. G. Selement and B. C. Woolley, eds., "Thomas Shepard's *Confessions*," *Colonial Society of Massachusetts Collections* 58 (1981): 76–79.

I am most grateful to Dr. Charles Cohen for drawing my attention to this passage. S. Foster, "Heresy in New England," *William and Mary Quarterly* 38 (1981): 652, suggests that the antinomian seducer was the notorious Captain Underhill. Winthrop's account of the affair, *Journal*, 1:275, has marked similarities, but, of course, Underhill was not a minister.

16 / Danforth's marginal note read 1662, but this must be an error.

17 / A Richard Cutter, aged forty-one, had been widowed in March 1662 and did not remarry until Feb. 1663. Savage does not record a namesake son, who might have been a more suitable bedfellow for Elizabeth. Cutter enjoyed middling economic status at this stage, but his growing affluence placed him in the top quarter of the Cambridge tax list in 1688. Faber, "Puritan Criminals" (see chap. 1, n. 43), 114, n. 71.

18 / Cf. *The Second Part of Unfortunate Jack* (London, 1681), reprinted in Thompson, *Penny Merriments* (see chap. 3, n. 49), 227–32: "His breeches 'twixt his legs were torn / His whim-whams they hung out."

19 / Illegible.

20 / Cf. Haskins, *Law and Authority*, 80; Thomas, "Puritans and Adultery," 261–62; Rogers was either Rev. Ezekiel of Rowley or Rev. Nathaniel of Ipswich.

21 / Sexual slang for private parts.

22 / Pulsifer 1:295; File 34.

23 / Flaherty, *Privacy* (see chap. 1, n. 7), 80; Sessions Records 1:87; File 170.

24 / Thompson, *Unfit* (see chap. 1, n. 15), chap. 3.

25 / The references by Langhorn are insufficiently precise to identify his source as *Aristotle's Problems* or *Aristotle's Master-Piece*. On both these hackworks, see Thompson, *Unfit*, 166–68; cf. O. T. Beale, "*Aristotle's Master-Piece*" (see chap. 5, n. 12), 207–22.

26 / See chap. 11 below. Bucknam had been married to Sarah, his second wife, for more than twenty years. He had bought twenty acres in Malden near the Charlestown line in 1649. Corey, *Malden* (see chap. 2, n. 55), 77.

27 / The daughter of Mr. Joseph Hills, magistrate and church elder.

28 / She was the wife of Joseph Hills, Jr.

29 / The complete list of women who deposed against Bucknam is: Margaret Greene; Elizabeth Webb; Rebecca, wife of Thomas Greene; the wife of Roger Kennicott; Hannah Barrett; Hannah Hills; Hannah, wife of Richard Stowers; Mary Tufts; Bridget Dexter; Margaret Pemberton; Elizabeth Felt; Tryal, wife of Walter Pore; Elizabeth Lareby; and Elizabeth Payne.

30 / Margaret Pemberton, aged fifty, had not reported his advances because "he came later and with sorrow promised amendment."

31 / Elizabeth Payne, the daughter of Edward Carrington, a turner, who was twenty-three in 1662, was found not guilty of sundry misdemeanors in Oct. 1685; the charges included reproachful speeches and drunkenness. The latter had already been proved before the Malden church of which she was a member. Pulsifer 4:187; File 119. She had previously shown an avid interest in the sexual exploits of Elizabeth Wells in 1669. File 52. Her later career is surveyed in chap. 11 below.

32 / Pulsifer 1:37.

33 / File 16, dated Dec. 1658.

34 / Pulsifer 1:272; File 31.

35 / Bucknam left £418. Wyman, *Charlestown Genealogies* (see chap. 1, n. 63).

36 / Savage, *Genealogical Dictionary* (see chap. 2, n. 56); Hazen, *Billerica* (see chap. 6, n. 23), 162. The complainant may have been Roger Toothaker.

37 / File 91.

38 / The Toothaker family, in financial and disciplinary trouble with the Billerica selectmen in 1683 and 1684, suffered severely during the witchcraze of 1692–93; Mary, the sister of Martha Allen Carrier executed at Salem on 19 Aug. 1692, was acquitted on 1 Feb. 1693. Roger, described as a doctor, had died in gaol in June 1692; two of their children Margaret and Jason were also accused. Koehler, *Search for Power* (see pref., n. 12), 488–89. Toothaker, who was fifty-eight in 1692, was accused of teaching Margaret supernatural methods of killing witches. Mary confessed to succumbing to the temptations of Satan in 1690 when he promised that "he would save her from the Indians." She was accused of afflicting Timothy Swan and Mary Warren. Mary Toothaker's worst fears were fulfilled on 5 Aug. 1695 when she was killed by Indians and her daughter Margaret captured.

39 / Perhaps on a medical visit. It is possible that some hostility existed between the Toothakers and Wilkinson by 1680 because of the latter's thwarted attempts to practice medicine.

40 / On the road between Woburn and Billerica, near the town lines.

41 / I.e., his penis was erect. Physical proximity of a pillion passenger probably contributed to this. See the cases of Phoebe Page and Jane Evans discussed below and Pulsifer 1:7, 62–63.

42 / This was the year of King Philip's War, 1676.

43 / File 91. Ruth Moore Shed had married on 5 July 1670.

44 / The Dane family had been connected with the Bulkeley family, leaders of Concord, at Odell in Buckinghamshire. Elizabeth was the wife of Joseph Dane, whose brother Thomas had escorted Mrs. Bulkeley to America and built the Bulkeley's house in Concord. C. H. Walcott, *History of Concord* (Boston, 1884), 1, 87. See below, note 47.

45 / Law had married Lydia (daughter of Roger Draper, convicted in 1657 of wife-beating) in 1660 and had four sons. He had been transported to Massachusetts as one of the Scottish prisoners of war and was a weaver by trade. Wheeler, *Concord* (see chap. 5, n. 28), 40.

46 / *The Womans Advocate, or Fifteen Real Comforts of Matrimony* (London, 1683, 3d ed.), 44, has a similar response by a woman taken by her husband in adultery. This edition was exported to Boston for Cotton Mather. It is possible that Law may have read an earlier edition. See Thompson, *Unfit*, 111–14, and idem, "The Puritans and Prurience: Aspects of the Restoration Book Trade," in *Contrast and Connection*, ed. H. C. Allen and Roger Thompson (London, 1976), 39, 42, 46.

47 / Mrs. Dane had threatened to call Edward Bulkeley, the minister.

48 / Probably Thomas, brother of Joseph who was Edward Bulkeley's fellow minister at Concord from 1667 to 1711.

49 / Pulsifer 4:19; File 95.

50 / Increase Mather, *Solemn Advice* (see chap. 4, n. 6), 48, quoted "one of the ancients" in an account of a "chast woman sollicited by a profane vile wretch to sin against God" who told him "to hold his finger in the flame for fifteen minutes." When he protested that this was unreasonable, she replied that it was "unreasonable for me to do that which leads to the perpetual flame." Dr. Charles Cohen informs me that Ames had

previously used this metaphor for hellfire. This exemplar may have been a commonplace of sermons. See chap. 4 above and Koehler, *Search for Power,* 100.

51 / Edward Iron, 7 Oct. 1650, Pulsifer 1:22. Capt. Carr, 17 Dec. 1661, ibid., 250. Thomas Watts, 2 April 1663, ibid., 260. Thomas Tally, 1 April 1673, Pulsifer 3:59. Tally had originally been complained of in Concord in 1670, where he had already lived for four years without his wife. Walcott, *Concord,* 142. William Hawford, 17 June 1673, ibid., 66. Watts, apparently sober and well behaved, was sent packing back to his wife in England after "marrying" Elizabeth Haddon of Charlestown. Cf. Morgan, "The Puritans and Sex" (see chap. 1, n. 27), 606.

52 / On Johnson's career and background, see Thompson, "The Puritans and Prurience," 38, 40.

53 / This news came in a long letter from his printer brother, Thomas. On the ephemeral street literature describing the low life of Restoration London, often printed by Johnson and so similar to what he here describes, see Thompson, *Unfit,* 57–65.

54 / The phrase comes from a testimonial presented to the General Court by President Charles Chauncey of Harvard. Pulsifer 1:240, 249, 295; Files 29, 34; Paige, *Cambridge* (see chap. 3, n. 45), 594.

55 / His wife was Ruth, daughter of Christopher Cane, the college caretaker. File 38.

56 / File 55; Wyman, *Charlestown Genealogies.*

57 / Her mother was Mary, daughter of Thomas Danforth. Solomon Phipps had had trouble in his household seven years previously when his Negro man Jock confessed in court to breaking into Lawrence Hammond's house in order to pay a night visit to Marie Negro. File 99. Solomon's sister had been convicted of premarital fornication with John Roy in 1663. See chap. 3 above.

58 / Either Hannah, born 1652, or Mary, 1656. The latter had been accused of improprieties with Benjamin Simons at Woburn in 1676. This evidence suggests that Walker had not arrived until the late 1670s. Pulsifer 3:158.

59 / Sarah had already given birth to two bastards by Stephen Geary in 1682 and 1685. The impression given in Phipps's testimony is that Sarah was regarded by some as the town whore. Pulsifer 4:44, 177, and chap. 2 above.

60 / The wife of William Hurry and a church member, aged about fifty. She was presumably one of those referred to in the selectmen's returns of Feb. 1679 on education provision in Charlestown: "English schooles kept by severall woemen." File 89.

61 / Edward Larkins had married Mary Walker on 1 Nov. 1688. Ten midwives and a doctor asserted the child of Mary Phipps was white.

62 / County Court Records 5:21; File 131.

63 / Mass. Hist. Soc. Photostats, Nov. 1699; Wyman, *Charlestown Genealogies.*

64 / Cf. Innes, *Labor in a New Land,* 129–33.

65 / Pulsifer 4:103; Files 108, 111, dated 1 April 1684. Woodward later served the town as highway surveyor in 1686 and selectman in 1702 and 1712. Savage, *Genealogical Dictionary;* Faber, "Puritan Criminals," 141.

66 / Sessions Records 1:74, 75–76, 77, 87.

67 / File 55.

68 / County Court Records 5:91; Files 143, 157.

69 / Pulsifer 1:100.

70 / Ibid., 64.

71 / See chap. 6 above.

72 / Convicted of harassing Elizabeth Dickerman on the sabbath in 1681. Pulsifer 4:13.

73 / Pulsifer 1:7. See chap. 11 below.

9. Unfaithful Wives

1 / Pp. 14–15, quoted in Morgan, "Puritans and Sex" (see chap. 1, n. 27), 592.

2 / Hoffer and Hull, *Murdering Mothers* (see pref., n. 12), 12.

3 / Quoted in Stone, *Family* (see pref., n. 9), 197.

4 / Cotton Mather, *Ornaments for the Daughters of Zion* (Boston, 1692), 47.

5 / Davis, "Sacred Condition of Equality" (see part 2, n. 9), 573; Thompson, *Unfit* (see chap. 1, n. 15), chap. 6; Koehler, *Search for Power* (see pref., n. 12), 28–36.

6 / Koehler, *Search for Power,* 148.

7 / See chap. 8 above.

8 / Thompson, "Popular Reading" (see pref., n. 7).

9 / Koehler, *Search for Power,* 47; cf. *Martin v. Long,* chap. 11 below.

10 / See e.g., Pulsifer 3:290

11 / See chap. 11 below.

12 / Thompson, *Unfit,* 98.

13 / She was the seventeen-year-old daughter of James Cutler of neighboring Cambridge Farms, later Lexington.

14 / Cf. Robert Montgomery who also tried to combine business with pleasure, chap. 4 above. Buss was also ensign of the militia and innkeeper of Concord.

15 / E.g., Thompson, *Penny Merriments* (see chap. 3, n. 49), 277–79, 280–82.

16 / See chap. 8 above.

17 / Hazen, *Billerica* (see chap. 6, n. 23), 189, 208.

18 / E.g., Thompson, *Penny Merriments,* 260–76, 280–82, 289–91.

19 / Pulsifer 3:332, 4:1; File 91. See chap. 11 below.

20 / Koehler, *Search for Power,* 151.

21 / See chap. 7 above.

22 / Wyman, *Charlestown Genealogies* (see chap. 1, n. 63).

23 / Pulsifer 3:12; File 57.

24 / File 45; File 57; Pulsifer 3:12; Pulsifer 4:177; Sessions Records A, 6, 17.

25 / *Court of Assistants* (see intro., n. 15), 1:70.

26 / "Suffolk Records" (see intro., n. 4), 1061.

27 / Ibid.

28 / Pulsifer 4:49.

29 / Sarah Everton, the daughter of the Charlestown miller, John Fownell, was admitted to the church in 1677.

30 / Either Abigail wife of John, or Mary wife of Samuel, both of neighboring Medford and both in their late twenties. Savage, *Genealogical Dictionary* (see chap. 2, n. 56).

31 / Recently married wife of Benjamin.

32 / Miriam, granddaughter-in-law of the famous Captain Edward, also in her late twenties. Elizabeth Robinson was the wife of the disreputable Andrew, which dignifies this attack with a certain poetic justice.

33 / John Long was a disreputable young man, to be met in chap. 11; Stephen Geary had fathered two bastards on Sarah Pore and had a string of other convictions, Pulsifer 4:44, 45, 173; Files 102, 113. John Betts had had a dispute with Everton, and Hannah Salter had been a witness against Brown ten years previously. Seven witnesses appeared for the defense. File 99. Everton was convicted in Oct. 1683 of illegal liquor sales and fined five pounds, Pulsifer 4:45, 81.

34 / John Wing was a wealthy Boston shopkeeper and an officer in the artillery com-

pany. He owned a tavern on Hudson's Lane, Boston. M. Halsey Thomas, ed., *The Diary of Samuel Sewall* (New York, 1973), 4 Dec. 1687.

35 / Boston merchant and soldier, born 1640. On this puritan family see Bailyn, *New England Merchants* (see intro., n. 3), 35, 59, 156.

36 / Twelve miles west of Boston, on the route to Sudbury and Marlborough.

37 / Daniel Henchman, schoolmaster in Boston from 1666, was on the 1665 committee for the survey of the new plantation at Worcester and later a proprietor. As a captain he achieved distinction in King Philip's War and died in 1685.

38 / County Court Records 5:40; Files 131, 139.

39 / Corey, *Malden* (see chap. 2, n. 55), 304.

40 / See chap. 4 above; Pulsifer 3:158; File 82. By 1692 Simons was sufficiently reformed to be appointed a Woburn tythingman. Sewall, *Woburn* (see chap. 5, n. 26), 50.

41 / See chap. 2 above; Sessions Records 1:53, 67.

42 / Frothingham, *Charlestown* (see chap. 5, n. 32), 1–246.

43 / Breen, *Good Ruler* (see intro., n. 5), 187.

44 / Frothingham, *Charlestown* (see chap. 5, n. 32), 220–21.

45 / E.g., Mercy Miller, Sarah Park, Catherine Ford, and Mary Harris, single women and unmarried mothers of sailors' children. Sessions Records 1:9, 41, 46.

46 / Sessions Records 1:9, dated 3 Jan. 1693.

47 / Pulsifer 3:76, 87, dated 7 Oct. 1678. The father was Zechary Crispe, departed seaman.

48 / Wyman, *Charlestown Genealogies* (see chap. 1, n. 63).

49 / Probably John Fowle of Charlestown.

50 / Pulsifer 4:130, 140; File 109.

51 / Born Elizabeth Brooks, the mother had married Mancer in 1670. The Ives family, originally of Watertown, had moved to Boston in 1641. Savage, *Genealogical Dictionary;* Wyman, *Charlestown Genealogies.*

52 / County Court Records 5:8; File 133.

53 / She was the daughter of Sarah Crouch and Thomas Jones; Wyman, *Charlestown Genealogies.* See chap. 2 above.

54 / A John Smith of Charlestown, son of Thomas the butcher, was a mariner who died at Jamaica on 22 July 1688, aged nineteen; his brother Thomas died at sea in 1690, aged twenty-five. However it seems inconceivable that news of these deaths would not have reached Charlestown by the end of 1695. Savage, *Genealogical Dictionary.*

55 / When Rear Admiral Sir Francis Wheeler had arrived with his squadron in Boston on 12 June 1693 after an unsuccessful expedition to the West Indies, Mary Harris was on board. He sailed for Newfoundland without her on Aug. 3. *Dictionary of National Biography* (hereafter cited as *DNB*).

56 / Her naming of Whiting rather than Carter may have been motivated by the need to secure maintenance from a native. Her arrival with the Royal Navy and her admitted promiscuity suggest that she may have been a seasoned prostitute. Whiting's other sexual exploits will be encountered in the Martin case, chap. 11. Sessions Records 1:46, 47, 48, 49, 57, 58, 62; Files 162, 201.

57 / Murrin, "Trial by Jury" (see intro., n. 13), 181.

58 / Thompson, "Popular Reading," 658.

59 / See chap. 6 above.

60 / See chap. 11 below.

61 / Francis Flashego, a black married man, reported in 1654 that Hannah Smith "would jeere him because he had noe children." File 9. Cf. Thompson, "Popular Reading," 661–63.

10. Domestic Relations

1 / Wrigley, "Reflections" (see pref., n. 5), 72–73.

2 / See chap. 2 above.

3 / See chap. 7 above.

4 / Testimonies of Danforth and Corbet, File 25.

5 / Henretta, "Families and Farms" (see chap. 3, n. 6), 32

6 / Demos, *Little Commonwealth* (see chap. 1, n. 29), 149.

7 / E. L. Page quoted in Koehler, *Search for Power* (see pref., n. 12), 136.

8 / Quaife, *Wanton Wenches* (see pref., n. 13), 15.

9 / See chap. 2 above.

10 / Pulsifer 1:62–63.

11 / Pulsifer 1:200, 201; testimony of James Barrett, File 25. The deputy governor was Richard Bellingham.

12 / Pulsifer 3:276; File 84.

13 / County Court Records 5:51, 62; File 135. Mitchell, in his late twenties, was also convicted at the same session for resisting the constable confiscating his goods for unpaid rates.

14 / Files 38, 42.

15 / Thomas Crosswell, in his early fifties in 1691, was married to Priscilla Upham, that daughter of Deacon Upham who had been illicitly courted by the disreputable Paul Wilson in 1658 when she was fifteen. Pulsifer 1:156. Both were church members, and they had twelve children. Wyman, *Charlestown Genealogies* (see chap. 1, n. 63).

16 / She was the wife of Henry Pounding of Boston and the widow of John Lee. She was the youngest of nine children of Michael Long of Charlestown. Goodwin was the son of another Christopher and had probably lived all his forty years in Charlestown. He was a mason and had married Mercy Crouch, sister of Sarah, in 1672 when she was nineteen. Both were church members. Wyman, *Charlestown Genealogies.*

17 / The son of a feltmaker of the same name.

18 / The wife of George Broughton of Boston and daughter-in-law of Thomas, a wealthy merchant and Maine land speculator. Frothingham, *Charlestown* (see chap. 5, n. 32), 147; Bond, *Watertown Genealogies* (see chap. 4, n. 29).

19 / They were Katherine Ford, aged nineteen, who was convicted of fornication with a sailor from H.M.S. *Nonsuch* in Sept. 1695. Sessions Records 1:41. She had been acquitted of accidental murder the previous October. Superior Court Records, 1692–95 (see chap. 3, n. 53), 129. The other maid, Abigail Cogin, aged eighteen, was Rebecca Pounding's niece.

20 / Formally complain to authority.

21 / This gloss was given by Daniel and Naomi Crosswell Dana, who impugned hostile evidence from the Smith family.

22 / James Oliver of Cambridge had been graduated from Harvard in 1680. He visited Rebecca two weeks before she died.

23 / One of these, Hannah Call, was related to the Crosswells by marriage.

24 / Just before Thanksgiving, several witnesses had seen her fall "backwards upon the low causeway . . . she was allmost drownded . . . and complained of pains in her neck."

25 / County Court Records 5:142; File 157. Cf. the Franklin case in 1644 and the Betts case in the Court of Assistants in 1653. Chapin, *Criminal Justice* (see intro., n. 9), 114–15.

26 / Corey, *Malden* (see chap. 2, n. 55), 120–21.

27 / Testimonies of William Hunt, John Redyat, Mehitabel Redyat, Files 38, 42.

28 / County Court Records 5:52.

29 / Pulsifer 3:106, 120; File 23. The full list of Creete's misdeeds is printed in Morgan, *Puritan Family* (see chap. 5, n. 2), 125–27.

30 / Koehler, *Search for Power*, 358.

31 / Ibid., 13.

32 / *Five Hundred Points of Good Husbandry*, ed. Geoffrey Grigson (Oxford, 1984), 115, 160, 165, 237, 269, 278–79, 297.

33 / *A Compleat Body of Divinity* (Boston, 1726), 614.

34 / *Puritan Family*, 124; cf. 77–78, 104–05, 108.

35 / *Little Commonwealth*, 116–17.

36 / See chap. 11 below.

37 / Mass. Hist. Soc. Photostats, Nov. 1699.

38 / File 55.

39 / File 18. Cf. Pulsifer 1:63; testimony of Josiah Wood in Wells and Tufts case, File 51; testimony of John Hore, File 49; testimony of Hobart et al., File 162.

40 / See chap. 2 above.

41 / See Thompson, "Adolescent Culture" (see chap. 5, n. 1), 128–29.

42 / See chap. 3 above.

43 / Pulsifer 1:71.

44 / Stone, *Family* (see pref., n. 9), 163–64.

45 / Greven, *Protestant Temperament* (see chap. 6, n. 44), 37.

46 / E.g., Lloyd de Mause, *The History of Childhood* (London, 1976), chap. 1.

47 / Alan Macfarlane, *The Family Life of Ralph Josselin* (Cambridge, 1970), 116; Levin, *Cotton Mather* (see chap. 5, n. 36), 12, 32, 183; Elizabeth Schlesinger, "Cotton Mather and His Family," *William and Mary Quarterly* 10 (1953): 181, 183–84; Thompson, *Women* (see chap. 2, n. 17), 151.

48 / Linda Pollock, *The Forgotten Children* (Cambridge, 1983), 23, 111, 128, 137, 151, 204, 208, 236, 271. Cf. Wrightson, *English Society* (see chap. 5, n. 34), 104.

49 / Macdonald, "Napier Casebooks" (see chap. 2, n. 27), 15–16; cf. Macfarlane, *Josselin*, 165.

50 / Philip Greven, *Child-Rearing Concepts* (Itasca, Illinois, 1973), 11–12.

51 / Thompson, *Women*, 148, 150; Schlesinger, "Cotton Mather," 187–88.

52 / Quoted in Greven, *Protestant Temperament*, 156.

53 / Morgan, "Diary" (see chap. 4, n. 9), 333, 335–36, 369, 375–76.

54 / See chap. 11 below.

55 / See chap. 2 above.

56 / See chap. 11 below.

57 / File 46.

58 / File 52.

59 / File 56.

60 / File 80. The fact that these sentiments were all expressed in petitions might render them somewhat suspect; it is, however, unlikely that petitioners would invoke feelings which were unfamiliar or unconventional to the court.

61 / Pulsifer 3:158; File 82. See chap. 4 above.

62 / Pulsifer 3:3, 26, 33, 41; File 59.

63 / Cf. Hugh Parson's similar inhumanity condemned in Springfield. Innes. *Labor in a New Land* (see pref., n. 17), 138–40.

64 / Pulsifer 1:260; File 30.

65 / See chap. 8 above.

66 / David D. Hall, "Towards a History of Popular Religion," *William and Mary Quarterly* 41 (1984): 53–54. See the relation of Nicholas Wyeth in Selement and Woolley, "Shepard Confessions" (see chap. 8, n. 15), 193.

67 / McGiffert, *God's Plot* (see chap. 6, n. 45), 58–60.

68 / Quoted from *The Necessity of Reformation* in Koehler, *Search for Power*, 342; cf. 358, 425.

69 / Wheeler, *Concord* (see chap. 5, n. 28), 19.

70 / Elliott, *Power and the Pulpit* (see chap. 5, n. 29), 159–97.

71 / E.g., Hannah Brackett living with Daniel Gookin or Mary Davis living with Henry Spring.

72 / Peter Laslett and Richard Wall, eds., *Household and Family in Past Time* (London, 1972).

73 / "Family History" (see pref., n. 4), 64.

74 / E.g., Frosts, Beales, Bloods, Pierces, Grants, Cutlers, Hastingses, Varnums, Greens, all met in preceding chapters.

75 / File 167.

76 / "Danforth Letters," *Mass. Hist. Soc. Procs.* 13 (1874): 305–06.

77 / Selement and Woolley, "Shepard Confessions," 136–38.

78 / Cf. Miranda Chaytor, "Household and Kinship" (see pref., n. 5), 45–48 on the importance of extended kinship in Ryton, County Durham.

11. Community Control

1 / *World We Have Lost* (see pref., n. 2), 79.

2 / Kenneth A. Lockridge, *A New England Town* (New York, 1970), 4–5.

3 / Nourse, *Lancaster* (see chap. 1, n. 23), 27–28.

4 / Heyrman, "Specters of Subversion" (see chap. 6, n. 47), 73.

5 / Greven, *Protestant Temperament* (see chap. 6, n. 44), 195.

6 / Michael Zuckerman, "The Fabrication of Identity in Early America," *William and Mary Quarterly* 34 (1977): 194.

7 / Powell, *Puritan Village* (see intro., n. 3); Allen, "In English Ways" (see intro., n. 17).

8 / E.g., Nicholas Danforth of Framlingham in Suffolk. John N. Merriam, "Nicholas Danforth, the Puritan Layman," in John Booth, ed., *Nicholas Danforth and his Neighbours* (Framingham, Mass., 1935), 5.

9 / Anthony Fletcher, *An English Community in Peace and War: Sussex 1600–1660* (London, 1975), 162.

10 / Winthrop, *Journal* (see chap. 1, n. 50), 1:290; Breen, *Good Ruler* (see intro., n. 5), 5, 59, 60.

11 / Lockridge, *New England Town*, chap. 1.

12 / Michael Zuckerman, *Peaceable Kingdoms* (New York, 1970); Lockridge, *New England Town;* Breen and Foster, "Social Cohesion" (see chap. 6, n. 10).

13 / Shorter, *Modern Family* (see chap. 4, n. 2), 68; Stone, *Family* (see pref., n. 9), 146–49, 194, 217; Quaife, *Wanton Wenches* (see pref., n. 13), 25–37.

14 / Larzer Ziff, *Puritanism in America* (New York, 1973), 165, 245–46.

15 / Demos, *Little Commonwealth* (see chap. 1, n. 29), 136–39, 145–50; Stone, *Family*, 176–77; John Demos, "Underlying Themes in Witchcraft," *American Historical Review* 75 (1970): 1320–26.

16 / Smith, *As a City* (see intro., n. 14), 137–38; Warden, "Law Reform" (see intro., n. 12), 619.

17 / Chapin, *Criminal Justice* (see intro., n. 9), 141.

18 / Konig, *Law and Society* (see intro., n. 1).

19 / Warden, "Law Reform," 677; Murrin, "Trial by Jury" (see intro., n. 13), 153.

20 / Pulsifer 3:332; File 91. See chap. 9 above. Cf. Heyrman, "Specters of Subversion," 67.

21 / See chap. 2 above.

22 / See chap. 3 above.

23 / Noyes had been a selectman of Sudbury for twenty-eight years since 1662 and was a member of a leading founding family of the town. Brown, a deacon and representative, was related to the first minister of the town. Savage, *Genealogical Dictionary*.

24 / The Goodenows were founder-leaders of Sudbury having migrated from Wiltshire in 1638. John's father Edmund often had been selectman, twice deputy, and captain of the militia and an honored military leader during King Philip's War in which he died. John had eight children and a wife still living in 1699. The Goodenows had been married about forty years. Savage, *Genealogical Dictionary* (see chap. 2, n. 56); Powell, *Puritan Village,* 91, 110, 123.

25 / The deposition is torn here.

26 / I.e., her pudendum was visible. The words italicized were added in Joseph Lynde's handwriting.

27 / Sessions Records 1:87; File 170.

28 / Cf. Wrightson, *English Society* (see chap. 5, n. 34), 54, 157 for similar informal procedures in the old country.

29 / Chapin, *Criminal Justice,* 132.

30 / This may explain why fewer suits were brought in Middlesex by "the middling sort and the stable respectable poor to mark their behaviour off from that of the disorderly or ungodly poor" which has been advanced as a major reason for the rise of defamation suits in England. James Sharpe, *Defamation and Sexual Slander in Early Modern England* (York, 1980).

31 / Demos, *Entertaining Satan* (see chap. 4, n. 5), 312.

32 / Macdonald, "Napier Casebooks" (see chap. 2, n. 27), 47–48, 54; Flaherty, *Privacy* (see chap. 1, n. 7), 92–108.

33 / *Othello,* act 3, sc. 3, lines 157–63.

34 / See, e.g., William Bucknam case, chap. 8 above; Bartlett case, Sessions Records 1:95; Demos, *Entertaining Satan,* chap. 2.

35 / File 34.

36 / File 27.

37 / File 131.

38 / File 157.

39 / File 43; he referred to James Taylor.

40 / See chap. 9 above.

41 / Robert Calef, *More Wonders of the Invisible World* (London, 1700), reprinted in G. L. Burr, ed., *Narratives of the Witchcraft Cases* (New York, 1914), 373. Cf. Thompson, *Witches of Salem* (see chap. 7, n. 11), 88.

42 / See chap. 8 above.

43 / Files 42, 157.

44 / C. A. Haigh, "Slander and the Church Courts in the Sixteenth Century," *Transactions of the Lancashire and Cheshire Antiquarian Society* 78 (1975): 8, cited in Sharpe, *Defamation,* 26. Dr. Sharpe doubts the validity of this hypothesis.

45 / See Thompson, " 'Holy Watchfulness' and Communal Conformism," *New England Quarterly* 56 (1983): 504.

46 / Chapin, *Criminal Justice,* 131. See *Mousall v. Tirrell and Fosdick* below.

47 / Mellings had married into the Dexter clan in 1658; he was probably therefore in his late twenties or early thirties. Goodwife Barlow was in fact Sarah and John's elder sister Mary. Savage, *Genealogical Dictionary.*

48 / Jade: a term of reprobation applied to women, *OED.* The word often had strong sexual undertones.

49 / Pulsifer 1:283; File 35.

50 / Savage, *Genealogical Dictionary.*

51 / John Mousall, aged thirty-three, was a member of one of Charlestown's leading families. His wife was twenty-nine.

52 / This was an offense carrying a five pound fine under the law of 1649. Smith, *Colonial Justice* (see intro., n. 7), 103. Fosdick later moved to Malden, where his second wife Elizabeth was accused of witchcraft in 1692.

53 / Words bracketed have been canceled by a different contemporary hand and replaced by italicized words, either in the margin or interlined.

54 / Pulsifer 1:286, 291; File 34. In 1671 James Fosdick, John's eldest son, aged twenty-two, was fined ten shillings for rude carriages toward others in Malden and for contempt. Pulsifer 3:13.

55 / Thompson, *Witches of Salem,* 119.

56 / *Cambridge Town Records* (see chap. 1, n. 23), 63, 108.

57 / S. A. Green, ed., *The Early Records of Groton* (Groton, 1880), 28.

58 / See chap. 2 above.

59 / Savage, *Genealogical Dictionary;* Wyman, *Charlestown Genealogies* (see chap. 1, n. 63).

60 / Jonathan Poole of Reading had been born in 1634 in Cambridge. He married about 1655 and later became a leading militia officer in King Philip's War and a representative in 1677.

61 / A tailor of Boston, a married man, and a church member.

62 / William Knap, patriarch of the notorious Watertown family, who died on 30 Aug. 1658, "aged about eighty years." Savage, *Genealogical Dictionary.*

63 / Her parents were John Page, aged sixty-four, a founding member of Watertown and a church member, and Phoebe, née Payne, aged sixty, whose sister Elizabeth Hammond and brother William had also emigrated to Watertown.

64 / Pulsifer 1:6–8, 10, 14. Phoebe eventually married, but not until the early 1660s and then to a twice-widowed man, James Cutler, who was at least twenty years older than she. His land was at Cambridge Farms, later Lexington. Savage, *Genealogical Dictionary.*

65 / Chapin, *Criminal Justice,* 46.

66 / Corey, *Malden* (see chap. 2, n. 55), 119. William Bucknam sued William Marble.

67 / Did this have some sexual connotation?

68 / Pulsifer 1:37, 45; File 7. This method of inhibiting sexual temptation was often employed by English magistrates. Haskins, *Law and Authority* (see intro., n. 17), 83.

69 / Corey, *Malden,* 393.

70 / Testimony of Sarah Bucknam, File 31.

71 / Another Sarah Bucknam, this Sarah's daughter-in-law, was indicted for adultery with Peter Cole of Charlestown in July 1676 before the Court of Assistants, during King Philip's War. They were found not guilty of the indictment, but guilty of "unlawfull and uncivill accompanying . . . being in bed together." They were both sentenced to stand

238 Notes to Pages 179–82

on the gallows haltered and to receive thirty-nine stripes at the cart-tail. *Court of Assistants* (see intro., n. 15), 1:73. In September, Sewall was shocked at their behavior on the gallows: "Four others sate on the gallows, two men and two impudent women one of whom at least laughed as several testified." It is possible that the shock of cuckoldom accounted for an affliction described by the diarist on 30 Dec. 1696: "Mr. Wigglesworth tells me that one John Bucknam of Malden, aged above fifty years old, has been perfectly dumb near 18 years and now within about three weeks has his understanding and speech restored. He is much affected with the goodness of God to him herein." Bucknam had fought in the war; in 1694 he had been unable to sign a deed concerning his father's estate "by reason of his present distraction." Corey, *Malden,* 324, 393.

72 / Defense of Sarah Bucknam, File 7; Corey, *Malden,* 119.

73 / Corey, *Malden,* 119.

74 / File 31.

75 / The others were Alice Larkins, Margaret Greene, and Margaret Pemberton.

76 / James Greene and the Whitmores.

77 / George Knower; Corey, *Malden,* 122.

78 / Elizabeth Webb married Thomas Greene, widower of Margaret, in 1667. Rebecca Greene was daughter of Joseph Hills; a daughter of Hannah Stowers married Abraham Hills in 1666. Elizabeth Lareby was daughter of Elizabeth Felt, another witness.

79 / Rebecca Greene, Elizabeth Lareby, Hannah Stowers, Mary Tufts, and Hannah Hills.

80 / Slater, the son of a feltmaker in Surrey, England, had been brought to Concord in the 1650s to learn a trade, but had been "sold often from one too another without respect to his trade whereby the said youth is much wronged." File 19, dated 1657.

81 / Pinion lived in neighboring Sudbury.

82 / *Furor uterinus* was a commonplace of bawdry in the seventeenth century, see Thompson, *Unfit* (see chap. 1, n. 15), 74, 76, 108, 114, 123–24; idem, *Penny Merriments* (see chap. 3, n. 49), 256, 260.

83 / Vagina.

84 / In the sense of puncturing or inserting a sharp object.

85 / A push, thrust, or shove against a resisting body. *OED.*

86 / The intention here seems to be scatological rather than an invitation to oral sex, a taboo topic confined to the most advanced French pornography at that time. Thompson, *Unfit,* 32.

87 / Vagina

88 / Used for enemas; here, with obvious phallic implications.

89 / Slang for testicles.

90 / This may have been a reference to the oft-reprinted works of David Dickson, a Scottish covenanter and divine, who greatly influenced Michael Wigglesworth. *DNB;* Corey, *Malden,* 232.

91 / File 36.

92 / Cliché for sexual intercourse.

93 / Again this suggestion seems to be scatological.

94 / Pulsifer 1:229, 233; File 28.

95 / See Thompson, *Unfit,* 117 and idem, *Penny Merriments,* 280–82.

96 / F. G. Emmison, *Elizabethan Life: Disorder* (Chelmsford, 1970), 71; cf. a long libelous rhyme prosecuted in 1583 and a shorter lampoon of 1588, quoted on 68–69; also see two Middlesex cases, dated 1597 and 1601, quoted in idem, *Elizabethan Life: Morals and the Church Courts* (see chap. 1, n. 52), 53. Cf. Ingram, "Ecclesiastical Justice" (see

chap. 1, n. 27), 102, which describes an obscene libel in 1611 against Rev. Francis Greatrakes and his wife and two daughters. He had roused popular resentment by removing the "Kynge House," a bower in the village of Keevil used for dancing and revels; E. R. Brinkworth, ed., "The Archdeacon's Court: Liber Actorum 1584," *Oxfordshire Record Society* 23 (1942): 12.

97 / The author was Thomas Stebbing, Jr. Smith, *Colonial Justice,* 109.

98 / Elizabeth, née Trumbull, was the forty-year-old wife of the captain of *The Blossom,* Richard Martin. She died on 6 Oct. 1689, and her widower remarried six weeks later. He wrecked his ship off the Kentish coast in 1690. His estate was valued at £561. Their daughter Elizabeth had married in 1679. Margaret Martin married Stephen Fosdick in 1686. Savage, *Genealogical Dictionary;* Wyman, *Charlestown Genealogies;* Mass. Hist. Soc. Photostats, 25 Oct. 1690.

99 / Hannah Long, born on 29 Dec. 1657, was daughter of Michael Long, aged sixty-eight, church member and tythingman, and granddaughter of Robert Long, a wealthy innkeeper, who was a selectman and close friend of Rev. Zechariah Symmes, minister of Charlestown. Wyman, *Charlestown Genealogies.*

100 / The jury's verdict may have been affected by counterevidence that Margaret had simply had a fever and that no one could testify to having actually seen the miscarriage taking place.

101 / Goody Martin's protestations that one visitor was ill and so had to decline her invitation to go to meeting, and that the servant had locked the chamber door and gone away with the key so that she could not get her cloak did not jibe with the ferryman's evidence that he called for the men in the evening but was sent away without them or an explanation.

102 / The seventy-one-year-old wife of John Trumbull, church member, sometime shipmaster.

103 / In 1696 he was accused of fathering a bastard on Mary Harris in the Smith case; see chap. 9 above. He was Richard Martin's grandson and wore his crowned hat. He also sported a speckled hair band and a red lined coat worn inside out.

104 / Probably the twenty-five-year-old son of John, the innkeeper of "The Two Cranes" after his father, Robert's, death. The elder John was a church member and had taken the daughter of Increase Nowell as his second wife in 1674. The younger John had already been in trouble with the court for window-breaking and swearing. File 45. Ruth Long and Elizabeth Drinker who both gave evidence against the Martins were sisters of Hannah.

105 / This was presumably a libel alleging the Martins' sexual availability.

106 / These were all Charlestown church members. Ann Foster, aged fifty-three, was the wife of the wealthy merchant William who had returned to Charlestown in Nov. 1673 after two years' captivity with his son under Turkish corsairs. Wigglesworth wrote a thanksgiving poem to celebrate their release. Crowder, *No Featherbed* (see chap. 2, n. 38), 151–52. Another son, Isaac, graduated from Harvard in 1671 and had just become minister of Hartford in 1680. Savage, *Genealogical Dictionary.*

107 / Hannah Lawrence, Hannah Capen, Elizabeth Drinker, and Mary Smith.

108 / Honor Hall, Elizabeth Coulter; Pulsifer 4:25, 32.

109 / See chap. 9 above.

110 / Ibid.

111 / Pulsifer 4:187; File 119.

112 / Stephen Payne was a church member from 1665 and a tythingman from 1679. In 1683 an Elizabeth Payne, spinster, was indicted before the Court of Assistants for will-

fully murdering her bastard on 6 March. The jury found her not guilty but "greatly negligent in not calling for help for her child's life" and the court sentenced her to twenty stripes. She may have been a daughter of Stephen and Elizabeth. *Court of Assistants*, 1:228.

113 / Pulsifer 1:272; File 31.

114 / File 52.

115 / In 1692 along with Elizabeth Fosdick, also of Malden, she was accused of witchcraft. Apart from the Salem Village accusers, Peter Tufts was the main complainant "for acts of witchcraft committed on his negro woman." By 1698 she had become the Malden midwife and gave evidence in the Sprague–Mellings case. File 169.

116 / Letter of Increase Mather dated 8 May 1679, quoted in Crowder, *No Featherbed*, 212.

117 / "Some Grounds and Reasons for laying down my Office Relation," quoted in ibid., 219.

118 / Mather letter, quoted in ibid., 214.

119 / See chap. 9 above.

120 / Corey, *Malden*, 219.

121 / Ibid., 218.

122 / Edward Carrington was Payne's father; ibid., 158.

123 / See chap. 5 above and Paige, *Cambridge* (see chap. 3, n. 45).

124 / Cotton Mather, *A Faithful Man* (Boston, 1705), 24; Corey, *Malden*, 260, 267, 279.

125 / E.g., Pulsifer 1:200, 241; File 36.

126 / See e.g., Sharpe, *Defamation*, 23; B. H. Cunnington, ed., *Records of the County of Wiltshire* (Devizes, 1932), 64, 79–80; Emmison, *Disorder*, 69, 108; N. Z. Davis, *Society and Culture* (see chap. 5, n. 41), 140, 141, 301; Macdonald, "Napier Casebooks" (see chap. 2, n. 27), 48. "Suffolk Records" (see intro., n. 4), 602, has an example of riding the stang.

127 / In French country districts in the early modern period widowers who married young women were subjected to the ridicule of charivari. Davis, *Society and Culture*, 116; cf. Shorter, *Modern Family* (see chap. 4, n. 2), 218. The suspected bigamist was John Squire, slandered in 1665 by Richard Liver's statement, "If he should marry again in this country he would have him hanged within half a year." File 38.

128 / See Sharpe, *Defamation*, 20–21; cf. D. G. Hey, *An English Rural Community: Myddle* (Leicester, 1974), 228.

129 / Flaherty, *Privacy*, 151.

130 / Rev. John Angier, quoted in R. C. Richardson, *Puritanism in North-West England* (Manchester, 1972), 104.

131 / D. Levin, ed., *Bonifacius: An Essay upon the Good* (Cambridge, Mass., 1966), 85.

132 / File 28.

133 / File 7.

134 / Macdonald, "Napier Casebooks," 43.

135 / *Entertaining Satan*, 309.

136 / Chaytor, "Household and Kinship" (see pref., n. 5), 49.

Conclusion

1 / "Puritans and Sex" (see chap. 1, n. 27).

2 / Anglo-Saxonisms were almost invariably used by people with criminal records or under communal suspicion.

3 / See Quaife, *Wanton Wenches* (see pref., n. 13); Ingram, "Ecclesiastical Justice" (see chap. 1, n. 27); Emmison, *Elizabethan Life: Disorder* (see chap. 11, n. 96) and idem, *Elizabethan Life: Morals* (see chap. 1, n. 52); Sharpe, *Defamation* (see chap. 11, n. 30).

4 / Perry Miller and Thomas Johnson, eds. *The Puritans* (New York, 1939), 7.

5 / Petition of Jane Bowen, File 30.

6 / Letter to Thomas Prince, Mass. Hist. Soc. Photostats, 12 Jan. 1665.

7 / J. M. Sosin, *English America and the Restoration Monarchy* (Lincoln, 1980); Richard R. Johnson, *Adjustment to Empire* (Leicester, 1982).

8 / Konig, *Law and Society* (see intro., n. 1); Murrin, "Trial by Jury" (see intro., n. 13), 197.

9 / Charlestown had to cope with thirty refugee families in 1676. Frothingham, *Charlestown* (see chap. 5, n. 32), 218.

10 / Henretta, "Morphology" (see pref., n. 8), 396–98; Pope, "New England and *The New England Mind*" (see chap. 6, n. 12).

11 / Pope, "New England and *The New England Mind*"; idem, *Half-Way Covenant*, app., table 2.

12 / Henretta, "Morphology," 389, 396.

13 / Cf. Laslett, *World We Have Lost* (see pref., n. 2), 32–33.

14 / Only nineteen Middlesex people were accused, mainly from Reading, Billerica, and Woburn. Koehler, *Search for Power* (see pref., n. 12), 480–91.

15 / Chapin, *Criminal Justice* (see intro., n. 9), 139–42.

16 / Charles Hambrick-Stowe, *The Practice of Piety* (Chapel Hill, 1982), esp. chap. 1; George Selement, "Meeting of Minds," *William and Mary Quarterly* 41 (1984): 32–48; Hall, "Towards a History of Popular Religion" (see chap. 10, n. 66), 50–55; Demos, *Entertaining Satan* (see chap. 4, n. 5), 311; Pope, "New England and *The New England Mind*," 105–07; Caldwell, *Puritan Conversion Narrative* (see chap. 6, n. 13).

17 / Breen and Foster, "Social Cohesion" (see chap. 6, n. 10), 9, 13, 15.

18 / Faber, "Puritan Criminals" (see chap. 1, n. 43), 125.

19 / E.g., Thompson, *Women* (see chap. 2, n. 17), 60–81; Richard D. Brown, "Modernisation in Early America," *Journal of Interdisciplinary History* 2 (1971–1972): 201–28.

20 / Thompson, *Women,* 25–31.

21 / Rebecca Lee in the Crosswell Case, chap. 10 above.

22 / E.g., Macdonald, "Napier Casebooks" (see chap. 2, n. 27); Pollock, *Forgotten Children* (see chap. 10, n. 48); Macfarlane, *Josselin* (see chap. 10, n. 47); Wrightson, *English Social History* (see chap. 5, n. 34); David Cressy, unpublished paper on letterwriting delivered at Anglo-American Conference, London, 1982; P. G. Slater, *Children in the New England Mind* (Hamden, 1977).

Index